Women and Religion in Britain Today

Belonging

Edited by

Yvonne Bennett

Canterbury Christ Church University

Women's Studies

VERNON PRESS

www.vernonpress.com

In the Americas:
Vernon Press
1000 N West Street, Suite 1200
Wilmington, Delaware, 19801
United States

In the rest of the world:
Vernon Press
C/Sancti Espiritu 17,
Malaga, 29006
Spain

Women's Studies

Library of Congress Control Number: 2022939894

ISBN: 978-1-64889-222-6

Cover design by Vernon Press. Cover image by Bianca Van Dijk from Pixabay.

Table of Contents

List of Figures

List of Images

Acknowledgements

We would like to thank you all for reading our book... your beliefs matter.

Introduction

Yvonne Bennett
Canterbury Christ Church University

Keywords: belief, belonging, cultural, faith, gender, lived religion, religion, religiosity, ritual, spirituality, women, worship.

***

This book examines a range of ways in which religion continues to impact on the lives of women in Britain today. We aim to give women a voice in answering the question "What counts as religion?" (Beckford, 2003, p. 12). Yet the terms *religion* and *women* are complex in definition, each commanding debate. The continuing conversations surrounding both terms are multifaceted, particularly where they intersect.

The primary theme of this book is about women and the ways in which they *belong* to religious groups. We, therefore, begin by setting out how we have defined the term women. Schudson, Beischel and van Anders (2019) examined how individuals have used and understood the six gender/sex categories (man, woman, feminine, masculine, female, and male). Their results showed that understandings are less binary and more fluid than in the past with greater diversity in contemporary understanding. Gender is not a dichotomy; it is not a binary variable. For the purposes of this book, we use gender to mean man and woman as each contributor frames sex and gender according to how their research participants understand these terms, and at times there is clarification where experiences of cis-gendered people cannot reflect the experiences of trans or non-binary people.

At the time of research, our respective cohorts were not enmeshed in the current positioning of gender fluidity. Collectively, we acknowledge that the debate about how inclusive categories of sex should be has gathered momentum. Though our intention is not to rehearse these arguments here, contributors to this book support the work to deconstruct rigid binaries of sex and gender, though theoretical emphases may vary.

Religion can be viewed as a social construct, one which changes and adapts over time, holding different meanings for different individuals. Today, religion remains a term that is widely contested. As religion is a continuing process that has evolved and continues to evolve, there can be no one definition that carries the same meaning to all people. Religion is not a single phenomenon (Smart, 1998). With this in mind, we include spirituality within the parameters of religion, drawn to King's view that:

> [t]oday the notion of spirituality is applied across different religious traditions; it is used inside and outside particular religions as well as in many inter-faith and secular contexts. Thus, spirituality has become a universal code word to indicate the human search for direction and meaning, for wholeness and transcendence. (2017, p. 668)

Linda Woodhead (2011) proposed that religion can be defined by situating it within five separate dimensions: culture, identity, relationship, practice, and power. We are of the opinion that these dimensions enable us to examine religion from a spiritual plane which allows us to incorporate beliefs that do not include an omnipresent being. In whatever way we wish to define it, religion continues to play a part in the lives of many of Britain's women. This book examines the lived religious experiences of women using ethnographic and holistic frameworks. This contemporary study of religion is multidisciplinary; therefore, through various academic fields, we look to gain an understanding of the religious and spiritual beliefs, practises, and everyday experiences of women. We examine religion as a lived experience, utilising the term *lived religion* to describe how people practise or experience religion and spirituality in their everyday lives. This may or may not include worship in a religious setting and can be formal or informal. The following chapters relate to each of Woodhead's five dimensions, exploring the ways religion and spirituality continue to impact on women's lives, offering a heterogeneous look at religion in the twenty-first century.

As this book looks at religion as a lived experience, we wanted to expand the boundaries beyond religion as a social and cultural construct. To explore the essence of belief and its relationship to belonging, we focus on the religiosity of women, in terms of worship, doctrinal adherence, ritual and experience. Bergan and McContha (2000), Holdcoft (2006) and Smart (1998) point out that religiosity is also not a simple concept to define. It is as difficult for an agreement to be reached as it is to agree on a definition for religion. One problem is that words such as religiousness, belief and faith are used as replacements for religiosity. However, as Holdcroft is quick to point out, these are measurements of religiosity rather than synonyms. Religiosity can be defined similarly to Woodhead's (2011) definition of religion, and Holdcroft suggests that these dimensions cover knowledge, faith, and ritual. What one must note is that it is possible to exemplify one dimension whilst being deficient in the others (Holdcroft, 2006). A sound religious knowledge does not necessarily equate with a cast-iron belief. For this book, we have defined religiosity as: faith, knowledge, belief, and practise. This definition encapsulates spirituality allowing us to examine the close relationship between faith and spirituality through knowledge, belief, and practise (King, 2017).

Saroglou et al. (2020) propose that spirituality/ religiousness is composed of four elements: believing, bonding, behaving, and belonging, with each element holding emotional, social, cognitive, and moral connotations. The individual chapters in this book study the element of *belonging* which Saroglou defined as:

> [t]he social aspects of religion, insertion into a community, continuity with a tradition, and the search for collective identity and social self-esteem by belonging to a group with a glorious past and an eternal future. (2020, p. 553)

Belonging is an important social motive; the need for acceptance and belonging is a fundamental concept that drives behaviours. Exploring how we belong grants an understanding of how choices are made, both by the individual and the group. Through belonging we are able, as individuals, to ground – or orientate ourselves in different social groupings. We add to our identities that of, amongst others, child, parent, friend, colleague, neighbour, and peer. Schudson, Beischel and van Anders noted that "belonging and bonding were uniquely associated with increased life satisfaction" (2019, p.552). This book examines the factors which underpin the need to belong, set the rules the group adhere to, and in some cases, the impact non-belonging can have. As Baumeister and Leary argue, people "have a pervasive drive to form and maintain at least a minimum quantity of lasting, positive, and significant interpersonal relationships" (Baumeister and Leary, 1995, p. 497). For many women in Britain, religion remains an essential aspect of their lives, and belonging helps foster meaningful interpersonal connections.

Chin makes an interesting point that although belonging frequently appears as a concept in academic literature "it is rarely defined generally" (Chin, 2019, p. 717). We are therefore using four dimensions to explore belonging within this book:

- Recognition: not only must the individual must recognise they belong to a group, but the other members must also recognise the individual as a co-member.

- Identity: an individual takes on the identity of the group; understanding their place within it.
- Strength: the extent to which an individual emphasises their place within the group. Some groups will demand more of a commitment than others.
- Setting: belonging occurs in a variety of groups. For this book, all groups are of a religious or spiritual nature.

Taking the above dimensions into account belonging is a common bond between individuals, it is the glue that holds groups together. It is the aim of this book to explore contemporary women's spirituality and religiosity in Britain by bringing together an interdisciplinary collection of voices to address this subject. Each chapter will look at belonging in a different religious setting, from a different academic standpoint.

The chapters contain threads that run through and connect them. Belonging is examined in relation to women's only spaces within religion and religious settings. From the women-only rituals the fictional character *Aisha,* in chapter six, is exposed to, to the women-only groups that those of the Gàidhealtachd, in chapter three, join. Within organised institutional religions, the use of such spaces grants women a degree of autonomy within the strict confines of a male-dominated orthodoxy. Conversely, within some church parishes, women clergy are denied access to religious spaces and/or denied the right to lead religious sacraments. The way women navigate exclusion is examined in chapters two and three. We have studied the space women inhabit in religious institutions, their practices, and beliefs with a focus on the impact these have on women's lives and their approaches to belonging.

The social aspect of religion through ritual is a common theme throughout the book, from the fields of law and sociology to literature. The importance of a religious marriage for many Muslim women is discussed in chapter four. The ritualistic aspect of the marriage ceremony brings with it a visible sense of belonging. The use of ritual is further examined in connection to birth and the welcoming of a new life within Humanism. The legal, emotional, and social aspect of rituals are examined with reference to being a wife and mother. The idealised role of wife and mother is a theme in both fiction and academic research. Infertility is blamed on *Aisha,* her infidelity portrayed as a stain on her *good Muslim* identity. My own research (2020) revealed that, within conservative Presbyterian communities, women were perceived as the instigators when a man committed adultery, he "[w]as portrayed as a man pushed into the affairs by a wife that was failing to care for her husband, the bad wife, and pulled into the affairs by temptresses." (2020, p. 165). Rituals may serve as a visual sign of belonging; however, that sense of belonging, that acceptance into a group or community, as will be discussed throughout this book, requires, at times, a degree of compromise from the women.

Reference List

Baumeister, R. and Leary, M. R. (1995) "The need to belong: Desire for interpersonal attachments as a fundamental human motivation." *Psychological Bulletin*, 117(3), pp. 497-529.

Beckford, J. A. (2003) *Social Theory and Religion.* Cambridge: Cambridge University Press.

Bennett, Y. H. (2020) *"Because the Bible Tells Me So": Gender and authority in conservative Presbyterianism on the Isle of Lewis (Scotland).* PhD Thesis, Canterbury, Canterbury Christ Church University.

Bergan, A. and McContha J. T. (2000) "Religiosity and Life Satisfaction." *Activities, Adaptation and Aging*, 24(3), pp. 23-34.

Chin, C. (2019) "The concept of belonging: Critical, normative and multicultural." *Ethnicities*, 2019, 19(5), pp. 715-739.

Holdcroft, B. (2006) "What is Religiosity?" *Catholic Education: A Journal of Inquiry and Practice*, 10(1) September, pp. 89-103.

King, U. (2017) "Spirituality" In Hinnells, J. R. (ed.) *A New Handbook of Living Religions 2nd Edition.* New Jersey, Wiley Blackhall, chapter 6.

Saroglou V., Clobert, M., Cohen, A. B., Johnson, K. A., Ladd, K. L., van Pachterbeke, M., Adamovova, L., Blogowska, J., Brandt, P-Y., Çukur, C. S., Hwang, K-K., Miglietta, A., Motti-Stefanidi, F., Mufioz-Garcia, A., Murken, S. and Roussiau, N. (2020) "Believing, Bonding, Behaving and Belonging: The Cognitive, Emotional, Moral, Social Dimensions of Religiousness across Cultures." *Journal of Cross-Cultural Psychology*, 51(7-8), pp. 551-575.

Schudson, Z. C. Beischel, W. J. and van Anders, S. M. (2019) "Individual variation in gender/sex category definitions." *Psychology of Sexual Orientation and Gender Diversity*, 6(4), pp. 448-460. Available at: https://psycnet.apa.org/record/2019-42958-001. Accessed: 12/6/ 2022.

Smart, N. (1998) *The World's Religions.* Cambridge, Cambridge University Press.

Woodhead, L. (2011) "Five Concepts of Religion." *International Review of Sociology* 21(1), pp. 121-143.

List of Abbreviations

BHA	The British Humanist Association
CAS	Complex Adaptive Systems
CRT	Complex Reflective Technê
DH	Department of Health
IHEU	International Humanist and Ethical Union
IMI	The Inclusive Mosque Initiative
NICU	Neonatal Intensive Care Unit
NHS	National Health Service
NICE	National Institute of Clinical Excellence
ONS	Office of National Statistics
SBNR	Spiritual but Not Religious
UK	United Kingdom
USA	United States of America
WHO	World Health Organisation

Chapter 1

Realising Potent Complexities of Women Being Spiritual and Healthy

Nicole Holt
Canterbury Christ Church University

Miles Greenford
Independent Scholar

Abstract: This chapter explores women's spirituality and the way it can assist with the attainment of healthy belonging in the myriad of groups that frame women's lives. This chapter is situated around a series of dialogues between the authors Nicole Holt and Miles Greenford. This has been an ongoing succession of conversations spanning many years in which they discuss the relationship between public health and spirituality. The conversations explore this subject professionally, academically, and practically.

The central premise of this chapter is that women can learn to identify problems with their own spirituality, problems that are impacting on their healthy belonging. This leads to an understanding and an ability to prioritise issues. The authors propose that this problem solving involves complex dynamics which they think of as a *technê*, craft. To gain a more in-depth understanding, they act as *guides* introducing the reader to the emerging technique of *Complex Reflective Technê (CRT)* and explain how women can apply this in practise. This technique is conceived within a philosophical home of an emerging *complex critical realism* influenced by Stegmaier (2019).

As a practically applied method, Complex Reflective Technê (CRT) enables a modelling of overt realisations of complex systematically nurtured reflections. CRT influences and potentially transforms our local and wider practises, learning, thinking and actions – a complex praxis network of adaptive agents. Holt and Green guide the reader through the process of CRT by using practical exercises for readers to action. As they propose that a philosophical aspect permeates and influences all inquiry, they began their investigation into the value of CRT by asking the co-authors of this book to undertake the exercises. The results are discussed in chapter seven as a reflexive process.

Keywords: adaption, adoption, autonomy, behaviour, complex adaptive systems, complex reflective technê, critical realism, dialectic, discernment, health, heuristic, mapping, meditation, orientation, phenomena, philosophy, reality, reflection, reflexivity, spirituality, systems.

***

Introduction

This chapter presents a significant philosophical development from an ongoing research dialogue by us, the authors, into spirituality and health and their promotion. Our ongoing dialogue currently extends back more than seven years and involves mutually beneficial academic peer support and supervision. Together we introduce you to our emerging approach for inquiry into the phenomena of spirituality and health, and spiritual health promotion. We refer to our evolving approach as Complex Reflective Technê (CRT).[1]

We chose to accept the offer of contributing to this book due to the diversity in subject matter and the varied academic backgrounds of our fellow authors. We took into consideration the depths of our own perspectives, knowledge, experiences, and skills relating to the theme women being religious in contemporary Britain. We recognise and value the complex diversity that reflects the dynamic reality of women as they are, simultaneously, individuals and peers, belonging to communities, and wider societies. We recognise and respect that there exist inherent tensions, whether within, through an understanding of self, identifying as being women by birth sex, by gender. Or, vicariously through identifying with, respecting, and highly valuing attributes generally given to and sometimes owned by women. Being across a spectrum, from outright rejection of the imposition of societal perceptions on what it means to be a woman to being fully cherished and highly valued by both self and others.

This chapter is informed and influenced through knowledge and experiences within our field of interest, philosophy. Our response to the significant philosophical influence includes our ongoing active engagement with a host of diverse philosophies alongside our interactions as we nurture and grow our own

---

[1] Technê, a term used by the ancient Greek philosophers is, in present times, usually defined as technique. A practical technique which enables us, with complex systems, to practice and craft attempts at influencing and realising personal perceptions of being.

philosophical approach. To fully understand the critical realities of women's spirituality and health, we recognise that any philosophical tool must be responsive to the transcendent complexities of religiosity.[2] We locate our approach within our emerging philosophical home (ecos) of complex critical realism. We recognise the need to be able to reliably orientate and reorientate ourselves when it comes to the field of spirituality and health. As a result, we endeavour to engage with some of these complexities by using a broader, general, application of Complexity Theories alongside our application of John Holland's (2012, 2014) works on *Complex Adaptive Systems (CAS)*. In so doing, we enable, and engage, a reliable complex adaptive system together with a complex reflective technê. These act as a channel for the emergence and evolution of reliable orientation and mapping. Throughout this chapter, we use an emergences approach that has been adopted from our Complex Reflective Technê (CRT) in our presentation style. The information presented emerges and aggregates from a range of different topics we treat as adaptive agents and networks, interacting together within sections and across the chapter, as well as with ourselves and readers.

We aim to furnish you, the reader, with the tools to critically reflect on your spirituality and the emotional health of your belonging by understanding and engaging with CRT.[3] To make this chapter achievable, we need to concentrate our efforts on the cluster of Complexity Theories, to the works of Holland in the field of complex adaptive systems (CAS). Recognising that his work is within a dominant philosophical home, Holland's work is relatively easy to follow when starting our journeys into Complexity Theories and, as such, a good introduction. Sultan (2019) suggests ways to heuristically inquire about our direct personal perceptions of being, which is highly precinct given the title of this chapter and theme of this book. For Sultan, heuristic research "makes for a very personal and communal journey of discovery" (2019, p. 3). As such, how we orientate and guide ourselves, and possibly others, permeate throughout the arts and sciences of heuristics. We also touch on the way spirituality has evolved from the use of meditation and discernment by the early Christians to these methods of orientation being viewed by some, in present times, as lying outside organised institutional religious practices.

This chapter is created to enable approaches that not merely identify and describe or simply subtract or add objective parts. It engages systems and complexity, accumulating gains beyond ideas and commentary shared within

[2] We are referring to health in a multiple of spheres, physical, mental, and spiritual.

[3] We must point out at this juncture that to engage with this chapter you do not need to self-identify as a woman. Our Complex Reflective Technê is inclusive of all gender identities.

this chapter, capable of being realised to further the notion of women being spiritual and healthy. We, encourage you to actively engage with some of the ideas here. Some form of a log or journal needs to be maintained, combined with willingness, to participate authentically in good faith. Authentic, in this context, is applied as a characteristic of Heuristic Inquiry. You are in control and can switch back to the role of passive reader whenever you wish, for whatever reasons.

Please could you record in your log your responses to the following question:

> **"What are some of the complexities of belonging as a spiritual and healthy woman in Britain?"**

Your responses can be from personal or professional experiences, from personal or professional considerations. There are no right or wrong answers.

Orientation and Mapping

Maps and mapping are valuable tools, especially when applied in conjunction with orientating and orientation. Orientation is one set of systems we frequently use to position ourselves when faced with, and experiencing, uncertainty "[o]rientation is usually understood as an achievement in finding one's way in a new situation.... A function of orientation is to give stability, a hold when disorientated" (Stegmaier, 2019, p. 1).

It is important to note that he adds:

> [h]owever, orientation must also be capable of adapting to unpredictable and surprising situations as well, for example, it must be able to change if the situation changes. The achievement of orienting oneself astonishes less by giving a permanent hold or stability than by keeping up with changes. For this purpose, it needs to establish flexible structures [and systems] that indeed provide a hold and stability, but only for a certain time. (Stegmaier, 2019, p. 1)

Rather like wading across a river, where the water is always in a range of flux, currents, and eddies. With changes in the riverbed or its banks, variations in weather conditions and the effects (including emotional) on those personally in the river experiencing it. Orientation is a complex system used as an aid in guiding ourselves. As orientation technical strategies go, heuristics is commonly and enduringly engaged (Kahneman, 2011).

We can see in the above quotes that Stegmaier utilises systems, networks, and resilience, adapting, and recognising them as unpredictable. When clustered together and used this way, it indicates their increased likelihood of being used as key concepts within a Complex Theory. Orientation, maps, and the way they are applied become increasingly valuable through use, as individuals become proficient in their use these tools become more reliable (Stegmaier, 2019). The prerequisite for a mutually beneficial symbiotic relationship between orientation, mapping and engagement is actioned via our continuing development of our evolving CRT.

Reflective practices, including journals and logs, can be highly objectified and, as such, more frequently encountered in fields engaging in quantitative research. We are adapting our technique to be versatile as a tool in both quantitative and qualitative research. For our inquiry, we are concentrating on it qualitatively, specifically, adapting and applying Sultan's Heuristic Inquiry work:

> [t]oday's qualitative research resides at the highly complex intersection of human experience, perception, memory, language, history, culture and other social systems, relational interactions, and social justice. In that sense, engaging in qualitative research in today's world is an act of hope and resilience and a quest for deliverance and reimagination. (2019, p. xiv)

Immediately apparent are the commonalities expressed between Sultan and our endeavours. In actioning our CRT, we actively encourage engaging "hope and resilience and a quest for deliverance and reimagination" (2019, p. xiv).

We also recognise the notion of women being spiritual and healthy continues to be highly complex. Our adaptation, and application of Holland's (2012) CAS system, provides us with a means to engage, apply, and dynamically interact with some of this complexity. Holland's interest lies in objective behaviours. Certainly, a legitimate dimension of reflective practise relates to our objective behaviours in practise, including our performances. We are not willing or prepared to restrict our interest in this chapter to purely our complex adaptive systems of our objective behaviours. This would do a disservice to our topic of interest, women, spirituality, and health. We also want to be able to identify our models of complex adaptive systems relating to our experiencing *being*. This includes our meaning, our meaning-making and meaning's resilience. Applying our adapted approach to Sultan's (2019) Heuristic Inquiry enables us to achieve this and guides you to apply this theory into practice.

We asked our fellow authors to use CRT as a reflexive exercise. This helped test the effectiveness of our philosophical tool as they looked at their own spiritual health, as academics, as women and as belonging to a new peer group.[4] It is therefore important that before moving on to discuss our complex reflection tool, we define technê and the way we are applying it. We realise that what we provide here is merely a current public snapshot of our understanding and use of technê. Our broader context is our engagement with it using a nurturing approach. In this context, we view technê as a multitude of organic inter- and intra-relating adaptive agents which are evolving within networks of highly complex adaptive systems. We propose that complexity comprises of four simultaneously evolving and symbiotic phenomena:

- Complex Critical Realism philosophical ecos (home).
- Complex Reflective Technê.
- Spirituality and Health.
- Sustainable and Resilient Spiritual Health Promotion.

The above four phenomena, we recognise and value, interact and influence one another. Each is a highly complex adaptive system and forms a wider network together as complex adaptive systems. We are acutely aware that the field of complexity theories and studies is vast and still evolving through informative, reflective scanning and scoping review exercises.

Over the years, our dialogues have formed a series of inquiring exercises to discover if there are any significant conjunctions between complexity and our area of interest, the development of evidence-based spiritual health programs within community/public health nursing. We qualitatively measured the significance of spiritual health by reflecting on the apparent extent of reliability and sensitivity towards the afore mentioned phenomena. Holland's (2012, 2014) works on complex adaptive systems (CAS) studies seem to be most applicable. Holland writes that CAS "concern themselves with elements that are not fixed. The elements, usually called agents, learn, or adapt in response to interactions with other agents" (2014, p. 8).

Agents learn or respond to changing conditions (Holland, 2014). We cover CAS in more detail in our complexity section, but for now, we can consider them to include:

- Adoption
- Adaptation

---

[4] Their responses, both before and after engagement with this chapter, can be found in Chapter 7.

- Mutation
- Hybridisation
- Extinction
- Aggregation
- Evolution

We are also attempting to cultivate our four phenomena through a mutually beneficial symbiotic relationships approach. Doing so in our attempt to enable reliable reflections and heuristic metamorphosis to be gleaned and recorded. These phenomena and recordings have the potential to influence and enable us to orientate, map, and be more reliably informed when considering prior, present, and future actions. We try to do so through the development of dynamic and mutually beneficial symbiotic relationships with the four phenomena and ourselves. Complex critical realism as we are currently applying it seems to be more sensitive and responsive to spirituality and health, and sustainable resilient spiritual health promotion, than a plethora of other philosophies, their methodologies, and methods. Our current conclusion is being reached through a combination of our examining, reflection, and reflexive discourse.

Technê

Our current snapshot of technê involves our recognising it as a craft. This is not without contention with the relevant debates and critiques it raises, including technê's place and value within communities, cultures, and societies. We are currently adopting and adapting from Bolton's (2021) work on technê, work influenced by Aristotle, as an emerging concept. Bolton engages dialectic as one of the examples considered by Aristotle in relation to technê. Through the acquisition of appropriate training and repeated practise, in relation to technê, combined with the gradual embedding of good subconscious and embodied habits, methods can be practised with varying degrees of proficiency. Appropriate training and repeated practises are needed to acquire both habituation and *trained memory* to underpin the degrees of proficiency with the relevant methods within a given technê "this shows the importance for Aristotle of habituated memory access to groups of similar past examples for the skilled practise of the technê" (Bolton, 2021, p. 157).

Our adaptation includes dialectic within complex reflective practices, hence, our technê becomes a complex reflective technê. We do so in recognition that dialectic is a technê within complex reflection. There are similarities and differences in dialectic and other reflective practices within a broader field of complex reflection, which enables us to identify dialectic as one amongst a cluster of reflective practises that continue to evolve over time. These practices, synthesise a range of different practices clustered close enough to be considered as a single domain or ecos (home), that of CRT. However, doing this also requires an analysis of their differences and similarities to improve the reliability of their placement within this cluster and to keep the complexities, including systems, active.

We also acknowledge the need for increasingly skilful proficiency that clearly demonstrates nurturing and finesse as competencies in the practises of CRT. These demonstrations become practise qualities of proficiency indicators, evolving from relevant topics and systems. Initially, the skills and practises necessary will be slow, cumbersome, and highly unreliable, growing from a robotic-like practise to an organic-like practise. As proficiency becomes increasingly more reliable, deeper, richer, and increasingly organic, sensitive, and responsively engaging with increasing complexity, these become a means of recognising and valuing proficiency qualities within the practise of CRT.

To engage with critical realism within our philosophical ecos, we turned to Roy Bhasker, who worked closely with, and influenced, Margaret Archer. We have adopted and applied some of Archer's work in relation to critical realism and Hegelian dialectics as a complex reflective practice. More specifically, we focus on practise as exampled in Hegel's methods of complex reflection, discourse and, importantly, dialectics. It is from Hegel's dialectical methods that he disclosed his deliberations of his internal dialogue involved a contradictory process between opposing sides of an argument. This was adopted and further adapted by the eighteenth-century German philosopher, Johann Fichte, and expressed as a method we generally recognise, as thesis-antithesis-synthesis. Archer et al. recognised the complexity and non-linearity in the practices of Hegel:

> [n]ow Hegel's practice is not in fact conceptually uniformly linear and there is no reason in principle why any term in an organic totality should not be reflected into any other, including compounds of such. In fact, perspectival fluidity and multifacetedness is an essential requirement for any concrete (and, a fortiori, totalising) inquiry, particularly in the socio-sphere. (1998, p. 622)

This is a significant point of conjunction between complexity and critical realism and given our hybridisation evolving application of both in our philosophically located practices that these are not only linear simple practices or processes, reflection and critical reflection can also be complex and non-linear.

With our emerging CRT, we have identified the following clusters which help us with critical reflective practice and orientation:

- Complex Reflection
- Modern Reflection
- Discernment
- Meditation (and Contemplation)
- Discourse
- Heuristics
- Reflexivity
- Biases (Systematic Errors)

Complex Reflection: We recognise that complex reflection is an organically diverse cluster that constitutes an evolving group of past and present skilled practices.[5] These practices require, or significantly engage, reflection. We aim to demonstrate the critically real presence of the cluster, and in so doing, we can start to consider it as emerging and aggregating complex reflection. We are engaging complex as shorthand for our application of some of Holland's studies into CAS and critical realism. Holland does not mention reflection in the context of looking inward. We actively engage some of Holland's work on CAS, adopting, and adapting this with the works of Archer et al. (1998). From this emerges a complex critical realism philosophical eco within CRT. Hartwig includes, in his book *The Dictionary of Critical Realism*, the following proposal:

> [i]n the human embodied person, it [reflection] is the (prime) personal emergent power (PEP) – transcendentally necessary for genuine accountability, presupposing the causal efficacy of reasons – to self-consciously monitor our activities and deliberate internally upon the always already natural, practical, and social context in which they occur. It is thus irreducible to the social or the biological, constituting rather the mediatory process between "structure and agency" that arises from our practical transactions with the objective, above all the natural, world. (2007, p. 408)

For Archer, reflection in critical realism is important and is the prime personal emergent power. However, it is qualified by complex adaptive systems studies, whereby adaptive agents are generally considered semi-powerful,

[5] Cluster in this chapter means a group of things.

semi-autonomous. Autonomy is partial "in the sense that their activity is only modulated by surrounding activity rather than being completely controlled by it" (Holland, 2014, p. 39). Similarly, internally, where complex internal activities modulate rather than completely control our experiences. This gives us power and autonomy as being semi and contingent, closer to our complex critically real experiences of being human. Our accountability is complex, inner, embodied, enriched and temporal, it is contextual and partial. We also must also consider mental and physical illnesses and the influence these have on individuals and the societies they live in alongside any personal accountability. Accountability thus becomes, in complex critical reality, semi-accountable. Our ability of complex reflection is contingent, but not reducible, to the biological or social. Our ability to undertake complex reflection constitutes practical transactions between our complex adaptive systems inherent within our embodied selves and our experiencing life within our niches, and temporal locations.

Modern Reflection: Within complex reflection we identify modern reflection. This is presented and advanced by Schön (1987, 1994) and is, we propose, an obvious initial adaptive practice from earlier systems of reflection. We can also locate critical reflection as a hybridisation of modern reflection where theorists, such as Brookfield (2011); Lawson (1985); Rolf, Freshwater, and Jasper (2001); Fook et al. (2016) and Thompson and Thompson (2008), have adopted and adapted other critical theories. Doing so alongside Schön's works. The works by these theorists highlight the significant influence philosophy has on our *being* and by situating modern reflection as an inner cluster of complex reflection, we identify an inner subcluster we refer to as modern critical reflection.

More recently, creativity (and imagination) has re-emerged as a niche in some modern critical reflection literature. It appears to be associated with criticality, knowing, believing, emotions, reality, imagination, ethics (including morality), and actions (including critical judgement, behaviours, and attentiveness). Where once dominant words were critical reflection, creativity is gaining ground as exampled in works by Bassot (2016); Bolton and Delderfield (2018); Johns (2017) and Moon (1999). There appears an ongoing emergence within the modern reflection, of creativity interacting with criticality. Creative and critical reflection is a growing subcluster very closely allied with the critical reflection subcluster.

A further notable hybridisation comes from the works of Mezirow et al. They suggest critical reflective practices are weighted in action, actions associated with learning as transformational (Mezirow et al., 2000, 2009). We can also witness the growth of inquiry as relates to complex reflection through drift. Autoethnography drifting into the cluster of complex reflection where the subject and field of inquiry is ethnographically located in the self of the inquirer as noted by Adams, Jones, and Ellis (2015); Coffey (1999) and Throne

(2019). This is an important consideration as some of this book's following chapters have an auto-ethnographic component. We consider complex reflection as an organic broad family cluster within which are an ongoing emerging evolutionary network of confluences, conjunctions, disjunctions, genetic roots, etc. Further members, we cluster within complex reflection, are meditation (and contemplation), and discernment.

Discernment: Discernment has been associated with some early Christian practices and continues to involve the interpretation of our internal being. This is specifically the interpretation of the spirits involved in the movements of the soul as debated by academics such as Njeri (2012); Orsy (2020); and Rich (2007). Ignatius of Loyola's discernment is an ability to differentiate between good and bad spirits.[6] This does not involve the use of reason or rationality but instead uses inner spiritual judgment (discernment). The official International Jesuit website describes discernment as follows:

> [d]iscernment is about finding the voice of the Spirit of God speaking to us in the ordinary and practical details of our lives. It is a key gift that St. Ignatius brought in the Spiritual Exercises. By trying always to listen to the Spirit, without being attached to our own desires and ideas, Jesuits wish to find where the Spirit of God is leading and respond with humility and joy. (Society of Jesuits, 2022)

Ignatius formulated a strict rigorous 22 rules-based systematic method involving a selected number and range of deliberate exercises that needed the individual to carry out through self-discipline (Loyola, 1914). Without proficiency in these spiritual exercises, discerning the good from bad spirits that are influencing one's soul becomes highly problematic and extremely challenging. The exercises, as formulated and directed by Ignatius of Loyola (1914) include mixtures of stated meditations. These are contemplations that enable the practitioner to be trained to tell the difference (discern) between inner communications between good and evil. They can then act on these discernments appropriately. Proficient discernment is experienced as an inner sense of judgement emerging through the proficient combined

---

[6] Ignatius of Loyola was a Spanish Catholic priest and theologian, a founding father of the religious order of the Society of Jesus (Jesuits). His discernment involves prayer and weighing facts and feelings about the several good choices which ultimately leads to a choice about what is the best fit for an individual. This includes a seven-step process, openness, courage, interior freedom, praying as reflective practice, priorities and not confusing the ends with the means.

systematic practices of mediation and contemplation. Contemplation was different for Ignatius than for other Christian orders of contemplatives of his time and remains so today. Discernment in this way is not rational intellectual judgement, nor intuitive judgement. It appears to be deeper inner senses that can resonate or dissociate but to a degree whereby they are experienced as something immanent and transcendent. This is significantly beyond normal emotional and intuitive feelings and thoughts (Lahav, 2018). With intensive and extensive proficient practice, these exercises become habituated.

Daydreaming and pondering, alongside being attentive, were highly significant for Ignatius:

> Ignatius was convinced that God can speak to us as surely through our imagination as through our thoughts and memories. In the Ignatian tradition, praying with the imagination is called contemplation. (O'Brian, 2022)

Discernment and discerning practises already existed within strict contemplative practices, which Ignatius was aware of. He adopted and adapted these practices hybridising them into his unique system of discernment which promoted daydreaming, pondering, imagination, and attentiveness. These internal actions influence choices and decisions that lead to further actions, including possibly further discernment. Orsy (2020) offers a similar approach, whereas Njeri (2012) proffers his hybridisation of Ignatian Discernment with Aristotle's Virtuous Action. Rich (2007) explores discernment as it relates to the Christian Religion commonly referred to as *The Desert Fathers.*[7] This demonstrates a highly significant evolutionary route through a spiritual-religious practice, to modern current sciences, as the religious and spiritual are gradually removed from discernment and mediation, becoming viewed as spiritual exercises. We see the stripping out process start in Descartes' meditations, where he is trying to discern through mediations using purely simple sceptical logical rationalism/reason. This is an early enlightenment emergence of what we come to know of today as modern reflective and critical reflective practices.

We, therefore, recognise and locate within discernment a complex critical reality of dynamic interactions between knowing, believing, emotions, reality, imagination, ethics (including morality), and actions (including critical

---

[7] Desert Fathers were early Christian hermits whose practice of asceticism in the Egyptian desert formed the basis of Christian monasticism. Following the example of Jesus' life of poverty, service, and self-denial, these early monks devoted themselves to vows of austerity, prayer, and work.

judgment, behaviours, and attentiveness). We also recognise discernment is organic and evolutionary, involving adoption, adaptations, and hybridisation. We note the gradual evolution of different scientific methods, methodologies, epistemologies, and ontologies as they emerge and evolve out of different philosophies. Remember, we make no claims to our Complex Reflective Technê (CRT) as being a science as CRT is, for us, a craft.

Meditation (and Contemplation): Approximately 90 years after Ignatius formalised his spiritual exercises for discernment, a 10-year-old student, Rene Descartes, entered one of the colleges run by the Society of Jesus (Jesuits) and studied there for 8 years. Descartes continued his involvements with members of the Jesuits in higher education establishments throughout his life. Thus, for meditation (and contemplation), we think here of Descartes (1641) *Discourse on Method and the Meditations.* Renowned for its influences on reasoning, applying in conjunction, uncertainty through doubt (scepticism) reasoning, famously reaching and expressing his first principle in the quote "*I think, therefore I am*" (Bauer, 2021). It appears that Descartes adopted Ignatius meditative, contemplative, and discerning practices, interacting with, and hybridising them into his own system. Descartes initially focused on reasoning doubt (sceptical). However:

> I am a thing which thinks, that is to say, which doubts, affirms, denies, knows a few things, is ignorant of many, which loves, hates, wills, does not will, which also imagines, and which perceives. For, as I noted above, although the things I perceive and imagine are perhaps nothing at all outside me and in themselves, I am nevertheless assured that that these modes of thought, which I call perceptions and imaginations, in so far only as they are modes of thought, certainly reside and are found in me. And in the little that I have just said, I believe I have stated all I really know, or at least, all that up to now I have observed that I know. (Descartes, 1968, p. 113)

We are cognisant of the complex critical reality of there being simultaneously multiple other forms and systems of meditation and contemplation.

Discourse: Discourse as an approach also becomes located within the complex reflection cluster, as its own subcluster. Within discourse, exists dialogues between two or more characters. These characters are identified within a dialogue, a dialogue which expresses their inner meditations, contemplations, and discernment. This form, and system of dialogue, then becomes located within discourse as an inner subcluster. We also identify dialectics as these are often used as a way of presenting two characters with opposing characteristics in dialogue. It is important to recognise that dialectics can also exist out with a dialogue approach. As Archer et al. noted "it should go without saying that Hegelian dialectic purports to be the constellationally completed reflection on reflection" (1998, p. 622). We therefore locate dialectics and dialogue as inner subclusters within a discourse cluster.

Heuristics: We have also placed heuristics within our CRT cluster. There are many common characteristics we have so far observed which are also recognisable in heuristics. These include reflective meditative and contemplative practises. Different systems and forms of heuristics are influenced by its evolutionary roots in the ancient Greek word *heuriskein* and how it's been translated, transliterated, and applied down through history. There is a consensus that heuristic means "to discover or to find" (Moustakas, 1990, p. 9).

Moustakas positions the self of the practitioner as present throughout his heuristic research method. The centrality of self is placed in a mutually beneficial symbiotic relationship between increasing depth of understanding of a phenomenon under inquiry, and the practitioner also experiencing growing self-knowledge and self-awareness, with "heuristic processes incorporating creative self-processes and self-discoveries" (Moustakas, 1990, p. 9). We can observe the similarities in Moustakas heuristic and others we have already mentioned in our current complex reflection cluster. This is an example of drift, as no references are made by Moustakas to Schön and his work. However, we are of the opinion that Moustakas shares some commonality with others we have located within our family cluster of complex reflection.

Sultan published her work involving heuristics, motivated in part arguing that, "the heuristic approach has been essentially 'lost' due to lack of precision and detailed description of the underlying processes" (2019, p. xiv). Sultan is more specific when it comes to acknowledging reflection's role in her heuristic systems. Reflection itself is mentioned as deep thought, in relation to journaling as it involves both reflective (deep thought) and reflexive (self and other) processing of experience" (2019, p. 136). She further notes that:

> [a]lthough it is not explicitly identified as one of the seven processes of heuristic inquiry, it is implicitly understood that journaling is a primary method for documenting each of seven heuristic processes, as well as each of the six phases of heuristic research. Journaling honours the social constructivist, autobiographical, exploratory, process-focused, intuitive, introspective, creative, and humanistic facets of heuristic research, eliciting deeper knowing and multidimensional perception. (2019, p. 136)

We can identify the breadth, depth and richness reflection and reflective practices brought to heuristic inquiry and the value placed on them by Sultan. We are also here introduced to reflexive, which, within our cluster of complex reflection, we locate as its own unique subcluster as this is where others start to become involved with self.

Reflexivity: Sultan views reflexivity as being on a continuum of experiences, from internal through to external. Furthermore, Sultan presents her own concept she calls embodied reflexivity:

> [w]hile reflection tends to operate specifically within the cognitive domain, I view reflexivity as an embodied venture that includes multidimensional ways of being and knowing, as well as our multifaceted ways of making sense of the contextual dynamics. (2019, p. 169)

Within our cluster of complex reflection, we can locate embodied reflexivity as an inner subcluster of reflexivity. We can deliberate on the way we can consider reflexivity and embodied as implicit fundamental systems of both autoethnography and first-person action research. Both research methodologies are situated on a spectrum with other forms of ethnographic and action research methods. There are with varying relational degrees of internal thought and personal experiences emphasis, from the personal towards other and wider others. This spectrum emerges and diverges out of reflexivity of an initial emphasis on the personal.

Given we are now considering our dynamic embodied socially, environmentally, and temporally located complex adaptive system that is our experience, it is important to acknowledge the issue of biases and prejudices. We all have them and must acknowledge that we do before we move on to recognise them before considering what actions, if any, we want and will take.

Biases (systematic errors): We turn to Kahneman (2011), internationally recognised as prominent in the field of bias and heuristics. Kahneman's interests involve the making of sound judgements and undertaking decision-making (including when uncertain). This is in relation to heuristics and their predictable biases (systematic errors), and the reliability of these heuristically formed judgements and decisions when made and enacted:

> [w]e did not ask ourselves whether all intuitive judgements under uncertainty are produced by the heuristics we studied; it is now clear that they are not. In particular, the accurate intuitions of experts are better explained by the effects of prolonged practice than by heuristics. We now draw a "richer and more balanced picture, in which skill and

> heuristics are alternative sources of intuitive judgements and choices." (Kahneman, 2011, p. 7)

Over many years, Kahneman, through his approaches and collaborations, has been able to identify a range of heuristic system errors. He highlights the parts emotions, and their influencing abilities play on rational intuition in relation to systematic errors in judgement and decision-making. Priest (2019) has complied, from Kahneman's works, a simple collection of 100 impairing cognitive biases and heuristics that enables easy reference to common practical examples in action.

Where Sultan seeks to value living experiences expressed as heuristic inquiry:

> not to abandon or reject the foundations of how we do empirical research and share findings with our colleagues and the general public, nor is it to undermine rigor. Instead, the aim is to ground our research process in real life by giving a voice – through relational and empathic dialogue – to those who have shared the experience we are researching. (2019, p. xiv)

Kahneman recognises the value and identifies inherent risks in living experiences expressed purely heuristically:

> the focus on error does not denigrate human intelligence, any more than the attention to diseases in medical texts denies good health. Most of us are healthy most of the time, and most of our judgements and actions are appropriate most of the time. As we navigate our lives, we normally allow ourselves to be guided by impressions and feelings, and the confidence we have in our intuitive beliefs and preferences is usually justified. But not always. We are often confident even when we are wrong, and an objective observer is more likely to detect our errors than we are. (2011, p. 4)

Although we recognise heuristically engaging with either of the above viewpoints, we mostly use variations of both Sultan's (2019) and Kahneman (2011). We live in complex dynamic multilevel variations of interpenetrating subjectivity and objectivity. We are constantly, by our actions and interactions, influencing and being influenced. This includes our highly complex heuristics, which can be fallible and biased. Importantly, it is not as simple as saying heuristics are always fallible and biased as this depends on the context of the inquiry being undertaken. A first-person inquiry into what emerges following a deep dive into a topic could result in a personal heuristic moment. Is this then judged as a system error or as evidence? From Kahneman, we appreciate heuristics is complex. This presents an emerging complex heuristic subcluster within the complex reflection cluster. In relation to a complex reflection cluster, the judgement or decision of bias is complex and relational.

We consider biases significant enough to be identified as potentially inherently relevant to each subcluster within our cluster of complex reflection and CRT, with sometimes profound effects and affects. A simple example being our personal exploration of how we react emotionally. We can inadvertently show bias in a reflective exercise by automatically applying a particular form of favoured or habituated practised rationalism. This could result in a dispassionate third-person object study of emotional experiences as fits the rationalist system applied. It may well screen out the irrationality and complexity of the experience resulting in a simple rational description. This is where CRT increasingly comes into its own when practised with increasing proficiency.

Complex Adaptive Systems: We have initially identified, within complex reflection, a cluster of practices that grew and evolved over 2500 years of history.[8] These are expressed in a Complex Reflection Hierarchy as can be viewed in Figure 1.1. below:

Modern Reflection	Discernment	Meditation and Contemplation	Discourse	Heuristics	Reflexive
Modern Critical Reflection			Dialogue	Complex Heuristics	Embodied Reflexivity
Modern Critical and Creative Reflection					
Transformat ive and Action-Driving Critical and Creative Reflection					

Figure 1.1. Complex Reflection

---

[8] We are aware that we have discussed these practices within Western cultures. Time and word constraints prevented us from studying the practices in relation to other world cultures.

Figure 1.1. appears to be an emerging complex adaptive system. It is important that we understand what we mean by this term. This understanding enables us to recognise and put subsequently into practise. First, we need to recall that we have embedded CRT in a complex critical realism philosophical ecos. To make complexity manageable within the boundaries of our chapter, we have utilised a crude representation of Holland's (2012) Complex Adaptive System (CAS). When we examine complex and complicated these are easily recognised as being on the extreme end of a descriptive spectrum. However, towards the middle of the spectrum, it becomes far more difficult and problematic, unclear, and arbitrary (Holland, 2014). Hence, Holland goes on to state:

> [f]or these reasons, complexity, like life and consciousness, does not have a rigorous definition. However, as with life (biology) and consciousness (psychology), this lack does not forestall a rigorous approach to the subject matter. Better yet, emergence ("the whole is more than the sum of the parts") helps distinguish complex systems from other systems. (2014, p. 3)

Holland's interest in emergence is not as a holistic phenomenon, impossible to be reduced to the sum of its parts. Rather, Holland "concentrates on interactions where the aggregate exhibits properties not attained by summation" (2014, p. 4). These interactions of interest are not simple and linear, they are both complex and non-linear.

Some reflective practices can be very crude, requiring little proficiency, but they can ease access into CRT. An example of adoptions, adaptations, emergences, and aggregations in reflection can be seen in Descartes' *Discourse on Methods and the Meditations.* Reflection, as practised by Descartes, appears to be the application of a simple combined linear analysis. This involved a system of critical reflection of himself and his world, commencing with his initial scanning and identification of his being through reflective practice. This was his attempt to achieve certainty of reality and truth. It was, and remains, highly effective and powerful. Arguably the most popular result of it is, "*I think, therefore I am*" (Bauer, 2021).

There are similarities between Descartes's Reflective Technê and those of Ignatius's meditations and contemplations, for example trying to discern knowledge of God, soul, and reality, through a combination of reasoning and filtering out doubt (scepticism). A fundamental difference, however, is in the reflective nature of the two. Descartes's reflections describe his own application of his own variation of reflective practices presented in Ignatius' *Spiritual Exercises.* These, we argue, can be viewed as heavily directional and highly structured. Furthermore, Descartes specifically states that he applies doubtful reasoning to remove imagination, senses, and other recognised and valued means of discernment. These were used by Ignatius and other groups, such as Jesuits, as forms of meditation and contemplation. We are going to sidestep a debate about which practices within CRT are simple and linear and which are complex adaptive systems as we cannot give it the depth it requires in this chapter. However, there needs to be recognition of and emphasise on the vitality of relative proficiencies in these applied practices.

Holland's focus is on the aggregates from emergences that are greater than the sum of their parts. Within CRT, simple linear processes are also included within a hierarchy of practices up to and including non-linear CAS practices. Examples of non-linear CAS include the emergent aggregate of intuition and insight. Each of these is more commonly associated with heuristic research inquiry approaches. Insights and intuition are also associated with some meditative and contemplative practices and most, if not all the subclusters within CRT. We are interested, not only on individual aggregates, but their interaction. We have looked for evidence of laws of organisation, how they work and where they are situated.[9] Selected aggregates with their laws at one level, become the building blocks for properties at a higher level to emerge. This gives us hierarchies of aggregates and their emergent properties. We consider CRT to be within such a hierarchy as emergent from CAS. Holland cites Herbert Simon (1981):

> [c]omplex systems will evolve from simple systems much more rapidly if there are stable intermediate forms...The resulting complex forms.... will be hierarchic. Among possible complex forms, hierarchies are the ones that have time to evolve. In hierarchic systems we can distinguish between interaction among subsystems...and the interactions within subsystems.... The interactions at different levels may be, and often will be, of different orders of magnitude. (2014, p. 3)

We do not go into detail here as that is beyond the scope and aim of this chapter. The top-down and bottom-up effects of complex reflective practices adapting over time is a pervasive feature of CAS. To re-iterate, relative proficiency with CRT practices is vital.

---

[9] When we look at the world, we usually perceive complex scenes composed of many groups of objects. These objects themselves consist of many parts which in turn have smaller parts. Max Werheimer, Wolfgang Kohler and Kurt Koffka proposed five laws of perceptual organisation are used to make sense of complexity. These are: the Law of Similarity, the Law of Pragnanz, the Law of Proximity, the Law of Continuity, and the Law of Closure. (see Ash, 1998)

Agent, agency, and boundaries are highly significant in Holland's (2012, 2014) works. Studies of CAS concern themselves with elements that are not fixed. Holland states "[t]he elements, usually called agents, learn, or adapt in response to interactions with other agents" (2014, p. 8). We witness this pervasive phenomenon in CRT and the way its cluster of complex reflective practices interact with each other and with their philosophies. Developing CRT as a tool to be used in spirituality and health and sustainable resilient spiritual health promotion depends, as Holland states "on a deep understanding of the interaction of adaptive agents in CAS (Complex Adaptive Systems)" (2014, p. 9). We propose this may help enhance the immune system, assist with mental health, and encourage innovation.

We can consider the reflective practices subclusters within CRT as complex adaptive agents. We recognise, over time, their convergences to states of balance or single best strategies as being, even momentarily, unusual, Holland (2014). However, mostly we witness them converge and diverge in relative degrees of ongoing dynamic flux. As our cultures and societies continue to change some of these changes interact with complex reflection, complex reflective practices and we propose this can also include CRT "[a]s the agents adapt to each other, new agents with new strategies usually emerge. Then each new agent offers opportunities for still further interaction, increasing the overall complexity" (Holland, 2014, p. 9).

Interactions of our subcluster of complex reflective adaptive agents have, in some instances, become increasingly entangled with some modern sciences such as Social Sciences (Heuristics, Critical Reflection). Entanglements between complex reflection and philosophy appear to be ongoing recognisable systems. An example is modern reflective practice, when reflecting on our actions, including experiences, as a means of obtaining information. This information is emerging from the combination of experience and applied reflective practice. The emergent information may stay with the practitioner internally; remembered or forgotten. It may also be external, recorded in a log or journal. This may lead to a progression where it informs an individual's theory and/or practise. The emergent information is considered simultaneously as an adaptive agent and as a network within a complex adaptive system "[a]ll CAS exhibit similar entanglements, each new agent offering possibilities for still other agents. The complex feedback loops that form make it difficult to analyse, or even describe, CAS" (Holland, 2014, p. 9). If analysis or description are made difficult in entangled CAS, so too are reliably causal predictions. For Holland, the analysis of such CAS pivots almost certainly on recognising recurring patterns in the ever-changing system's configurations. Before we move on to draw out one such pattern emergent across the current subclusters within our current complex reflection and CRT, we must visit how our use of adaptive agent relates to agency.

Holland proposes that autonomy is the concept closest to agency. He suggests those autonomous systems are driven by current stimuli and self-governance. In this concept, autonomy becomes an emergent aggregate with a higher standing than the stimuli a practitioner is acting and responding to. In relation to CRT, attention, and motivation alongside the practitioner's ability to control these, become vital resources. One must be able to control and use our attention and motivation as resources. This is necessary for proficiency in all reflective practices within the currently identified cluster of complex reflection. These abilities also require degrees of autonomy to enable conscious and subconscious/habituated controls to be identified, germinated, nurtured, and grown. These abilities have the potential to evolve. We also need to have the option of being able to recognise and identify the active stimuli from which the relevant autonomy emerges and aggregates:

> [i]n the sense that their activity is only modulated by surrounding activity rather than being completely controlled by it. Such autonomy allows the CAS to run internal activities that go beyond the current stimulus. More complex loops allow the CAS to "look ahead", examining the effects of various action sequences without actually executing the actions. (Holland, 2014, p. 39)

Holland further highlights that autonomy in agents "is closely associated with loops and recirculation in networks" (2014, p. 80). The recirculation can be observed, however, in tangled networks, it is difficult to determine the changes in autonomy brought about by adding even a few extra loops. Holland's approach involves comparing observations in easy cases to difficult cases "may suggest ways of transferring techniques for control" (2014, p. 80).

Here, we take an immersive, informed, and influenced by CAS and Complex Reflective Technê (CRT) complex heuristic leap. Our complex heuristic leap is akin Kahneman's complex two heuristic systems:

> System one operates automatically and quickly, with little or no effort and no sense of voluntary control.
>
> System two allocates attention to the effortful mental activities that demand it, including complex computation. The operations of System two are often associated with the subjective experience of agency, choice, and concentration. (2011, p. 20)

Within our own emerging approach, we broadly employ system two alongside the interactions of both systems in reaching our conjecture. Our complex heuristic leap of conjecture also transcends from Holland's engagement with language:

> we get a hierarchy of niches: idiolects, dialects, language communities, and language groups. Within this hierarchy, language provides long-range anticipation and increased agent autonomy, so that an agent's behaviour is not conditional on current stimulus alone. Instead, current stimulus only modulates ongoing internal activity (such as playing through possible scenarios mentally). That is, an agent can "run" an internal model that permits "lookahead" and an internal exploration of options.... Salient cues within an internal model strongly influence the overall interpretation of utterance sequences (Five Grades 2009). Thus, communication often consists of prefabricated sequences based on anticipations, rather than word-by-word choices. (2012, p. 202)

Our nurturing of CRT as it is philosophically niched within complex critical realism enables us to test our conjecture. We do so by locating and understanding the complex reflective practices as an emergent aggregate network. This network supports the semi-autonomy of practitioners applying it. We also recognise the more proficient in complex reflective practices a practitioner becomes the value of our technê of complex reflection increases.

Before we move on to *Complex Heuristic Adaptive Agents Network*, we first need to identify what we mean by networks. We briefly discussed adaptive agents to provide an understanding of networks. We need to be aware that every adaptive agent interacts and thus has performance capability. Our complex reflection becomes simultaneously an adaptive agent with an internal network cluster of various interacting adaptive agents. These adaptive agents are within a hierarchic network that can be viewed in Figure 1.2.

We can observe, within the CRT adaptive agent hierarchical levels, an adaptive agent called *complex reflection cluster*. There are other interactive, adaptive agents within CRT although our current interest is in the complex reflection cluster adaptive agent.

Within the network of the complex reflection cluster we have, to date, identified seven significant interacting adaptive agents. There are rules active within and across these hierarchies and adaptive agents that, at this stage of our research, are only just emerging discernibly. These rules emerge from observable patterns, these patterns we apply to test in our following Complex Heuristic Adaptive Agents Network. In relation to our current complex reflection cluster, each of the seven adaptive agents is fanouts from the cluster (properties fanning out from the cluster adaptive agent). Holland notes:

> [t]he study of networks in terms of fanout leads to the definition of communities within the network. A community is a set of nodes (adaptive agents) where the connections of each node in the set largely lead to other nodes (adaptive agents) within that set. The qualification of "largely" determines the "tightness" of the community. A large set of nodes with 50 per cent of the connections leading to other members of the set is a quite different community from a small set of nodes with 90 per cent of the connections leading back into the set. Indeed, a loose community may contain several tight communities, leading on to community-orientated definition of hierarchical organisations. (2014, p.38)

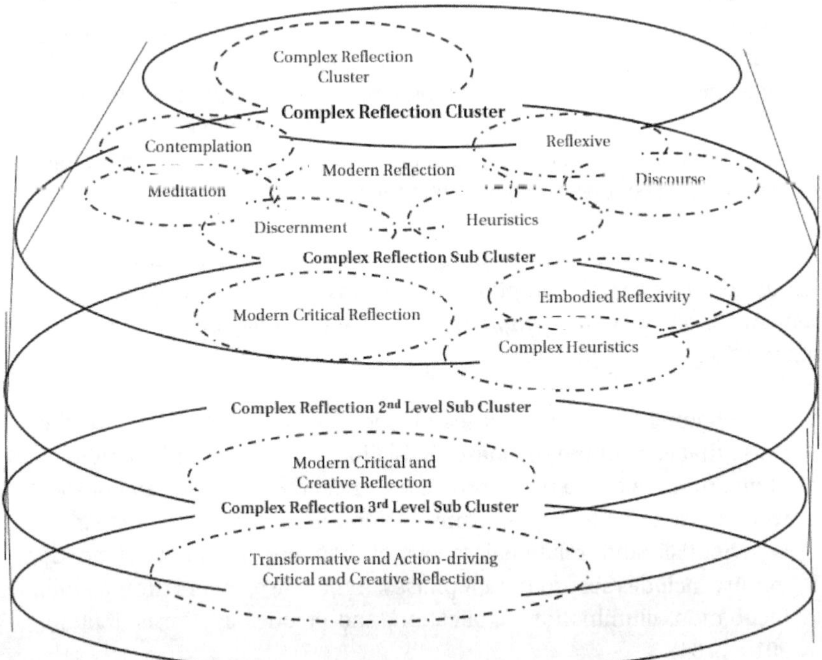

Figure 1.2. Complex Reflective Techné (CRT)

Our cluster can be considered a set of adaptive agents and the question that follows is the identification of connections. We considered those within our complex reflection cluster for connections involving common characteristics. We identified those common characteristics along with their connections to each other that start to emerge and aggregate a Complex Heuristic Adaptive Agents Network.

Complex Heuristic Adaptive Agents Network

As means of orientation, we are not restricted to solely gaze outward, we also gaze inwardly upon ourselves. We reflect, bend back, on ourselves to inform our orientations and actions. However, we need to reflect our engagement of complex reflection, and its use of critical realism with complexity, in our current working definition of complex reflection. We are therefore adopting and adapting Hartwig's (2007) definition (see page 16) to the following:

> [c]omplex reflection is the prime personally emerging and aggregating relative semi-autonomy in the temporally located, niched environmentally, ecologically, and socio-culturally, embodied experiential living human being. Proficiencies in complex reflection relative to our (in)actions are indicative of and necessary for genuine accountability, self-consciously monitoring our activities and deliberating upon the contexts they are in inter and transactions with. Complex reflection is a proficiency-related mediatory complex adaptive system that arises from our need to orientate ourselves and our (in)actions within our personal phenomena of mindfully experiencing our being, to our phenomena of interest.[10]

We recognised some of our emerging active patterns are also present in Sultan's as an emerging complex dual-systems approach engaging actions for heuristic inquiry. Sultan employs a relatively simple heuristic process in conjunction with six phases:

> as a channel for the six phases of this research methodology in the sense that each of the six phases is facilitated through implementation of one or more of the seven processes. Thus, the processes and phases work in concert to support the exploratory, introspective, creative, experiential, and relational facets of heuristic research. Heuristic inquiry includes six prominent phases: initial engagement, immersion, incubation, illumination, explication, and creative synthesis. (Sultan, 2019, p. 94)

These phases may or may not unfold in a sequential fashion, depending on the needs of your study. We have devised Figure 1.3. below as a visual representation of Sultan's approach.

---

[10] This is our own working definition of complex reflection.

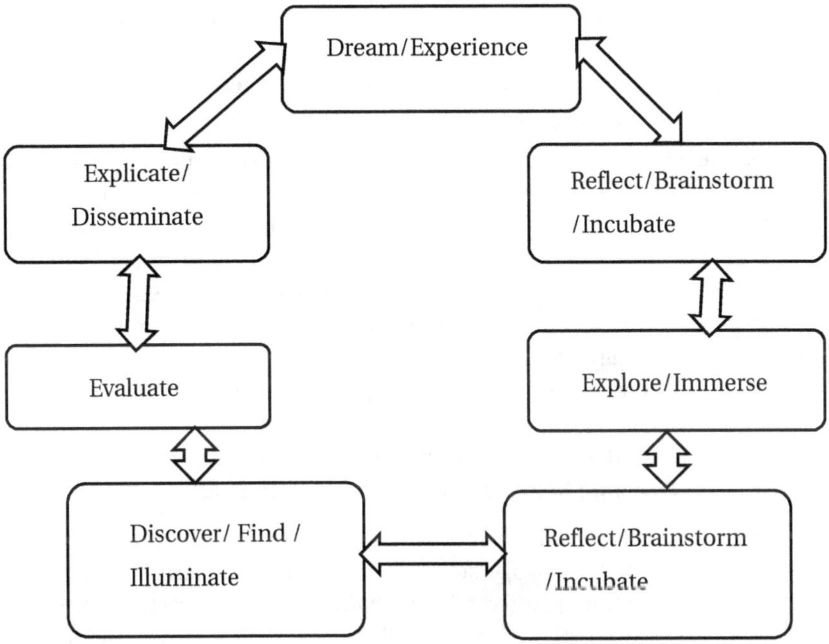

Figure 1.3. The Heuristic Research Process

For Sultan (2019) each of the seven boxes can be viewed as *being-in-the-present* as orientated processes within a simple practice. This approach does not preclude pre-planning, as to adopt this process requires familiarity with it, and possibly other approaches. We can reflect on these possibilities, on planning, adopting, both with and without adaptions. We can do so before and during early practises and drafting exercises. This occurs across all complex reflective practices within complex reflection and CRT. From practical experience, it is possible, and sometimes helpful, to recognise the above cannot be restricted to just being practised as illustrated in Figure 1.3. Complex interplays and non-linearity, akin to neural networking, are more reliable representative descriptors of what can also occur.

Semi-autonomy is both necessary and required in practise. Complex reflection and CRT are not restricted to a relatively simple prescriptive series of feedback processes and phases. With increasing proficiency, we can recognise, in certain contexts, that the phenomena/phenomenon being inquired about, warrant the execution of practises not only from a single boxed action in a single layer, but to a range of actions, across and through multiple layers. Actions, considered by us as adaptive agents in an action-orientated heuristic network of adaptive agents. We also recognise in the patterns and our experiences with complex reflection that sometimes we are required to move across these adaptive agents, damping or extinguishing some, whilst increasing relative power to others. There is not a universal application in the ordering of Figure 1.3.

We also recognise and value there exists a critical spectrum of proactively (forward-planning) and reactively (to a sudden interaction or aggregated emergences). This proactively/reactively active spectrum is required to enable and support any necessary deviation (even if temporary) from our current position. Our complex reflective practices are recognised and valued, varying from relatively simple processes to highly complex adaptive systems, sometimes beautifully creative and innovative; craft-like – technê. This is highly dependent on the proficiency of the practitioner of CRT.

Applying the model of a Complex Reflective Adaptive Actions-Oriented Learning Network in Complex Reflective Technê

We realise the combination of our descriptive approach and Figure1.3. can be adopted and adapted to engage active patterns. These patterns are currently identified in our combined interaction with Kahneman's heuristic system one and system two (see page 25) as well as applying CAS as highlighted throughout this chapter. Some of these active patterns have also been identified by Sultan in her heuristic inquiry approach. We adopt these and adapt them by including what we consider are absent in Sultan's (2019) work. We do so to innovate and germinate our practical schematic model of a complex reflective action-orientated learning network in Figure 1.4. below.

Figure 1.4. shows CRT does not always necessarily have to default to rational or empirical causality, rational or empirical causality is contingent on the complex reflective practitioner's active engagement and proficiency with CRT.[11] Rational or empirical causality may or may not be a phenomenon or phenomena of deliberation within the current niche of the practitioner; rational or empirical causality is contingent on this too.

CAS of interactions between the motivations and attention of a practitioner interact with their semi-autonomy and these in turn interaction with wider embodied niched temporally located, experiencing human being. Again, contingency is active. Furthermore, their phenomena or phenomenon of deliberation may across a spectrum to, may not be, of their personal maximal semi-autonomous choice but may be forced upon them against their own semi-autonomy. Temporarily restricting some of the practitioner's semi-

[11] We now refer to the complex reflective practitioner as practitioner.

autonomy and requiring them to commit and engage in ways and means they need to in the current short or medium-term for potential future or longer-term expectations. Once again, contingency in action. Is the phenomena or phenomenon of deliberation fluid or is it highly fixed with no potential for adaptations to interactions occurring that influence the practitioner, including their broader temporally located and niched semi-autonomous experiencing human being? Or is the highly fixed nature of the phenomena or phenomenon purposeful? Such that its purpose is to bring into their gaze, or change, or enforce something/s, system, or process within the Complex Reflective Practitioner and/or their person and/or their niche? Once more, contingency is clearly and demonstrably highly active.

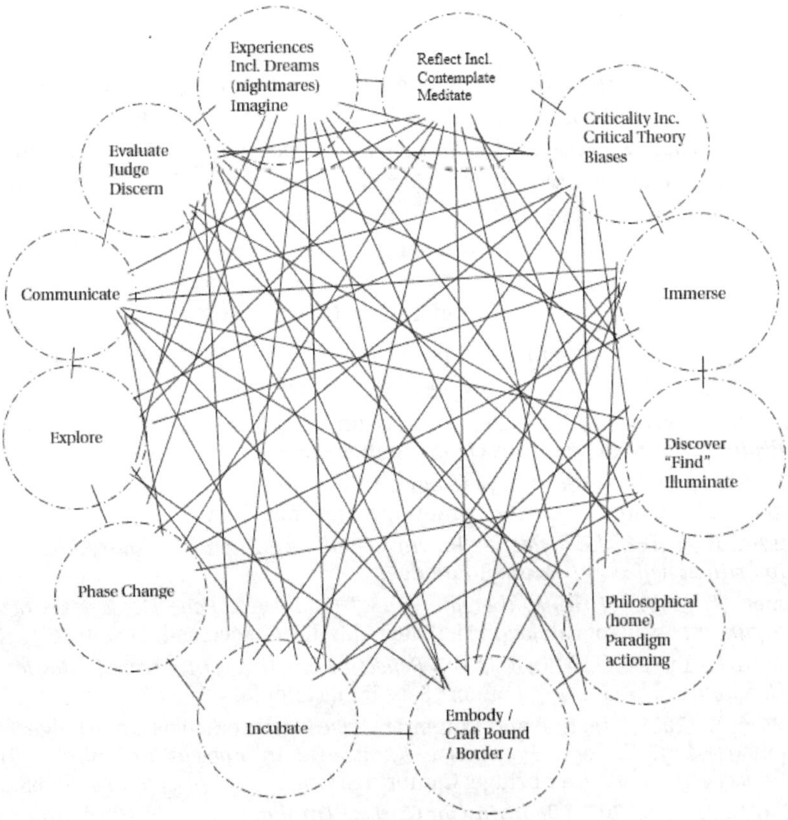

Figure 1.4. Schematic Model of a Complex Reflective Adaptive Actions-Oriented Learning Network

Conclusion

Our chapter has been compiled with the intent to share an introduction, through a brief review of Complex Reflective Technê (CRT). These processes emerge and aggregate an orientational aid, a sketch map (Figure 1.4.) showing how it can start to be applied in practise. We are of the opinion that CRT is sensitive to the experiences expressed by individuals. We are developing, nurturing our process. As we do, we are looking to see its potential in benefitting the spiritual health of individuals.

We ask you to review your attempts at actively applying what you have learned in this chapter by returning to the question we posed at the beginning:

> **"What are some of the complexities of belonging as a spiritual and healthy woman in Britain?"**

What did you learn through your exercises of attempting to actively engage with and apply our introduction to Complex Reflective Technê? When you compare your two answers how do they, if in fact they do, differ? We aim to give more details about applying Complex Reflective Technê in later works with some real-life case study logs and participatory action research (Action Learning Teams) to the question we posed here.

Reference List

Adams, T., Jones, S. and Ellis, C. (2015) *Autoethnography. Understanding Qualitative Research.* New York: Oxford University Press.

Archer, M., Bhaskar, R., Collier, A., Lawson, T. and Norrie, A. (1998) *Critical Realism. Essential Readings.* Oxon: Routledge.

Ash, M. G. (1998) *Gestalt psychology in German culture, 1890-1967: Holism and the quest for objectivity.* Cambridge University Press.

Bassot, B. (2016) *The Reflective Practice Guide. An Interdisciplinary Approach to Critical Reflection.* Oxon: Routledge.

Bauer, N. (2021) *"I think, therefore I am" Explained. René Descartes' Cogito Argument.* Available at: Jacob N. Bauer – Medium. Accessed: 1/6/2022.

Bolton, G. and Delderfield, R. (2018) *Reflective Practice. Writing and Professional Development, 5th Edition.* London: Sage Publications.

Bolton, R. (2021) "Technê and Empeiria. Aristotle on Practical Knowledge." In Johansen, T. K. (ed.) *Productive Knowledge in Ancient Philosophy. The Concept of Technê.* Cambridge: Cambridge University Press, pp. 131 – 165.

Brookfield, S. D. (2011) *Teaching for Critical Thinking. Tools and Techniques to Help Students Question Their Assumptions.* San Francisco: Jossey-Bass.

Coffey, A. (1999) *The Ethnographic Self. Fieldwork and the Representation of Identity.* London: Sage Publications.

Descartes, R. (1968) *Discourse on Method and the Meditations.* Translated from the French by Sutcliffe, F. E. London: Penguin Books.

Fook, J., Collington, V., Ross, F., Ruch, G. and West, L. (2016) *Researching Critical Reflection. Multidisciplinary Perspectives.* Oxon: Routledge.

Hartwig, M. (2007) *Dictionary of Critical Realism.* Oxon: Routledge.

Holland, J. (2012) *Signals and Boundaries. Building Blocks for Complex Adaptive Systems.* Cambridge, MA: MIT Press.

Holland J. (2014) *Complexity. A Very Short Introduction.* Oxford: Oxford University Press.

Ignatius of Loyola. (1914) *Spiritual Exercises of St. Ignatius or Manresa.* Translated from the Autograph by Elder Mullan. New York: Pantianos Classics.

Ignatian Spirituality (2022) *Discernment of Spirits.* Available at: Discernment of Spirits - IgnatianSpirituality.com. Accessed: 12/6/2022.

Johns, C. (2017) *Becoming a Reflective Practitioner, 5th Edition.* Chichester: John Wiley and Sons.

Kahneman, D. (2011) *Thinking Fast and Slow.* London: Penguin Books.

Lahav, R. (2018) *Philosophical Contemplation. Theory and Techniques for the Contemplator.* Hardwick: Loyev Books.

Lawson, H. (1985) *Reflexivity. The Post-Modern Predicament.* Reprint. London: Hutchinson.

Mezirow, J. and Associates. (2000) *Learning as Transformation. Critical Perspectives on a Theory in Progress.* San Francisco: Jossey-Bass Inc Publishers.

Mezirow, J., Taylor, E. W. and Associates. (2009) *Transformative Learning in Practice. Insights from Community, Workplace and Higher Education.* Hoboken: Jossey-Bass Publishers.

Moon, J. (1999) *Reflection in Learning & Professional Development. Theory and Practice.* London: Kogan Page.

Moustakas, C. (1990) *Heuristic Research. Design, Methodology, and Applications.* London: Sage Publications.

Njeri, G. (2012) *Discernment: An Ignatian complement to Aristotle's Virtuous Action. Beyond Aristotle.* Saarbrücken: Lambert Academic Publishing.

O'Brian, K. (2022) *Ignatian Contemplation: Imaginative Prayer.* Loyola Press. Available at: Ignatian Contemplation: Imaginative Prayer – IgnatianSpirituality.com. Accessed: 13/6/2022.

Orsy, L. (2020) *Discernment. Theology and Practice, Communal and Personal.* Collegeville: Liturgical Press.

Priest, H. (2019) *Biases & Heuristics. The Complete Collection of Cognitive Biases and Heuristics that Impair Decisions in Banking, Finance and Everything Else.* London: Amazon.

Rich, A. (2007) *Discernment in the Desert Fathers. Diakrisis in the Life and Thought of Early Egyptian Monasticism.* Milton Keynes: Paternoster.

Rolf, G., Freshwater, D. and Jasper, M. (2001) *Critical Reflection for Nursing and the Helping Professions. A User's Guide.* Basingstoke: Palgrave MacMillan.

Schön, D. (1987) *Educating the Reflective Practitioner.* London: Jossey-Bass.

Schön, D. and Rein, M. (1994) *Frame Reflection. Toward the Resolution of Intractable Policy Controversies.* New York: Basic Books.

Simon, H. (1981) cited in Holland, J. (2014) *Complexity. A Very Short Introduction.* Oxford: Oxford University Press.

Society of Jesuits. (2022) *Discernment.* Available at: Discernment | The Society of Jesus (jesuits. global). Accessed: 12/6/2022.

Stegmaier, W. (2019) *What is Orientation. A Philosophical Investigation.* Translated from the German by Mueller, R. G. Berlin: De Gruyter.

Sultan, N. (2019) *Heuristic Inquiry. Researching Human Experience Holistically.* London: Sage Publications.

Thompson, S. and Thompson, N. (2008) *The Critically Reflective Practitioner.* London: Macmillan International Higher Education.

Throne, R. (2019) *Autoethnography and Heuristic Inquiry for Doctoral – Level Researchers: Emerging Research and Opportunities.* Hershey, PA: IGI Global.

Chapter 2

The Trickster Priest and the Gift of Non-Belonging for Ordained Women in the Church of England

Sharon Jagger

York St John University

Abstract: On the 12th of March 1994, 32 women were ordained into the priesthood of the Church of England. However, many in the Church remained opposed to the ordination of women and, to help prevent schism, the Church's structure was split to accommodate those who wished to avoid the ministry of ordained women. Parishes may vote to only accept the ministry of male priests and to seek oversight from bishops who have never ordained a woman. In 2020 The Church of England's Ministry Statistics reported that over 33% of those in ordained ministry were women, however:

> [t]here were 590 parishes in which a resolution under the House of Bishops' Declaration on the Ministry of Bishops and Priests had been passed at the end of 2020, accounting for 4.8% of all parishes. (2020, p. 32)

It is evident that the battle for parity and acceptance continues, and after 30 years of women's ordination into the Church of England, Sharon Jagger's research suggests that female priesthood is constructed as problematic by institutional discourse and structure, and that the notion of an exclusively male priesthood is protected and legitimised. She argues that the Church's structure, originally known as *the two integrities*, is experienced by ordained women as masculine domination (Bourdieu, 2001), which keeps female priests in a state of theological and doctrinal precarity and liminality. Whilst many women priests are resistant to, and challenging of, theological positions that undermine their ontological existence, this research highlights stories of gendered power being exercised at multiple levels of the organisation, manifesting as *ambivalent sexism* (Glick and Fiske, 2011). Drawing on interviews with 26 female clergy in the Church of England, Jagger explores their relationships with male clergy who do not accept women's ordination and how women priests often play a *trickster* role, (Hyde, 2008) to subvert and challenge the boundaries that prevent full belonging. The question explored in this chapter is whether women can shape their own belonging in the priesthood of the Church of England to circumvent the structural liminality in which they currently reside. Ultimately, Jagger suggests that belonging in the priesthood of the Church, since its maleness has not been deconstructed, is not a goal for women priests. Rather, non-belonging is a gift that yields a far richer and more creative religious experience.

Keywords: Act of Synod, (non)belonging, Church of England, clergy, discrimination, feminist, gender, heretical, hierarchy, institution, liminal, misogyny, ordination, power, priest(hood), sexism, sexuality, theology, tradition, trickster, two integrities.

***

Introduction

How people belong in the Church of England has, in recent years, become the focus of discussion both inside and outside the institution. The Church faces multiple challenges to its institutional discourses and positioning around sexuality (Ledbetter, 2017; Shepherd, 2018), race (France-Williams, 2020), trans and nonbinary identities (Beardsley and O'Brien, 2016), class and regionality (Rooms and Wort, 2021), and elitism that shrinks the boundaries of belonging (Brown and Woodhead, 2016). Rosi Braidotti's (2013) notion of the zero degree of difference helps us to understand the construction of an ideal norm of the White, heterosexual, middle-class male, a norm that creates degrees of otherness as people diverge from these characteristics. My proposition is that the Church of England is an exemplar of how this norm is reproduced through theology, doctrine, and structures. The Church has periodically responded to criticisms of its barriers to belonging – see, for example, the Church of England publications; The Pilling Report, 2013, which discusses the Church's response to issues around sexuality; and From Lament to Action, 2021, the latest response to evidence of institutional racism in the Church. However, work to make the Church inclusive at an institutional level is seriously stymied. Since the inclusion of women in the priesthood in 1994, the Church has perpetuated a structure that allows ordained women to be treated differently to male clergy and theologies and doctrines that construct the priesthood as exclusively male are given institutional legitimacy. The impact of the Church's systemic gendered discrimination on how women priests belong is the focus of this chapter. I also wonder whether the goal of belonging for women priests needs to be reconfigured and I explore below whether forms of non-belonging are more fruitful and creative than they appear at first glance. I agree with feminist theologians who have misgivings about the basis on which women enter the priesthood and who argue that clericalism has dubious masculine foundations; while it remains un-deconstructed, women would be wiser to avoid being drawn in (see, for example, Radford Ruether, 2011; Althaus-Reid and Isherwood, 2007). However, my task here is not to rehearse these anti-clerical arguments, but to tease out how belonging in the priesthood is troubled by gender and how women priests re-calibrate what belonging means.

My research has developed from a curiosity about how women clergy manage their relationship with the Church, given the institution's official and unofficial gender differentiation and discrimination in the priesthood. As a young, active, and committed member of the Church in the 80s and 90s, I observed (and more importantly, experienced) how femaleness and femininity are constructed through theology, doctrine, and institutional discourses. Open discussions about women's incompatibility with the priesthood did not sit easily with my developing feminist worldview. Daphne Hampson's (2002) journey to post-Christianity made a significant impression on me and I borrow from her in establishing a post-insider critical viewpoint in my research. The theme of belonging therefore has personal ramifications; for me, belonging to the Church of England was problematised by being female and working class. As I reflect on my own experience, I suggest it is unsurprising that the theme of belonging has come to dominate my research with ordained women in the Church of England. The stories of lived experience I have collected suggest that for women, belonging in the priesthood is complex, and made contingent at structural, social, and individual levels.

I conducted 26 semi-structured interviews with ordained women over a period of a year.[1] The participants were self-selected and at various stages of their Church careers, including a deacon waiting to be ordained as a priest and two retirees. The majority had parish experience, though some had moved into chaplaincy work. I did not aim to establish a representative sample of women priests in terms of theological traditions; however, such alignments became an important feature in the analysis. Just over half of the cohort identified as Anglo-Catholic, with the remainder split between evangelical-leaning and what is commonly referred to in the interviews as *middle-of-the-road* (suggestive of a more pragmatic and flexible approach to theology and doctrine). These positionings are highly significant when exploring

[1] All names have been changed for anonymity and confidentiality.

definitions of belonging. Anglo-Catholic beliefs about the priesthood focus on ontology and sacrament (raising the question, for example, of whether a woman can represent Christ), which form the basis of the structural arrangements that differentiate women clergy. Within the context of these traditions, belonging can be talked about in terms of status, institutional boundaries, and the discursive; in other words, belonging is dependent on where the power lies to name and affirm who is a priest and who is not. Belonging can also be discussed as part of the affective economy (Ahmed, 2004), how and whether women priests feel they belong, something which is fluid, but nonetheless an important part of their lived experience, and some of my discussion alludes to the emotional as well as the structural. I explore both aspects of belonging below with specific reference to the Church's structure, but women priests also negotiate everyday social micro-barriers to belonging because of their sex. Several studies involving women priests explore the gendered environment of the Church and identify ways sexism is systemic (see, for example, Bagilhole, 2006; Page, 2014; Robbins and Greene, 2018). Projects such as "Eva's Call" (Davies, 2018) – an art installation made up of sexist comments made to women priests – give voice to the chronic misogyny women encounter, made more visible because they are priests. My research reveals that whilst women priests wrestle with sexist symbolic, social, and discursive practices that compromise their belonging, they are ultimately faced with a fundamental differentiation at the structural level, whereby the Church legitimises discourses and theologies that construct women as differently human to men.

Whilst belonging for women priests is problematic in multiple ways, in this chapter, I focus on how the structure of the Church creates liminality for women priests and how they often find themselves at the margins of the Church. This non-belonging bears a cost for women clergy; however, I also argue that being in liminality is a fruitful place from which symbolic and social change can be activated. Equally, operating at the margins of the Church, though not a comfortable place to be, can produce novel praxis and creative thinking. Moreover, women priests, I argue, must be subversive as they negotiate a place in an institution and symbolic order that continually creates doubt around femaleness in the priesthood. To frame and explore instances of subversion, I use the trickster archetype as a thinking tool (for a methodological explanation, see Priyadharshini, 2012). I discuss below the ways women priests negotiate marginality and precarity, with the last section devoted to the Trickster Priest – an imaginative framing of women priests who find ways of bending, breaking, and dissolving boundaries. Before examining the specific stories from my research, I will briefly explain the trickster archetype and its symbolic usefulness.

Carl Jung (2016) describes the trickster as a pan-cultural mythical character allowing a reversal of hierarchies, boundary-play, and shapeshifting. Paul Radin (1956) and Lewis Hyde (2008) point to the trickster's creativity to emphasise how culture is stretched and developed in new ways, generating social change from chaos and disruption. Trickster myths, whilst often described in masculine terms, employ gender fluidity to cross boundaries and to create new identities, making the archetype useful for deconstructing gendered hierarchies. For the purposes of this discussion, I lean on Ricki Tannen (2007) who applies the trickster archetype to women challenging boundaries as outsiders and who operate in marginal spaces. She suggests women with trickster energy are serious and purposeful about rebellion, rather than enacting the more chaotic mischief credited to the archetype; indeed, women priests are (perhaps in involuntary ways) revolutionary because their presence disrupts and overturns a dominant ideology, which might explain the continued resistance to their presence in the Church. Women priests do suffer in their non-belonging, as my research indicates (such as stalled career progression). However, I want to explore how cheating boundaries, seeking unorthodox positions, and shape-shifting their way around the structure and culture of the Church means that women priests are actively generating change, not in spite of their non-belonging, but because of it. The twist in the narrative is that the trickster does not seek to belong to the aggregated whole at all but disrupts the very concept of belonging. The trickster's tools include irony, the ability to juggle internal and external dualities, and the freedom that liminality allows; belonging is not necessary. The trickster is most at home in the in-between spaces that offer a useful outsider's perspective. Whilst some trickster motifs can be dark, bringing chaos and disruption, the trickster is also a liberatory figure. Most interesting for this discussion, is Jung's suggestion that in some forms the trickster has an "approximation to the figure of a saviour" (2016, p. 206) and this may become important to grasp for a declining institution like the Church of England. As I discuss the ways women priests do not belong in the priesthood, I weave in the trickster perspective to challenge the project of belonging; perhaps women priests do not seek belonging but are generating new liminal communities as alternative destinations.

The Liminal Priest

The vote in the Synod, the Church of England's governing body, that finally allowed women into the priesthood, succeeded by the narrowest of margins in 1992 (Furlong, 1998). The closeness of the vote and the strong resistance to women's ordination displayed during the preceding years of campaigning are signs that the controversy surrounding women's presence in the priesthood was unlikely to dissipate swiftly or easily. One bishop in favour of women's ordination highlighted the dominance of the male "tribe" after the entry of women into the priesthood (Selby, 1998, p. 78) and my research shows that the opposing voices, albeit in a minority, still have a significant impact on how women priests belong institutionally, socially, and symbolically. The divisions over women's place in the priesthood run deep, but the Church has reified these divisions within its structure, creating an environment where women are made to feel that the "whole difficult situation was their fault" (Furlong, 1998, p. 5). Messages that frame women clergy as the villains of the piece keep the issue live. Warner, a commentator against women in the priesthood, claims female priesthood is the causal factor in the tearing of the fabric of communion with the universal Church, the unravellers of the weft and warp of the Church's tapestry, something which is "very ominous" (2015, p. 8). The collective guilt that women priests are expected to carry is damaging, but the trickster generates chaos ultimately for the purposes of renewal and change. The guilt may be undesirable for women priests, but perhaps the disruption is not.

To accommodate women in the priesthood, the legislative process – the Act of Synod – created significant structural change in the Church. The goal was also to allow male clergy and their parishes who remain in opposition to women's ordination to avoid the ministry of female priests and to have episcopal oversight from bishops who have never ordained a woman – they came to be popularly known as *flying bishops* (see, for example, Butt, 2011). This parallel structure means that women priests are currently excluded from working in 590 parishes or 4.7% of the total number of parishes (Church of England, 2020). Authors who critique the Act of Synod highlight its focus on amelioration for a wounded minority who cannot accept women as priests, rather than providing unequivocal belonging for ordained women (see, for example, Percy, 2017). The structural arrangement was known as the *two integrities* and remains, in my view, the most significant barrier to belonging for women in the priesthood, not least because it attempts to give legitimacy and parity to beliefs that frame the priesthood as exclusively male. Alice, one of my interviewees, is a priest who is angry about how ordained women are framed as destructive and how the naming of the structure obfuscates the discrimination against women priests:

> That word "integrity". The appropriateness of the word integrity. As if there is equal integrity in both systems. As if that position has an integrity. As if they are the keepers of the tradition and we are the evil destroyers, usurpers.

Efforts to construct the part of the Church that rejects women priests as an equally legitimate alternative structure creates for Alice a powerful discourse that frames the female priest in negative terms. Her objection reveals the fear that the institutional protection given to those who oppose women's priesthood supports and legitimises a claim to male ownership of tradition, meaning women priests in their novelty assault a set of truths. As an Anglo-Catholic with an investment in the same tradition that is being shaped around the male, Alice is cut off from the source of her belonging. Tradition, significantly, is used by some to discern God's will for the Church and for Alice, to be seen as outside tradition, indeed, a usurper of tradition, is deeply alienating.

The structure now permanently supports the position of those opposed to women's priesthood, creating a situation of "apartheid" (Furlong, 1998, p. 8) and for some, it is "the institutionalisation of sexism par excellence" (Shaw, 1998, p. 18). The story of women's entry into the priesthood is, then, characterised by the "ambivalent invitation" to women priests (Walrond-Skinner, 1994, p. 7) and "the frostiest welcome imaginable" (Furlong, 1998, p. 17). Women priests I interviewed offered a more nuanced vision of their integration into the Church, but their everyday lives are punctuated with the need to negotiate the discourse of division and institutional wounding that women's ordination inflicts. These women's stories also reveal intense theological and pastoral creativity as a reaction to compromised belonging, an example of how, according to Jung (2016), destruction and creativity are two sides of the same coin for the trickster. It is only through a process of breaking and disrupting that women have been able to enter the priesthood, creating new space for the feminine within a paradigm previously entirely dominated by the masculine. In this sense, belonging may not be good for women priests, or ultimately the Church; rather the challenge generated by non-belonging makes possible the deconstruction of a brittle masculine system of thought.

There is irony, then, in how the two integrities were designed to protect the notion that the priesthood is ontologically and theologically male, yet it creates deconstructive potential by placing women priests into structural liminal space. Liminality, according to anthropologist Victor Turner, means being held at the boundary as "threshold people" who are "betwixt and between the positions assigned and arrayed by law, custom, conventional, and ceremonial" (Turner, 1969, p. 95). Liminal space is ambiguous, without the "consummation" or "aggregation" provided by the full passage through a process of claiming a legitimised new status (1969, p. 94). Ritual process is designed to resolve such liminality. Yet, despite going through the rite of ordination, women are not fully received as priests across the whole of the institution of the Church of England; there is something faulty in this ritual for women. Often, explains Turner, those in liminal spaces are regarded as "dangerous" and "polluting" (1969, p. 108) and in my research, women priests describe a discourse of pollution that circulates in some parts of the Church and how some male colleagues believe presiding women priests deconsecrate the altar. Liminality is made more complex by these discourses because even in spaces where women's priesthood is accepted, women still experience acts of rejection – such as congregants refusing the bread and wine blessed by a woman priest presiding over the Eucharist. Being placed in this liminal space makes belonging problematic; however, if the trickster priest can achieve a newly conceived type of belonging through subversive means, liminal space is the most creative of places where new common values are developed and shared (Tannen, 2007). Whilst life in liminal space can be challenging for women priests, I offer an exploration below into ways trickster energy derived from such non-belonging is brimming with potentiality.

The Marginal Priest

Marginality for the Church is made virtuous by some theologians (Rooms and Wort, 2021), who interpret the diminishing relevance of institutional Christianity as exile with Biblical overtones – divine purpose and spiritual capital are to be found at the margins of society. The obvious problem with this imagery applied to the Church of England is that its marginalisation is, in part at least, due to its own alienating practices and beliefs that reproduce White heterosexual male hegemony, increasingly out of step with social attitudes in the UK (that the Church is exempt from UK equality legislation is an indicator of this). Moreover, the Church produces its own internal margins, which require similar interpretation as holy places – a fractal-like image of margins within margins is attractive, but this alone does not challenge the structural discrimination of women priests. However, the idea of the margins being creative spaces for those alienated from the centre of power has trickster potential. Some women priests consciously work at the margins of the Church, both in terms of pastoral work with others who also see themselves as on the edge of belonging, and in terms of the symbolic margins that accompany unorthodox thought. For Sara Ahmed (2017), marginality is sometimes created by the undermining push of the orthodox crowd, a movement difficult to see and resist, and I will expand on this dynamic in the next section. Though the push to the margins may come from external forces, exploring the stories gathered during my research about what it means to be, and feel, marginal, I detect a space-creating dynamic.

As with liminal space, marginal space is where trickster energy can flourish because it brings with it the ability to develop a wider set of meanings. Dale Spender (1985) argues that occupying marginal space gives women an advantage over the male dominant group who have limited scope for meaning-making within their own, unchallenged, worldview. Marginal spaces may also provide an alternative sense of belonging: belonging as subject rather than object is not conferred by an externalised structure or set of rituals (which I have argued do not work effectively for women priests). The space-creating potential of marginality is, for some women priests, centred around the re-configuration of outside-ness into spiritual capital, a form of empowerment. Denise, a priest from a middle-of-the-road tradition, views working at the edges as social activism:

> That's a passion of mine. Marginal voices. Maybe because I've struggled, and I've fought, I've fought for other people and maybe I'll do that for all my ministry.

Rooms and Wort (2021) describe how developing belonging is challenging for church communities and that some people live in ways that do not fit into the Church's institutional practices (such as homeless people). Such groups of people fall into marginalisation, but sometimes find ways of establishing their own worshipping communities in which belonging is not contingent on particular social norms, but on shared marginality. For Rooms and Wort, supporting such groups at the margins is given spiritual capital. So, other people's marginality is a way for Denise to work with a self-confirmed legitimacy at the edges of the Church and this conscious move towards marginality re-orientates her towards rhizomatic voices, away from the (masculine) centre of gravity. Denise's comments reveal how women priests can stand in for all marginalised groups that have been othered by the androcentric Church, her female otherness is a proxy for all otherness. Tannen's (2007) description of the female trickster emphasises the social work that often lays at the heart of significant rebellion – this is not the same as aligning to socially constructed ideals of femininity (such as women as nurturers), but rather a leveraging of the energy and freedom found at the margins to benefit a wider community as well as assisting the journey to self-actualisation. The developing of a new set of communal norms creates a new place in which to belong and non-belonging within the institutional structure becomes less important. Trickster work is both social work and political work.

Whilst trickster social work can revolutionise how people belong, we should remember that this energy is created out of the pain of rejection when identities are constructed as varying from the ideal norm. Another of my interviewees, Carol, is a priest who is openly gay and sees herself operating at the margins, undertaking emotional labour on behalf of others. She tells me that "someone's got to be there" for those whose sexuality is constructed as a barrier to belonging in the Church. Carol's sense of marginality is only obliquely related to her sexuality and her gender and is tinged with perplexity:

> I feel a bit marginalised I think, and it's never been clear to me why that is.

The Church's heteronormative discourse (see for example, Church of England, 2017), is not explicitly named, but such discourses operate in the affective economy – Carol feels marginalised. However, her reluctance to name her marginality as the result of heteronormativity and the differentiation of women priests may also mean that she internalises the causes of her non-belonging as an individual problem rather than a systemic one.

For some women priests, the margin is a place where they are at ease, not least because it creates space to express priesthood in ways that do not conform to the masculinised hegemony. However, it is also a precarious place because the spiritual capital women see in these spaces is not valued in the same way by the institutional centre of power. Natalie, a priest who describes herself as being middle-of-the-road theologically, is concerned that her own work at the margins of the Church is being eclipsed by evangelical movements that "get bums on seats". She wonders if her work is in jeopardy because it does not conform to traditional models of religious production. She is dubious about how honest the Church hierarchy is about institutional imperatives being privileged over certain types of ministries:

> I think my question to [the hierarchy of the Church] is whether the ministry that people like me have, and presented to the Church twenty years ago, is still valid. And that question is live for me.

Natalie is clear that she does not want to label her less visible ministry as a typically female ministry – she refuses the stereotypes that it suggests. However, the evangelical mission-oriented movement in the Church, which she sees as being privileged because of the financial weight it brings (to reduce 'institutional panic' as she sees it), is "a big takeover of evangelical boys". Natalie might resist having her ministry identified as gendered, but there is a palpable threat from a type of ministry that is perceived as gendered, potentially harnessed to negative attitudes to the female place in priesthood.

The Precarious Priest

Liminality and marginality are spaces that are at once threatening and creative for women priests, with the potential to develop new meanings around belonging. At this point, I want to introduce another plot twist in this belonging narrative – as women priests navigate the waters of liminal and marginal space, they are caught between the *Scylla and Charybdis* of permanent non-belonging and precarious temporary existence. The longevity of the two integrities, and the continual ordaining of male priests who reject women's priesthood, implies an institutional desire to maintain the status quo. There is a sense of permanency around the structural liminality I have described above. None of my interviewees talked about overt campaigning against, or public complaining about, their structural discrimination (which has propelled me to explore the hidden ways women priests subvert the two integrities) and so, from my cohort at least, there is no direct internal pressure being put on the Church to change its arrangements. Whilst liminality appears permanently embedded, there is also a discourse of temporariness regarding female priesthood; the notion of reception (Avis, 2004). Until the doctrinal rightness of female priesthood is agreed more widely by the Christian Church (in particular the Roman Catholic Church), so the argument of reception runs, women's priesthood cannot be viewed as permanently accepted in the Church of England (though my argument is that women are not accepted at a structural and symbolic level). The creation of female bishops has not, for some, established a principle of permanence for the woman priest. One commentator emphasises: "there is no reason to believe that the ordination of women to the episcopate in the Church of England will bring to an end debate about the rightness or otherwise of such ordinations" (Podmore, 2015, p. xv). Polly, an evangelical vicar in her 60s, recognises reception as a cyclical argument that preserves the two integrities:

> I think there's a train of thought that this is just for the, you know, time being. What do they call it? Reception. But the worst thing that they did was after 1992, they should have insisted that those people who came forward for training would accept that they would have to work with women colleagues. And they didn't do that. So, they've divided training courses and colleges that are women-free zones and they're allowed to say.... and it's got worse with the bishops, about who puts hands on whose head.

Polly lives with the everyday discomfort the reception discourse brings and understands the double jeopardy of permanent "women-free zones" and the precarity of temporariness in the context of the wider Christian Church. The reception discourse stretches the boundaries of liminal space. Even if the two integrities within the Church of England were dismantled, there may be yet another threshold at which women must wait for full acceptance. The sensing of this precarity and the awareness that women priests are continually being discussed as anomalous, or a problem for the Church, is significant, since it affects how women priests feel about their belonging. Women priests are required to accept women-free zones as part of the price of their entry into the priesthood, and at the same time, they are aware that the discourse of reception threatens their status, as differentiated as it is.

Polly and several other interviewees point out that by continuing to ordain men who reject female priesthood the institution feeds the two integrities. Reception of women clergy within the Church of England is therefore delayed indefinitely; the institution is simultaneously seeking and preventing reception through its structural organisation. The desire to protect the male priest who does not accept female ordination creates a perverse struggle to ensure that both integrities are regarded as having equal legitimacy and in so doing creating precarity for women priests. The swirl of undermining discourses that keep women both in permanent liminality and in a precarious temporariness, are entirely gendered and it is difficult to see how women can find belonging without significant deconstructive work in the institution. I suggest some of this work is now being done by women priests who consciously trouble theology and doctrine, perhaps because non-belonging allows space and freedom to play with being non-orthodox. A brush with the concept of heresy stirs the creative potential of liminality and marginality.

The Heretical Priest

To talk about belonging for women priests in the Church of England is not simply a question about how they are able to move around the structure or challenge a *stained-glass ceiling* (Sullins, 2000). How ordained women negotiate their own belonging from a position of structural liminality and active marginality opens up the possibility that meaning-making in the priesthood does not rely on belonging in the same way as for male clergy. Ahmed's (2017) notion of the push of the orthodox crowd is especially potent in this context; value is placed on sharing a set of beliefs as part of the process of belonging and where these beliefs cannot be shared (or it is undesirable to share them) there is a social push to the margins. Women priests may find that the freedom liminality brings to challenge what is regarded as orthodox results in further marginalisation. Several women I interviewed identify strongly with Anglo-Catholicism and give especially vivid accounts of attachments to groups which shared in this tradition. And yet, within these narratives are stories of how women cannot fully belong where their sex challenges orthodoxy. Wendy, as an Anglo-Catholic priest, laments the separation from doctrine because she is a woman:

> Part of me would love to actually be able to say how wonderful Apostolic Succession [the uninterrupted male line of spiritual authority

> passed from the Apostles through bishops] is, that's my high church bit. But actually, I can't because it doesn't work for me, obviously.

She realises being a woman priest means she is unable to subscribe to some doctrines that are part of the tradition in which she claims her belonging. Women priests are required to eject some shared beliefs and symbols that are the source of their rejection, and this potentially frees women to challenge more generally. For some, women priests embody heresy; Tracy, a curate in the North of England, was told by a relative that female priesthood was "heretical". If a woman's claim to priesthood can be framed as heretical then she is surely free from obligations to orthodoxy. In my research, many of the interviewees expressed a rejection of the Church's stance on issues such as human sexuality, for example (and undoubtedly, many male clergy do the same). Another example is how some women make efforts to mine the symbolic potential of menstruation at the altar, which produces radical somatic theology. Alice, for example, wonders about the potential of menstrual blood serving as a feminine Eucharistic symbol. Operating from liminality forces women in the priesthood to think beyond orthodoxy. The cost may be further alienation from the aggregated whole, but some women priests are undeterred. Karen develops a somatic theology based on her motherhood and describes this as "incredibly dodgy". Una, with a middle-of-the-road theology, would like to open up the doctrinal dimension of the Church to include a broader range of beliefs, but immediately labels this as "probably heresy". Valerie, an Anglo-Catholic curate, whilst exploring what a female transfigured Jesus might mean for her sense of femaleness, asks (rhetorically) "is that utterly heretical, do you think?". Valerie plays the trickster priest by adding that she does not see the Bible as infallible and (light-heartedly perhaps) wonders if she risks being "thrown out of the Church of England". Using the word heretical flags up the possibility of subverting the liminal position by inferring a resistance to belonging to orthodoxy – there is a strong possibility that women priests do not wish to belong to a heteronormative masculinised symbol system but are seeking to generate a community which shares beliefs outside the Church's official doctrinal life. Such anti-orthodoxy is a mark of the trickster (Priyadharshini, 2012). The above comments from interviewees suggest a sense of playing with the notion of being outside orthodoxy to make sense of femaleness in the priesthood and in the Christian symbol system and my argument is that this becomes more possible when belonging to the masculine paradigm is no longer sought.

Perhaps a more fluid term for the female challenge to orthodoxy is heterodoxy. There is subversion in heterodoxy and as Ahmed (2017) argues, to dissent from orthodoxy is a wilful, feminist act. Such a description may surprise some of the interviewees in my research, who do not all align themselves with a feminist position (though some do). There are suggestions in feminist theology that orthodoxy is an inhibitor of inclusivity (see Greene-McCreighton, 2000) and so the struggle over difference takes place between the borders of orthodoxy and non-orthodoxy, another liminal space. Women priests like Valerie see orthodoxy as narrowly male-owned formulations that are actively differentiating the female priest. Heterodoxy is a way of challenging this hegemony, and by embracing heterodoxy and weaving an identity that does not require belonging, some women priests are creating spiritual capital at the margins. However, there are still yet more obliterating discourses that threaten the ontology of women's priesthood at a symbolic level and whilst women priests are being creative in theology and ministry, they must still negotiate those beliefs, and the accompanying praxis, that construct the priesthood as exclusively male.

The Fake Priest

I have discussed above how liminality, marginality and precarity are barriers to belonging for women priests, and at the same time, I am exploring how such non-belonging can generate meaning and a rhizomatic community of voices outside the formal boundaries of the Church. We now need to consider how the ontology of female priesthood is obliterated. Many women priests must continually face contexts where they are not recognised as priests by those in the Church who remain convinced of the divine intention that priesthood is male. As I have hinted in the discussion about the structural arrangements of the Church, there is power in the hands of the individual male priest to declare women as non-priests. Boundaries of belonging are drawn according to these individual beliefs. In one parish, a woman is a priest because the Church has ordained her, but in the next parish, she may not be recognised as such – and this disseminated power to reject the validity of a woman's ordination creates a peculiar existential situation where, not only is belonging troubled, but the ontological reality of women priests is made dependent on who observes them as (non)priests. Revd Judy Stowell (2019) has explained this situation for ordained women using the well-known allegory from quantum physics:

> We live in an environment that suggests we are perhaps "not quite" priests. I have often thought of us as Schrödinger's priests – like the cat, one day the box will be opened, but until then, it is perfectly OK to believe both that we are priests, and that we are not.

Several women priests I interviewed explained how they negotiate this power of individual male colleagues to place women outside the boundary of the priesthood and how women are required to bolster their status against theological discourses that disavow female ordination. For those at the Anglo-Catholic end of the theological spectrum, beliefs about the ontology of priesthood mean that some can claim female priesthood does not exist, since God has not participated in the ordination ritual to create ontological change. This pushes women beyond liminality, into a zone of non-existence, since the ritual is stripped of meaning and power to become an empty set of gestures. Women priests are dogged by this existential doubt. Alice, as an Anglo-Catholic, explains how she is surrounded by male clergy she believes see her as a fake priest:

> I think identity is a big thing.... particularly the men in my deanery who are not affirming of women's ministry. Although they are never unkind to me, there is, I know it, I know that they think that what I'm doing is made up almost.

The denial of the ontology of women's priesthood, even if it is a minority view, deconstructs the female priest into woman and non-priest. One of the key elements in Alice's story is that there is an alienation that is unspoken – she feels it and is conscious of it, but because she is not subject to outward hostility there is no hard edge against which to resist. The discourse of dubiety is silently at work and male clergy do not need to display open hostility for Alice to feel undermined. The sense that Alice's priestly actions are constructed as "made up" chimes with Tannen's description of the female trickster; women priests are at the crossroads of culture "cloaked in the appropriate drag" (2007, p. 3). This is an apposite description for the woman priest, who is simultaneously at the centre of change and occupying liminal space, taking on the performative appearance of the male priest and challenging the ontological meaning. Drag has been used as a shorthand for objections of some women priests to the masculinised look of priestly clothing (Oliphant, 2016). But the term also captures how the ontology of female priesthood is controlled by external forces to form women clergy as non-priests in priest's clothing, acting out a male-priest role.

The women I interviewed are resilient (and trickster) enough to bend and dance and play at the boundary of belonging. However, I detect in some stories a deadlock at the point a woman's vocational calling is questioned. Being called may not begin as a gendered discourse, however, as Greene and Robbins (2015) argue, the call to a religious vocation for a woman generates gendered meaning, as it contributes to her tendency to accept discrimination and institutional difficulties – and could be described as a "sacrificial embrace"

(Peyton and Gatrell, 2013, p. 86). A calling to a vocation is understood as prosocial, consuming, and arising out of a passion, though there is a darker side to the "psychic cost" of a calling (Madden, Bailey, and Kerr, 2015, p. 867). The psychic cost of women's calling is accentuated by conflict between the consuming nature of the draw to the priesthood and the burden of how women priests are made to feel shame and guilt about feeling such a call. When a male colleague believes God does not call women to the priesthood, how can women's calling be explained? Is it imagined or a form of deceit? The denial of a woman's call to ordination is not an uncommon event. When Pauline, at the start of her journey to priesthood, went to a male priest to say she had been called, his reply was: "No, you haven't. Have you thought about being a nun?". The accusation that she has heard incorrectly, invented her vocation, or is lying, is a significant weapon to use, since the anchor for many women priests is their faith in the rightness of the call and their trust that the Church recognises it. Although women priests have been through this process of legitimisation, the call remains a front on which women priests must defend their status. The undermining of a woman's call to ministry is heavily gendered since it is based on gendered beliefs about the priesthood. Individual men who believe they have been called to the ministry may not always have this call affirmed, but this would never be because of their sex.

The stories in my research about women encountering denial of their calling highlight the confusion and contradiction generated, both for women themselves and for men who struggle to reconcile their theological position with the working relationships they have women priests. It is poignant that some women experience the denial of their calling through collegiate relational interactions. In our interview, Wendy explains that she feels such denial is an attempt to separate her, in her femaleness, from a contract between her and God:

> The thing that got me the most was someone said, they were saying, "Oh your vocation isn't.... God hasn't given you this calling to the priesthood." They were sort of questioning my vocation, even though I'd been through three years of discernment, three years of training, the Church of England had recognised my vocation, but they were saying, "No, God hasn't called you to this." That was the hardest thing. Not so much the biblical arguments, which I don't agree with, but I can accept their integrity, their belief. But when someone says to you, "God hasn't called you to this" that was it, really.

To be called to the priesthood is the last word in validation for women priests and for Wendy it is an inviolable position, regardless of the beliefs that uphold the Church's split structure. Wendy is unable to accept the contradiction: the

Church recognises her call, which should make it an unquestioned aspect of her belonging, yet other clergy can legitimately deny this call. Not only does she see it as a personal attack on her integrity, but it jeopardises the discourse relied on by women to secure their priesthood status, whereby the divine call overrides erasing theologies and doctrines. There is a history of "negative space of female calling" in the religious context (Berkelaar and Buzzanell, 2015, p. 162), whereby female calling is afforded less worth than that of a male. Yet a calling is a device by which a woman priest might elevate herself (see Madden, Bailey, and Kerr, 2015), despite the institution holding her in liminality. When a woman's call is denied, as in Wendy's story, its worth – important even if it is complicated by gender – is destroyed. Even if women were willing to spend their time and energy engaging in theological and Biblical discussions with those who do not accept their priesthood, the denial that women can be called to the priesthood leaves them without solid ground from which to speak with authority. It is a device that obliterates belonging and one made more powerful because of the Church's desire to create legitimacy and parity for beliefs that exclude women from the priesthood. The confusion around belonging for women priests is created because a woman's call to the priesthood is recognised and legitimised by the Church, yet the structure itself continues to equally deny the call that women lay claim to. In this sense, I am arguing these denial events are not micro-aggressions that individuals must negotiate but belong to a systemic and structural disavowal of female priesthood. It is the ultimate conundrum that women priests experience: that the Church both legitimises their call and legitimises the power to deny it.

The outright denial of a woman's call causes pain and alienation, but some women experience more confusing encounters when male colleagues who oppose women's priesthood are willing to affirm an individual woman's call, a cognitive dissonance that is difficult to understand. Several interviewees tell this type of story, expressing puzzlement over how these two opposing positions can be held. It may be worth noting that two approaches are described by women in my research. Some male colleagues explain to them that if the Roman Catholic Church ordains women, this would be considered a rightful change of doctrine. Others maintain that it is more fundamentally and ontologically impossible for women to become priests. Still, other male clergy, more likely to be evangelical in their theology, hold that it is a biblical principle that women should not hold authority over men. Women priests are required to negotiate these nuances. Regardless of these differing rationales for women not belonging in the priesthood, if a male priest believes generally that women should not or cannot be priests but acknowledges that an individual woman can be called to the priesthood, his continued opposition in institutional terms is contradictory and makes no sense. The alternative is to admit that the male priesthood is a (male) human construction and is therefore entirely open to change. Fiona, a priest who runs several parishes, describes her confusion over how a male colleague can hold these two notions together:

> He doesn't theologically believe in women priests.... He went, "I know you're called by God." So, if he knows that, and he does know it, then why are they making these rules that only men can do it. It just all doesn't make sense... I really don't understand it. Once they got to know me, they're like "Yeah, we know you're called by God." Well, if that's the case, let me get on with it!

Whilst they can hold a general belief that the priesthood is male, Fiona discovers that male clergy can present contradictory beliefs about her calling because they know her as an individual. She is treated as an exception to a general rule. This may offer some relief and enable male and female clergy to work together on an individual basis, but it does not challenge the structure of the Church nor the general discourses that prevent women from fully belonging in the priesthood. When a relationship yields recognition of a woman's call to the priesthood, it is a gendered experience since a male priest does not need his call to be bolstered because his maleness does not create doubt. This contradictory positioning of some male clergy holds further precarity for women who rely, at times, on the generosity of male clergy. Alice, as part of the Anglo-Catholic community, enjoys spiritual patronage from oppositional male clergy, but begins to explore how this apparent contradiction – the belief in the maleness of the priesthood and the acceptance of an individual female priest – is possible, yet unfathomable "I didn't think those two could exist together and maybe on one level they can't.". There is also emotional labour involved for women as they process the contradictions in which they are asked to play a part. As Fiona's comment above suggests, women clergy can feel as though barriers are put in their way which are then negated privately by those who work to support the two integrities to keep themselves officially separated from women in the priesthood. Perhaps, in this instance, male clergy are using trickster strategies to cushion themselves from accusations of sexism, whilst being a more invisible part of the mechanism that keeps women liminal.

In Hyde's (1998) analysis of trickster methods, he observes that the trickster defeats immortal enemies by exploiting the vulnerability of the opponent's joints. Working with this analogy, the juxtaposition between the supportive male priest or bishop who holds on to theologies that reject female priesthood is a joint, an articulation that holds relationships together within a discriminatory context. The trickster metaphor helps us to position the woman priest as someone who can prise open the joint by illuminating the contradictions to which she is subject. A male priest who denies the subjectivity of the female priest can have warm and supportive relationships with female priests, and the woman priest can reciprocate – although in this reciprocation she is ready to reveal the discomfort that discriminatory theology generates in both male and female clergy. This joint work is powerful because it reveals rather than hides how women priests are held in liminality, and the important characteristic is that it operates through relationships. Louise, still in her training period as a curate, describes her relationship with a bishop who opposes women's ordination:

> but he's been very helpful, very supportive.... he has got a very good reputation from the women clergy. I don't know how he squares the circle himself personally, but he does it very effectively, being a bishop. He didn't take part in the ordinations of deacons or priests, but he was there and came bounding up at the peace and gave me a hug.

Personal support and affection are offered to Louise by the male bishop, who refuses to ordain women. The warmth around the relational is disconnected from actions and beliefs that deny her priesthood. A dissonance rings through Louise's relational experiences and she picks up the idea that there is a vulnerability at the joint between theological beliefs and relationships – she does not know how "he squares the circle" or how he is able to maintain both supportive and undermining positions articulated through relational interaction. Since Louise is completely aware of this set of contradictions, the joint begins to creak.

Louise's narrative brings out an interesting contingency in relationships. She understands that it is the Anglo-Catholic shared view of tradition, doctrine, and sacrament that acts as an entry point, the joint at which to work. She is in an interesting position: her femaleness finds resistance along the hard boundary of the two integrities, and her Anglo-Catholic beliefs differentiate her along the more pliant boundary of ecclesiology – and this is where she works on her belonging. Within this tradition, she believes there is scope for integrating the female priest:

> I remember this vicar saying.... one of the reasons why people in this tradition are wary of women priests is because they associate it with a certain liberal, very un-liturgically minded strand, and when they meet a woman priest that doesn't fit that mould and shatters that stereotype, things begin to shift.

Louise, because of her alignment with the Anglo-Catholic tradition, invested in liturgy and not "liberal" in the sense that doctrine is easily overturned, believes she can help influence attitudes. Importantly, it is the sharing of Anglo-Catholic beliefs in ritual and tradition that allows her to experience warm comradeship, support, and guidance helpful to her career from the very men who do not accept her priesthood theologically and ecclesiologically. There is more to Louise's story, since she has identified how "things begin to shift". Her ability to negotiate the boundary between the two integrities, to find some form of integration because of shared Anglo-Catholic beliefs, takes a surprising – and very trickster-like – turn.

The Trickster Priest

Using the trickster archetype interrupts the inclination to see belonging to the priesthood as the principal feminist goal for women priests; non-belonging may yield a richer and more liberating experience of ministry for women. In this vein, I see significant trickster energy at play at the boundary between the two integrities, whereby women priests can enter the space where their priesthood is rejected to do the joint work discussed above. Stepping over the boundary between the two integrities is not the same as belonging to the space, and it seems to require a temporary adjustment to how a woman priest presents facets of her identity. The space where women priests do not exist – because male clergy do not believe they can exist, given institutional legitimacy – is reminiscent of Mary Daly's (1978) discussion of toxic male caves. Her advice is that women should not linger too long in those spaces to avoid being subsumed into the masculine paradigm. To clarify, as discussed above, the spaces in the Church where women are not accepted as priests are toxic in the sense that they disavow women's place in the priesthood by constructing female as differently human in relation to the divine. But if we see these women-free zones as penetrable through subversive means, we can also trouble the power held over women by male clergy who reject women's ordination. Women are operating from liminal space and rather than seeing this in terms of lack and being stuck, I want to explore how trickster magic can happen, as women bend the boundary and find gaps through which to make raids into forbidden territory. Two stories, shared with me by Louise and Olive, both of whom are Anglo-Catholic priests, show the possibility of defeating the boundary in surprising, subversive ways. However, the price is that both Louise and Olive must diminish aspects of their identities to journey across into the opposing integrity. Things are left behind at the threshold.

As I have explored above, Louise's story focuses on how she cultivates a sense of belonging within the community of Anglo-Catholics. Seeing Anglo-Catholicism as a set of strong bonds, Louise uses her sense of attachment to the tradition to shift focus from the gendered character of the boundary between the two integrities to the non-gendered boundary of ecclesiological belonging, where she shares important beliefs about sacrament and liturgy. As an Anglo-Catholic, Louise understands she has more in common, theologically and ecclesiologically, with a bishop who will not ordain women than with her diocesan evangelical bishop who is theologically at ease with women's ordination. She is, though, aware that at times she is required to diminish her femaleness to facilitate some form of belonging along these lines. Not all male clergy in her tradition reject her priesthood, but the shadow of the two integrities requires Louise to see her femaleness as a site of contention, and for the sake of group cohesion, she finds it is collectively minimised. Whilst she is positive about relationships with male clergy who do not accept her priesthood, she is also aware of knotty contradictions as she negotiates the homosocial character of the group:

> I tend to band together with the Catholics, even though they're mostly blokes and actually, some of them don't accept my orders. Weirdly they seem to be able to perform an act of cognitive dissonance and see me as one of the boys. It's really odd. It's really, really odd. And if you start to think about it too much you.... it's simpler, because we've, even though we've got one thing that we differ very greatly on, in other ways where we're coming from is more similar. And I find that continuing tension of my ministry, particularly when it comes to church politics and questions, what my understanding of what happens at the Eucharist is much closer, probably pretty identical to .... Bishop North's [a bishop who does not accept women's ordination], you know it's a lot more in common with that than with the area bishop who is an evangelical. So, there's that oddity too.

Here, Louise is on the edge of something startling "if you think about it too much you...." Suspending the analysis of her position helps Louise to cross the boundary and she is willing to embrace the messiness and illogicality of the way she is perceived in the group where she belongs and does not belong simultaneously. She expresses the discombobulation – I use this word to capture the sense of shame and confusion – caused by being separated from the group because of gender yet drawn in because of shared beliefs. Yet this is a push/pull dynamic that complicates belonging, but also provides the energy behind Louise's own agency in carving out a type of belonging that blurs the boundary set up by the two integrities. By emphasising how she relates to Anglo-Catholic doctrine and theology, Louise can find a form of conscious belonging that still exposes the vulnerable joint – the cognitive dissonance that she sees. If she allows herself to fully explore the implications of her positioning, that some male colleagues believe the priesthood to be exclusively male, she may experience an unravelling in how she belongs to the Anglo-Catholic group (another form of precarity). This self-censorship, not just in speech and action, but in thought, may ensure she can hold in tension her priesthood and her femaleness whilst she dances around the boundary.

I see in this story the trickster device of shape-shifting as Louise allows herself to be perceived as one of the boys. However, we should remember that the labelling is done by those who are unable to accept women into the priesthood, and to cope with the conundrum, women priests like Louise are knowingly being fluid about identity. Another priest, Wendy, also Anglo-Catholic, recognises this shape-shifting as something that is external to her "the people who would look at me as maybe an honorary man would be the people who wouldn't recognise my priesthood". Male clergy treating women priests as one of the boys or an honorary man is an attempt to align the woman priest to the male-as-norm, whereby the degrees of difference are deliberately blurred to ensure there is fit of sorts. In Louise's case, this is for the benefit of the group, but it is also a way for women priests to achieve a sense of place.

The splitting of Louise's femaleness and her priesthood as she moves across the boundary of the two integrities may cause tension in her ministry, but Tannen (2007) suggests that such dualities held by women are useful. These inner contradictions can act as separate trickster characters, as though they are independent parts of the woman priest, and I wonder if this describes Louise's ability to put aside femaleness to become *one of the boys*. But I also wonder if the tension caused by the priest/woman duality is ameliorated by the ideological communitas (Turner, 1969 [2008]) of Anglo-Catholic tradition. I am borrowing Victor Turner's concept here to propose that the bonds created by shared practices and beliefs overcome (though do not eradicate) gendered boundaries; the flow experienced in Anglo-Catholic ritual provides strong, momentary communal connections. Communitas provides a gap through which the trickster priest can cross the boundary, and it allows some women priests to be subversive by their very presence in a fraternity. As Louise explains, the Eucharist is a pivotal ritual and communitas – the fellowship of numinosity – temporarily masks gender differentiation. Shedding femaleness could also be an act of rebellion against enforced status as a woman priest, where femaleness is the basis of liminality. Are women priests burdened by the continual emphasis on their sex? For women, the shape-shifting trick that suspends acknowledgement of gender relies on compromise and does not sit easily within some feminist perspectives. For French feminist philosopher Luce Irigaray (2002), the masking of sexual difference is at the heart of the masculine paradigm to which Christian thought has contributed and only by embracing the feminine divine and by abandoning masculine monotheism will sexual difference be revealed to produce subjectivity for women. The downplaying of femaleness in Louise's story is a manifestation of the more general denial of sexual difference in the paradigm described by Irigaray (and from this standpoint, femaleness must be recognised and elevated, but this is impossible for women priests given the current shape of the institution of the Church). But because Louise is conscious of the process of hiding sexual difference, she illuminates it – as a joint – and what is illuminated can be deconstructed. Of course, being one of the boys is not a panacea, but a temporary trick and at some point, the woman priest must confront the non-belonging that is generated by some aspects of ecclesiology.

The story above is an example of how femaleness is put to one side to cross the boundary between the integrities. Another trickster strategy is to temporarily shape-shift into a non-priest. Olive is a priest who holds a senior role and was invited to act as deacon (a role that does not have priestly authority) by a male colleague who does not recognise her as a priest. Olive agreed since the relationship is warm and cordial, indeed loving, and she sees no harm in undertaking the role in a church service. Using the trickster thinking tool, I argue that she holds on to her femaleness, but leaves her priesthood at the threshold – a reversal of Louise's strategy. Olive enters a space where she is not recognised as a priest and acts out her non-priesthood:

> I actually get on quite well with a number of people who are Forward in Faith [an umbrella organisation for those who oppose women's ordination] and when we work together, we sort of skip around each other in quite a loving way really. For example, [a male colleague of equal standing] "oh come along", he says. "Come and deacon for me".... I say, "Oh alright, why not?"

The power exercised within the context of a positive relationship leaves Olive as a non-priest. To *skip around each other in a loving way* hints at a trickster dynamic, one like a dance, a mutual set of choreographed movements which allow certain relational moves to veil the boundary's implications. But in trickster fashion Olive treats the character of the boundary lightly, not taking too seriously its implications for her own priesthood. Internally, Olive retains her understanding of herself as a priest but embodies her structural liminality by taking on the deacon role. The trade-off may be the nurturing of the positive relationship, important for women's sense of comfort in the priesthood, but the significant point for our discussion is that Olive is not being accepted on condition that her femaleness is diminished, but on condition that her priesthood is put to one side. The relational aspects of this story are entangled with the power to name a woman as non-priest, as I discussed above, and if Olive were to remain in this space, she would only ever be a deacon with no power to access sacramental symbols. The jump across the boundary can only be temporary. Olive appears to have a resistance to the toxicity of this space where her priesthood is denied and may not consider acting as deacon a risk to her own sense of belonging as a priest. She can act as deacon since she "knows" she is a priest, but shape-shifts to indulge a male colleague. As with Louise's story, however, Olive's account is about femaleness and priesthood accruing meaning in parts of the Church that create incompatibility between the two identities. Olive's compromise could never be experienced by her male colleague since there are no spaces in the Church where maleness is problematised in this way. I wonder if Olive would ever ask him to deacon for her and I wonder what the response would be.

Olive's story is complex and at first glance, it seems that she is colluding with power that seeks to strip her of her priesthood status. Returning to Ahmed's (2017) discussion about how feminist acts can be hidden and subversive, she reminds us that there is the possibility of becoming invested in that which is fought against, and this complex dynamic appears in several stories like Olive's, where women priests are highly invested in the Church and the legitimisation it gives their ordained ministry. Ahmed goes on, though, to provide a helpful exploration of how women might change an institution from within "she might pass as willing in order to be wilful" (2017, p. 83). Some women priests, as in Olive's story, appear as willing in their relationships across the boundary of the two integrities. As I see it, the willingness to act as deacon is not acquiescence, but an act of sabotage against liminality. Olive steps over the boundary by acting out a pretence of being a deacon. The shape-shifting is only superficial. She is passing as willing in order to be wilful.

Conclusion

In this chapter, I have attempted to divert us away from the reasonable feminist inclination to demand the same belonging for women as men in the priesthood of the Church of England. To be clear, I do maintain that the Church's structure is inherently sexist and produces gendered abuses that would be against equality legislation in a secular institution. The Church legitimises and supports beliefs that deny women can or should be priests and frame women as differently human, whilst at the same time ordaining those women. The inability of the Church to unequivocally accept women into the priesthood is an affront to the principles of gender equality and places women priests in an existentially impossible situation. So, my view is that if the Church of England wishes to lay claim to any social justice mission with integrity, the differentiating structure must be dismantled post-haste. For the purposes of this philosophical discussion, however, I am alerted by warnings from some feminist theologians such as Rosemary Radford Ruether (2011), who suggest that the priesthood is not something women should aspire to enter whilst ever it sits, un-deconstructed, in a masculine paradigm. We might, then, be wary of insisting on conditions that allow belonging until we are certain women are not constructed in masculine terms as one of the boys. I describe the boundary-play of the woman priest in trickster terms because she might be thought of as the proto-priest, as the trickster is a proto-identity, one that is capable of splitting into characters and is comfortable on the threshold. The woman priest may still be searching for authentic form, but ultimately, she is seeking ways of being a priest that speaks to her femaleness. The female trickster, for Tannen (2007), refuses to be a victim, but is adept at resistance. My intention has been to show that women priests are subversive in their relationship with the institution and with male clergy, and that belonging is given a new meaning that circumvents the institutional boundaries. Like the trickster, the woman priest often finds herself at the margins, where she aligns herself with other rhizomatic voices, and it is in these spaces that trickster social work can thrive. Women priests are investing in small acts that call for change and that each time a joint – a contradiction, an illogicality, an irrational practice – is illuminated by women priests' engagement, a shift occurs. The discussion in this chapter plots a course into more nuanced territory that, whilst challenging the desirability of belonging to the priesthood, shows liminality and marginality are places where women priests can forge more creative ideas about what it means to belong. The freedom to reject orthodox theologies and doctrines and to establish new praxis that reveals sexual difference, rather than masking it, may not be available if women priests were not liminal. I have used the trickster archetype as a thinking tool to help interpret women's stories from this angle, and it leads me to suggest that rather than seeking to resolve liminality, we should see it as a gift.

Reference List

Ahmed, S. (2004) *The Cultural Politics of Emotion*. Edinburgh: Edinburgh University Press.

Ahmed, S. (2017) *Living a Feminist Life*. London: Duke University Press.

Althaus-Reid, M. and Isherwood, L. (2007) *Controversies in Feminist Theology*. London: SCM Press.

Avis, P. (2004) *Seeking the Truth of Change in the Church: Reception, Communion, and the Ordination ofWomen*. London: T&T Clarke, Ltd.

Bagilhole, B. (2006) "Not a Glass Ceiling More a Lead Roof: Experiences of Pioneer Women Priests in the Church of England." *Equal Opportunities International,* 25(2), pp. 109-125.

Beardsley, T. and O'Brien, M. (2016) *This is My Body: Hearing the Theology of Transgender Christians.* London: Darton, Longman and Todd.

Berkelaar, B. L. and Buzzanell, P. M. (2015) "Bait and Switch or Double-Edged Sword? The (Sometimes) Failed Promises of Calling." *Human Relations,* 68(1), pp. 157–178.

Bourdieu, P. (2001) *Masculine Domination.* Stanford: Stanford University Press.

Braidotti, R. (2013) *The Posthuman.* Malden: Polity Press.

Brown, A. and Woodhead, L. (2016) *That Was the Church That Was: How the Church of England Lost the English People.* London: Bloomsbury Publishing.

Butt, R. (2011) "Archbishop of Canterbury Appoints Flying Bishops." *The Guardian* (Online) Available at: https://www.theguardian.com/world/2011/may/05/archbishop-canterbury-flying-bishops. Accessed: 12/6/2022.

Church of England (2013) *The Pilling Report: Report of the House of Bishops Working Group on Human Sexuality.* London: Church House Publishing.

Church of England (2017) "Marriage and Same Sex Relationships after the Shared Conversations A Report from the House of Bishops." Available at: https://www.churchofengland.org/sites/default/files/2017-12/opiv.pdf. Accessed: 22/6/2021.

Church of England (2020) *Ministry Statistics 2019.* Available at: https://www.churchofengland.org/sites/default/files/2020-06/Ministry%20Statistics%202019%20report%20FINAL_0.pdf. Accessed: 12/6/2022.

Church of England (2021) From Lament to Action: The Report of the Archbishops' Anti-Racism Taskforce. Available at: https://www.churchofengland.org/sites/default/files/2021-04/FromLamentToAction-report.pdf. Accessed: 12/6/2022.

Daly, M. (1995) *Beyond God the Father: Toward a Philosophy of Women's Liberation.* London: The Women's Press Ltd.

Davies, M. (2018) "Churches Accused of 'Institutional Sexism' on International Women's Day." *Church Times.* 9 March 2018. Available at: https://www.churchtimes.co.uk/articles/2018/16-march/news/uk/churches-accused-of-institutional-sexism-on-international-women-s-day. Accessed: 4/6/2022.

France-Williams, A. D. (2020) *Ghost Ship: Institutional Racism and the Church of England.* London: SCM Press.

Furlong, M. (ed.). (1998) *Act of Synod – Act of Folly?* London: SCM Press.

Glick, P. and Fiske, S. T. (2011) "Ambivalent Sexism Revisited." *Psychology of Women Quarterly,* 35(3), pp. 530-535.

Greene, A. and Robbins, M. (2015) "The Cost of a Calling? Clergywomen and Work in the Church of England." *Gender, Work and Organization,* 22(4), pp. 405-420.

Greene-McCreighton, K. (2000) *Feminist Reconstructions of Christian Doctrine: Narrative Analysis and Appraisal.* Oxford: Oxford University Press.

Hampson, D. (2002) *After Christianity.* London: SCM Press.

Hyde, L. (2008). *Trickster Makes this World: How Disruptive Imagination Creates Culture.* London: Cannongate.

Irigaray, L. (2002) "Divine Women." In Joy, M., O'Grady, K. and Poxon, J.(eds.) *French Feminists on Religion: A Reader.* London: Routledge, pp. 41-48. Originally published in *Sexes and Genealogies,* translated by Gill, G. C. (1993). Ithaca: Cornell University Press.

Jung, C. G. (2016) "On the psychology of the trickster figure." In Rothenburg, D. (ed.) *Symposium of the Whole.* California: University of California Press, pp. 206-216.

Ledbetter, C. (2017). "Sexuality and informal authority in the Church of England." *Theology,* 120(2), pp. 112-121.

Madden, A., Bailey, C. and Kerr, J. (2015) "'For this I was made': Conflict and Calling in the Role of a Woman as Priest." *Work, Employment and Society,* 29(5), pp. 866-874.

Oliphant, V. (2016) "Woman Priest Sexes Up Clothing for Women Clergy Fed Up with Looking Like 'Men in Drag'." *The Express.* (Online). 23 May 2016. Available at: https://www.express.co.uk/news/uk/672913/Woman-priest-launch-business-curvy-clothing-female-clergy-men-in-drag. Accessed 13/6/2022.

Page, S. J. (2014) "The Scrutinized Priest: Women in the Church of England Negotiating Professional and Sacred Clothing Regimes." *Gender, Work and Organisation,* 2(4), pp. 295-307.

Percy, E. (2017) "Women, Ordination, and the Church of England: An Ambiguous Welcome." *Feminist Theology,* 26(1), pp. 90-100.

Peyton, N. and Gatrell, C. (2013) *Managing Clergy Lives: Obedience, Sacrifice, Intimacy.* London: Bloomsbury.

Podmore, C. (2015) *Fathers in God?* Norwich: Canterbury Press.

Priyadharshini, E. (2012) "Thinking with the Trickster: Sporadic Illuminations for Educational Research." *Cambridge Journal of Education,* 42(4), pp. 547-561.

Radford Ruether, R. (2011). "Should Women Want Women Priests or Women-Church?" *Feminist Theology,* 20(1), pp. 63–72.

Radin, P. (1956) *The Trickster: A Study in American Indian Mythology.* New York: Schocken Books.

Robbins, M. and Greene, A. M. (2018) "Clergywomen's Experience of Ministry in the Church of England." *Journal of Gender Studies,* 27(8), pp. 890-900.

Rooms, N. and Wort, E. (2021) *Fuzzy Church: Gospel and Culture in the North of England.* Durham: Sacristy Press.

Selby, P. (1998) "Working the Act." In Furlong, M. (ed.) *Act of Synod – Act of Folly?* London: SCM Press, pp. 76-86.

Shaw, J. (1998) "Gender and the Act of Synod." In Furlong, M. (ed.). *Act of Synod – Act of Folly?* London: SCM, pp. 14-26.

Shepherd, C. A. (2018) *Bisexuality and the Western Christian Church: The Damage of Silence.* Cham: Springer.

Spender, D. (1985) *Man Made Language, 2nd Edition.* London: Pandora Press.

Sullins, P. (2000) "The Stained-Glass Ceiling: Career Attainment for Women Clergy." *Sociology of Religion,* 61(3), pp. 243-266.

Tannen, R. (2007). *The Female Trickster: The Mask That Reveals.* New York: Routledge.

Turner, V. (2008) *The Ritual Process: Structure and Anti-Structure.* London: Transaction Publishers. (Originally published in 1969).

Walrond-Skinner, S. (1994) *Crossing the Boundary: What Will Women Priests Mean?* London: Mowbray.

Warner, M. (2015) "In Love and Charity with Your Neighbour." In Podmore, C. (ed.). *Fathers in God?* Norwich: Canterbury Press, pp. 3-15.

Chapter 3

Seen but not Heard: Choosing to Belong

Yvonne Bennett
Canterbury Christ Church University

Abstract: The Church of Scotland has been ordaining women into the ministry since 1969. However, the conservative Presbyterian churches of the *Gàidhealtachd* (Highlands and Islands areas and communities of Scotland) are patriarchal in doctrine and practice. In these denominations, women hold no roles of authority, they cannot be ordained, nor be elders or lead prayer during worship. Yet women can, and do, hold jobs of authority on the island. Yvonne Bennett's chapter examines the way women navigate between the patriarchal church and equality-driven social spheres of their lives.

There are 45 active places of worship on the Isle of Lewis of which 37 are Presbyterian. There is religious freedom of choice for all who live on the island, this includes the right to identify as non-religious. Yet religion impacts those who live and visit the island be they religious or not as the island is one of the last bastions of Sabbatarianism in contemporary Britain.

There are no social penalties for the religious choices women make, but there are social consequences for those who do not uphold the rules surrounding the Sabbath as a day of rest. There are also costs for women of the conservative churches who are judged as not upholding the idealised roles of wife and mother. This chapter will scrutinise women's autonomy with reference to women-only zones and the authority ascribed to women through mission. The boundaries that prevent women having an equal role in the church are not challenged by the women but are reinforced by them, underpinned by creed.

Keywords: agency, authority, autonomy, Bible, Church of Scotland, choice, conservative, family, Free Church of Scotland, Gàidhealtachd, gender, mission, patriarchy, power, Precent, Presbyterian, religiosity, Sabbatarianism, sacred canopy, scripture, shaming, worship.

***

Introduction

Let your women keep silence in the churches; for it is not permitted unto them to speak; but they are commanded to be under obedience as also saith the law.
1 Corinthians 14:34, King James Version
Let a woman learn in silence with full submission. I permit no woman to teach or to have authority over a man; she is to keep silent
1 Timothy 2:11-12 King James Version

This chapter draws upon my ethnographic research on conservative Presbyterian church communities in the Gàidhealtachd. The Gàidhealtachd encompasses the geographical area of the Highlands and Islands of Scotland. However, it is more than just a land mass, it also includes the history, culture, traditions, language, music, and religious beliefs of the Gaels, the indigenous peoples of the area. My research focussed on women's autonomy when belonging to a patriarchal religion.

The participants lived in two communities on the remote Isle of Lewis.[1] The first community is a church congregation in the main town of Stornoway, the second is a small rural church community, a five-minute drive from the town. The churches that serve both groups are of the Free Church of Scotland denomination. The church in Stornoway is a new church, established in 2014 following a schism from the Church of Scotland over the ordination of gay clergy. Data were collected using semi-structured interviews and observations over a period of three years. Participants included those in the communities who identified as non-religious. My final fieldwork trip, planned for April 2020, was cancelled due to the Coronavirus pandemic.

Lewis lies off the northwest coast of Scotland and is the largest of the islands that make up the Outer Hebridean Archipelago. The island is, in my view, truly beautiful; from its white sandy beaches to the peat bogs that stretch as far as the eye can see. It is very exposed thanks to its flat terrain, and as a result, gales can prevail at any time of year. Thanks to the winds few trees grow on the island and few floral tributes adorn graves. Stornoway, the main Lewis town, is closer to Bergen in Norway than it is to London. Flights and sailings to and from the island are often cancelled due to storms but are no longer banned by Sabbatarianism. The Hebridean islands are perceived as being the last bastions of Sabbatarianism in Britain. After much protest, Sunday flights began in 2002, with Sunday sailings delayed until 2009.

[1] From this point it will be referred to as Lewis.

Traditionally the main industries were fishing, crofting, and weaving. Today, people are still employed in these industries, but these are now, in the main, second or part-time jobs.

Lewis has a combined population of around 19,658 of whom around 81% identify as white Scottish.[2] Lots leave the island as young adults for university or employment, many return later to raise their own children.[3] The majority of those who participated in my research project were from the indigenous community, with only one person, L., identifying as an incomer. The island has 45 active places of worship of which 37 are Presbyterian. There is one Roman Catholic Church, and a Mosque.[4] Women can hold no role of authority within the church, yet some hold positions of authority within their working lives. I was interested to discover how they rationalise these polar positions, especially as they have chosen to belong to this particular Presbyterian denomination. A significant amount of existing research on female inequality and religion focuses on Islam and Judaism, both in Britain and America. There is scholarship which examines Mormon women and the emphasis placed on the idealised roles of mother and wife (Leamaster and Bautista, 2018) with my research findings showing many similarities with their work. Within this chapter, I will discuss why women chose to belong to this conservative denomination and the way they navigate between the equality-driven social sphere and patriarchal church sphere of their lives. I examine the importance of Biblical authority and the sense of security belonging to a church congregation brings to many. Belonging in this chapter places the emphasis on identity and strength (Chin, 2019).

Patriarchy, Power, and Authority

I was drawn to Johnson's work (2005) where he used the image of a tree to describe patriarchy and the ways in which individuals relate to, challenge, and uphold it. The roots of the tree represent the core of patriarchy and because roots run deep it is difficult to challenge them. The trunk represents social institutions such as the church. The branches are our social groups and

---

[2] Population data is from 2011 Scottish Census.

[3] A large proportion of those leaving go to Glasgow. The city traditionally employed Gaels in shipbuilding, nursing, and teaching.

[4] In August 2018 the island saw the opening of a mosque. This has been controversial with the Free Church of Scotland opposing planning permission. The mosque serves Muslims from all the Outer Hebridean islands, although the majority live on Lewis. The island has been a part of a resettlement programme for Syrian refugee families, with an aging population, Lewis needs more families to move to the island.

our families. These are the ways in which we interact with the trunk and, ultimately, the roots. The leaves are us as individuals, nourished by the roots. Johnson wrote:

> [w]e can't avoid participating in patriarchy. It was handed to us the moment we came into the world. But we can choose how to participate in it. In this sense we are far more than passive leaves on a tree, for human beings think and feel and most importantly, make choices through which we either perpetuate or challenge the status quo. (2005, p. 19).

The women who participated in my research all made choices re belonging to a patriarchal religious congregation, the majority of which perpetuated the status quo.

Yet contemporary Scots live in a society that strives for equality between the sexes, with laws in place to prevent sexual discrimination. Between 2015-17 women led the three main Scottish political parties.[5] The more liberal Church of Scotland has been ordaining women since 1969 with four women being elected Moderator of the General Assembly, Dr. Alison Elliot being the first to hold the post in 2004.[6] When compared to the Church of England, the Church of Scotland has been at the forefront of clerical equality in Britain. What is of interest is that, despite this religious equality, no Church of Scotland congregation on the island has engaged a woman minister. My research suggested that the patriarchal aspect of the churches has its genesis not only in scripture but in the traditional patriarchal *clan* system.[7] The notion of men governing continues to this day with all councilors of the *Comhairle nan Eilean Siar* (Western Isles Council) wards, as well as the island's MP and MSP being

---

[5] From 2015 -2017 all three main political parties were led by women. Ruth Davidson was head of the Scottish Conservative Party, Kezia Dugdale, head of the Scottish Labour Party and Nicola Sturgeon, head of the Scottish National Party, SNP.

[6] The Moderator of the General Assembly is the minister or elder elected to chair the annual General Assembly of the Church of Scotland's Synod. Following this they spend a year as the symbolic head of the church.

[7] The word clan is from the Gaelic word "clann" or "clanna" for children. It describes a close-knit group of relatives. Clans were hierarchical communities who lived in the Highlands and Islands of Scotland. As well as kinship and a sense of identity and belonging, being part of a clan was an important part of survival throughout many troubled centuries.

male.[8] It is here that we can see the entanglement and entrenchment of religious and social traditions within the Gàidhealtachd. Patriarchy is being upheld by theology, doctrine, and cultural traditions.

As I analysed the interview transcripts, I explored the intersections between power and authority and began to understand them as having separate meanings. Authority is held by all men in the congregation, affording them the right to give orders, make decisions, cast judgement, and hand out punishment.[9] It does not afford them the right to direct or influence the behaviour of others, nor determine a course of events; power has the capacity to do all of that (Schüssler Fiorenza, 2006). This differentiation between power and authority relates with Berger's (1967) definition of power. Berger discusses power within society arguing that in this setting, power is coercive as it "directs, sanctions, controls and punishes individual conduct" (1967, p. 11). That the men hold power afforded to them by their positions of authority is not denied, however, I suggest that the women also hold some power, albeit within limited female spheres. This can be self-empowerment or, as will be discussed, can be used against others they see as behaving out with the edicts of their religion. Shaming is a power tool which is used, frequently obtaining the desired results. In this manner, women are empowered as they gain the ability to direct, sanction, control and punish other women, evidence that power does not need physical force. The power of women within conservative religions is limited, used in certain situations, and exercised in specific ways:

> a woman who lives up to the gendered cultural expectations of her religion is using her agency because she is achieving a status that she desires (observant, religious woman), even if these actions seem to restrict her. (Leamaster and Bautista, 2018, p. 143)

The women I interviewed did not see themselves as being submissive to men. It was not men that held authority but God, delivered through the pages of the Bible that gave them status, that enabled them to belong to the church community as observant religious women.

One participant had a different perspective of authority than the other Free Church of Scotland women participants and that was F., a university student

---

[8] MP: a member of parliament within the UK government; MSP: a member of Scottish devolved parliament.

[9] All the roles of authority in the church are held by men, from minister to deacon. However, all men have the authority to lead prayer and *Precent*. Precenting is where an elder will sing the first line of a psalm and the congregation will follow his lead.

living in Glasgow. What struck me most about her interview was the number of times she employed the word *power*, using it ten times. This was not a word that I or any of the other participants, used when discussing patriarchy. The word used in all other interviews was authority:

> There's just a massive sense of power that, with guys in the Free Church. I think it's why I get very concerned for how many young guys want to go to the ministry because it's that power, it's that I don't trust most of them. I'm not gonna lie.

Power, used here in relation to F.'s interview, conjured up, for me, a more sinister understanding; it was not legitimised. This is an example of masculine hegemony used as a control and it has left her with a different perspective, no longer recognising the validity of the patriarchy within the Free Church of Scotland.

However, F. remained an active member of The Free Church, joining Glasgow City Free Church of Scotland. This was surprising as the majority of those from Lewis attend Glasgow's other Free Church, Dowanvale. F. had made a choice based on two factors. Firstly, she could be more anonymous and secondly, this church congregation allows women to Precent the psalms and lead prayers at worship:

> and it was the first time, like when I was trying to decide which church to go to, I went to this one and then, I heard a woman Precent.... and I was like shook, I was like 'I'm staying'. That means I can continue going to the Free Church denomination but still feel like I've like I have control over that. I've got something to kind of contribute.

Glasgow City Free Church of Scotland's practice of allowing women to Precent and lead prayer compares with that of The Inclusive Mosque Initiative (IMI), which began in London in 2012.[10] This initiative "accepts women leading prayer and welcomes people of diverse gender and sexual orientation" (Nyhagen 2019, p. 3). When it comes to a conflict between religious and secular views, individual conservative religious organisations making changes to resolve gender inequality, affords women the choice to remain in their chosen religious denomination. F. remains a communicant of the Free Church of Scotland and this is important to her. She has agency without concession:

---

[10] See http://inclusivemosque.org/about/ for further information on IMI.

> even before I probably knew what the word was, I've always been a feminist. Like, I found it a really frustrating. It's actually why I chose the church even right now, because women actually get to do stuff.

I found her stance energising because, as Sharon Jagger notes "there is a difficult relationship between Christianity and feminism, and at times the [Anglican] Church has contributed to the backlash against feminism as a movement." (2019, p. 39).[11] F. has found a church which allows her to be both a feminist and a Free Church of Scotland communicant. Neither her faith nor her feminist beliefs have altered.

Doing Religion

Orvit Avishai's works (2008; 2016) on gender and agency, focused on American Orthodox Jewish women. I was particularly interested in her work on the ways in which women within conservative religions *do religion* in a secular world as this resonated with my own research findings. In both works, Avishai writes of the assumptions made by those outside of conservative religions about the subordination of women. Yet, what she highlights is that women do have a degree of agency, arguing against some feminist scholars who are of the notion that women are "bound by dominant ideological constructs of femininity" (2016, p. 265). These constructs only serve to highlight the perceptions of the dutiful daughter, the good wife and mother, that many conservative religions, including the conservative Scottish Presbyterian denominations, project.

For Avishai, there are three strategies that she argues women use, the first is that they undertake partial compliance. Here there is a gap between the edicts laid down by religious law and actual practise. The second strategy is that of strategic compliance; the woman in this situation is using religious compliance for "extra religious ends" (2008, p. 420). Compliance is entangled with rewards and punishments. The final strategy is noncompliance; within conservative religions this could lead to the woman being ostracised or being shamed into using one of the other two strategies. Avishai's first strategy correlates with Leamaster and Bautista's (2018) work on Mormon women. As with the churches on Lewis, The Latter-Day Saints place an emphasis on women being good wives and mothers. They are encouraged to be stay-at-home mothers. However, many do work, through choice and / or through

[11] Although Jagger was writing about the Anglican church her findings correlate with the findings of this research.

financial need. Leamaster and Bautista (2018) suggest that when this occurs, women overcompensate in their religious practice. They also noted the use of guilt as a control over women in conservative religions. They argued that "religion first induces guilt in women for not meeting gender expectations, and then offers a way to reduce the guilt through religious adherence" (2018, p. 143). In this situation, religious compliance can be viewed as a reward; complete religious compliance removes the guilt of not being a stay-at-home mother. I found examples of all three of Avishai's strategies when I analysed my data. As will be shown in later sections, all the women who identified as religious utilise Avishai's first strategy of partial compliance, no participants chose non-compliance and, interestingly, I, myself use her second.

On evaluating my fieldwork diary, I observed that I too was doing religion. I deduced that I navigated between my social and fieldwork spheres by utilising the second of Avishai's strategies. My response to the patriarchy was to "strategize and appropriate religion to further extra religious ends" (2008, p. 411). From my non-belonging standpoint, I was using strategic compliance, exercising religious observance to minimise my outsider position. When in the field, I upheld the rules surrounding Sabbatarianism. At worship, I took on the female gender-specific role; I remained silent and was led in prayer by men. On further analysis, I concluded that, during interviews, I did not challenge the men on gender inequality although I did challenge the women.

Throughout my fieldwork I did not want to be confrontational as I feared losing the participants. However, this concern was gender-associated, I was not being upfront with the men as I feared losing their support, yet I did not fear losing the support of the women. Throughout this research all the gatekeepers to the communities were men. Gaining and maintaining a good relationship with my gatekeepers was important and I did not wish to alienate them.[12] As I examined my actions, I understood that I challenged the women as I held the preconception that their actions were submissive, and as such, they lacked the power to close my access to the communities. Before I analysed the data from the transcripts, I perceived the women to lack agency. Ironically, by not challenging the men, I was relinquishing a degree of my own

---

[12] During my MA research fieldwork my gatekeeper, a family friend, decided that he did not like the topic of my research, and he "buried" all my questionnaires under paperwork on his desk until it was too late. My research question was "Do religious practices become more conservative as a means of preserving cultural identity in a rural island community when faced with a changing demographic?" I subsequently changed the focus to "Does Fundamentalist Protestantism flourish more in a remote community?" The research was based on the Inner Hebridean Isle of Skye.

agency. I continued to uphold the patriarchy by viewing the men as having the control and seeing the women, myself included, as having none. Examination through a reflexive process revealed that I had held unfounded opinions on which I had based my actions and interactions. By doing religion, I was upholding patriarchal authority, I did not challenge the status quo. I was at pains not to be "the secular other" (Etherington 2004, p. 423). I viewed the deep roots of the patriarchal tree as impenetrable. I wanted, for a short period of time, to belong.

One other way in which women's agency is assured is when the men are removed from the setting. Research has shown that women belonging to patriarchal religious communities form women-only groups (Brasher, 1998; Ibry, 2014; Nyhagen, 2019). On Lewis, there are women-only prayer groups, Fellowship, and women's Bible Study sessions. The Free Church of Scotland also has an organisation, Women for Mission, established over 100 years ago, to enable women to support missions both at home and internationally.[13] The excerpt below shows how much importance the people of Lewis place on mission. In the interview, I was asking L. and her husband A. questions about a special Fellowship meeting held in June 2018. The talk was by a man who had spent ten years in Afghanistan with his wife and three young children on a mission placement:

> **L:** "Yeah. Absolutely, I felt jealous."
>
> **Me:** "About going out to Afghanistan?"
>
> **A:** "Yeah, sometimes it's hard to, it's hard to accept what your [mission] is, you know."
>
> **L:** "because for a long time, my natural desire is to do something big, and exciting, but you know, I've got to remember my whole life isn't.... I've got two wee boys. We've got a family, and that is where, you know, the focus is at, just now, and there'll be time for other stuff."

My analysis of the above excerpt initially saw me make culturally specific assumptions, specific to my own cultural stance. However, I kept in mind that my analysis is not necessarily the participants' analysis (Jagger, 2019). Decisions are made on belief, knowledge and understanding and I am not a

---

13 The aim of Christian mission is to spread Christianity to new converts, both nationally and internationally.

party to all the knowledge the participants hold nor do I share their religious beliefs, therefore, I hold a different understanding. I saw the speaker, as well as L. and A., as thinking and behaving irrationally by placing themselves and their children in danger. For those in the church community, there was a belief that mission, no matter where to or the dangers involved, was a calling from God. L. and A. are waiting for that call, but until then, God has placed them in the important role of parents, their mission is familial.

F.'s reply to my question shows that a call by God to mission is equally important as being called to the clergy. She spoke of her younger sister who had spent a year on a mission before going to university:

> **Me:** "What if a woman is called? Your dad has three daughters, but if you were called?"
>
> **F:** "I mean, I'm never going to be called."
>
> **Me:** "What about your younger sister, if she is called?"
>
> **R:** "Oh, she already is. She's already doing it; she's been on mission. It's just like, I don't know in terms of like, ministry, like, there still isn't really space for it, but then again, I've gone to, like, mission meetings where women have led it. It's like women who have gone on mission and stuff, and they speak about it. Like that's happened plenty."

Once again, my initial judgement was socially specific as I viewed F's sister as having her true calling denied. However, undertaking a mission is not perceived as a lesser calling. Not all men are called to the clergy, the speaker had been called to mission and, as L. and A. explained to me, this is an honour and something they hope to be asked to fulfil in the future. For the participants gender equality was in God's calling; it was situational, differing between upholding the spiritual well-being of the congregation and spreading the message abroad. With mission, women perceive themselves as being given a gender-equal religious position.

I found parallels with the 1998 piece of ethnographic research by Brenda Brasher and her study of women from two fundamentalist Churches in America. Within conservative religions, men always govern mixed-sex groups. F's sister was able to undertake a mission on her own as part of the Women for Mission group. For L. to undertake a mission with A. she would have to wait until he was called. Ibry suggested that women-only groups offer "an autonomous women's sphere" (2014, p. 1272) and belonging confers a degree of agency. Any position of authority held in a women's only group in no way negates the patriarchal authority and governance of the rest of the church. Brasher (1998) and Irby (2014) however found that such groups offer women a place of solidarity. Although in the Free Church of Scotland, women are allowed to lead prayer at women's prayer group meetings, Bible Study is led by the minister. It is he, after all, who has been called by God to deliver the correct theological message.

Because the Bible Told me So

The Biblical passages at the start of this chapter were cited by members of the community as reasons why women's equality finds no place on the pews of the Lewis churches. The quotes below are indicative of the generational transmission of these beliefs:

> Jesus said to women to hold their tongues in church, to keep quiet, it is written in the Bible, and we must follow that. (S., 17, 2019)

> I believed and still do that the reason we have male ministers and elders is Biblical and although I do not doubt that women are perfectly able to perform these roles, the Bible is the source of our beliefs, and we need to remain steadfast and true to the guidance written in it. (J., 75, 2019)

Fundamentalist adherence to gender differentiation as laid down in the scriptures "determines which meetings they can attend, what offices they can hold, and how they are expected to relate to their God." (Brasher, 1998, p. 168). I was interested to discern if women agree with the patriarchy, as to do otherwise would be to question their interpretation of scriptures, such as 1 Corinthians, and make them take a degree of responsibility for their compliance with their lack of authority in the Church (Croatto, 1987; Brasher, 1998; Schüssler Fiorenza, 2006). Is it that the women require a degree of Biblical authority to obtain agency in the religious sphere of their lives? I maintain that by using the Bible as the ultimate authority, the women gain agency; legitimising their decision to belong.

The conservative Presbyterian churches continue to deliver a strong Christian message, demanding adherence to Biblical authority. Iannaccone proposed that the conservative churches have a strictness which benefits them in three ways "they raise overall levels of commitment, they increase average rates of participation, and they enhance the net benefits of membership" (1994, p. 1183). A similar point by Rose demonstrates the benefits of a strict Church, "where worship is highly ritualised...there are strong codes of behaviour or even dress" (2009, p. 35). People know what is expected of them and that brings reassurance. My findings corroborate Iannaccone and Rose's proposals. There were around 150-200 people in attendance at all the morning services I went to. The churches practise intergenerational worship with the pews full of people, from primary school children to the elderly. In the evening, there would be around 100, the majority of whom had been to morning worship. There were further prayer groups and fellowship meetings held throughout the week. I attended the Thursday fellowship meetings, where, once again, attendance was high. Belonging is reinforced by the strength of the church and the doctrine it endorses. Schudson, Beischel and van Anders (2020) wrote of the social aspect of belonging and there is an important social motive through attendance. Although no refreshments are served after Sunday worship, people do stand around chatting before and after the services. At weekday church events, refreshments are served and people can often be found socialising an hour after Fellowship has ended. Interestingly, it was at such social gatherings that my non-belonging to the island was most discernible when people spoke in Gaelic.[14]

The Free Church of Scotland's ministry has been exclusively male since its inception, underpinned by androcentric beliefs about the entitlement to authority as prescribed by the scriptures. The following is taken from the Free Church of Scotland website and exemplifies the Bible as the ultimate source of authority:

> Perhaps the most obvious feature of the Free Church is the centrality of the Bible in all that we do. The Free Church believes that the Bible is the inspired Word of God. (www.freechurch.org)

Despite its insistence on biblical literalism, the Free Church of Scotland takes a particular interpretation of male authority from the Bible, which has also been read in other ways. The Bible has historical and traditional authority in defining the role of women in a religious sphere. It is important to note that female inequality is not specifically mentioned in the Bible. Ward proposed that some of what is written in the scriptures has been taken as absolute, focusing on Paul's teachings on the subordination of women, which have been "read as giving men in general authority over women, and as such have been generally harmful to women" (1999, p. 213). However, as Paul also

[14] Gaelic has always been the language of the Gàidhealtachd. It is not the language of the Lowlanders, of which I am one. Not speaking Gaelic was not a problem as English is the national language with only 2% of Scots having a working grasp of Gaelic.

taught that all should be equal in the eyes of Christ it stands to reason that the subordination of women is unsubstantiated.

Scriptural teachings aside, there may be another reason why women have no positions of authority in the conservative denominations. As the Bible was written using male language for God, Radford Ruether proposed that this may result in "the view that males are more God like than females, that only males can represent God as leaders in church or society." (2002, p. 3). Writing of the ordination of female priests in the Church of England, Aldredge-Clanton pointed out that:

> down through history people have used the Bible to support the status quo…. some of those opposing the motion would say "I believe the Bible is literally true." However, they chose only a few verses from the passage to take literally. So, what they really mean is, "I believe that those portions of the Bible that I believe are literally true are literally true." (1990, p. 15).

Taking a literal interpretation of the scriptures may stop women, such as S. and J., questioning the interpretations laid down over the centuries, thus preventing them from rejecting the guidelines set down by God.

The Bible is an important part of religiosity for those who worship in the Free Church of Scotland. Those attending worship and Fellowship who do not bring their own Bible are in the minority. I made use of a Gideon Bible left in the bedside cabinet of my rental cottage. I did so after my first attendance at Sunday worship as I realised, I was in the minority by not having my own Bible, my non-belonging made visible. Primary school children bring their own copies to Sunday worship. The Bibles belonging to the older members of the congregation appear to be frequently used, with well-thumbed corners.

The participants all spoke of reading the Bible at home, a practice that goes back to the very heart of the Reformation. Luther argued that the Bible offered such clarity that all who read it could understand the edicts from God (Barton, 2019). Today, the messages found in the Bible hold as much relevance for those in Stornoway as they did during the Reformation. It was the Bible that L. turned to when the demands of new motherhood overwhelmed her:

> I'd read like The Baby Whisperer and was like, "It's nice, it's a bit wishy-washy, but it's nice," and Gina Ford [a British author of childcare books] was just a bit too scary, and I was like, "Do you know what? I know the Bible's right; I can't go wrong with that." So, he had this insight Bible has lots of you know, the easy sort of headings, and I thought, "Well, that saves me, sitting and reading passages, because I

> don't understand that." And there was like parenthood, and you know, anxiety and all these sorts of things. And I just started reading it, and I was like, "This is actually quite helpful."

L.'s use of the Bible as a means of support relates to Schüssler Fiorenza's view that "whether as a source of well-being or of a dependence on authority, the Bible is still central in many wo/men's lives." (2001, p. 83). For L. the unwavering message of the Bible eclipsed all secular parenting guides and, at times, conflicting advice.

The church in Stornoway has established youth Bible study sessions where the young people are encouraged to ask questions, debate the scriptures and their meanings. Barna Group's (2015) research into Christianity and Faith in Scotland looked at the importance of the Bible for Millennials. Their findings for this demographic related to my analysis, noting "[a]nother marker of engaged Millennials is how they see the Bible as an indispensable guide to navigating today's complex world" (2015, p. 72). Their findings showed that this cohort read their Bibles regularly with "96 per cent report reading the Bible at least once a week" (2015, p. 72). What also struck a chord with my research is that Barna Group discovered that debating the scriptures with their peers was key to maintaining engagement (Barna Group 2015). It may also be noted that for young adults:

> [m]ore open individuals might be more inclined to question rapture theology (premillenialism) and the supposition that the Bible is free of errors (inerrancy) by examining multiple sources and opposing data. (Bartoszuk and Deal, 2016, p. 150)

I met with a group of teenagers in a café and the group spoke of a book, *Evidence That Demands a Verdict: New and Revised* by Josh McDowell (2004), which they all professed to have read. They told me this book had given them a greater understanding of the Bible by enabling them to read the scriptures in relation to present-day situations. I purchased the book, a weighty tome, but found it difficult to navigate.

From my analysis and observations of this group, it was clear that their study group was using interpretation as a tool for maintaining structures of male domination. I wonder if using a different hermeneutic approach, a feminist exegesis may have granted them a better understanding of the importance of contesting patriarchal authority:

> there is much to be said for reading against the grains of the biblical text and learning strategies that neither deny the presence of texts that

> are violently hostile to women, nor collude with the sentencing of women to generations of destructive behaviour authenticated by institutional authority. (Gilfillan Upton, 2002, p. 110)

Challenging the patriarchy would not necessarily lead to them disposing it. Using a feminist critique may strengthen their views on religious gender inequality. By gaining a different perspective, the girls could be afforded a greater degree of autonomy as they consider the social and historical constructs of the scriptures (Gilfillan Upton, 2002).

One aspect of the Bible being used from the pulpit to endorse the patriarchal aspect of the church community came to light during F.'s interview. She spoke of the way the minister at her church made no reference to women when he preached:

> There are even issues with like even with the language used. Like, so there's a minister in my church, and he's like the least feminist guy I've ever met. Like even in his Bible and stuff when he reads it if it says like men and women in the Bible, he will only read the men part. Either that or he's got no Bible and likes changing it. It's like, yeah, it's just.... I don't know, it's really frustrating.

This minister is not only using the Bible to legitimise the silencing of women in church, but he is actively silencing them in the scriptures. I can only guess the reasons behind his removal of women from his readings. The vast majority of those at worship follow the readings in their own Bibles, so the absence must be apparent. I could only surmise that as women tend to appear as minor characters in the Bible, and are often silenced, any omission goes unnoticed.

The views of multi-generational women that gender roles were laid down in scripture is explored by an essay contained in Stacey and Gerard's work on contemporary Evangelical gender ideology. The essay title *We Are Not Doormats* draws on a direct quote from one of their research participants (1990, p. 98), rejecting the idea that women who belong to conservative religions do so through learned patriarchal submission. Stacey and Gerard argued that although the women were selective in their scriptural reading choices, to belong to a patriarchal denomination was an active choice. The women I interviewed on Lewis had all chosen to either belong to their Church or, in the case of one participant, to leave it.

Research shows that women's lives within conservative patriarchal religions are not necessarily dichotomous (Mahmood, 2012). One must consider that belonging to the Free Church of Scotland does not necessarily mean that a woman has become passive or submissive, it can be interpreted as a form of agency "agentival capacity is entailed not only in those acts that resist norms but also in the multiple ways in which one inhabits norms" (Mahmood, 2012, p. 15). One way in which women gain agency could be by meeting and embracing religious gender norms. As will be discussed, belonging to a Free Church of Scotland congregation appears to be reliant on accepting and portraying specific gender identities.

Idealised Gender Roles

Woman/man gender identity is a prerequisite when one belongs to the conservative Presbyterian Churches. From the start of this research, I was aware of the male authoritarian stance of the conservative Churches of the Gàidhealtachd. However, I was unaware that this encompassed all aspects of congregational life. I attended a fellowship meeting in a village Mission Hall during a fieldwork trip in June 2018. The meeting took the usual form; prayers, led by the men, a short Bible study and a concluding psalm, Precented by an elder. Following fellowship there was an AGM for the administration of the Mission Hall. I had assumed, correctly, that women would not hold a place on the Hall committee; what I had not expected was the women being seen but not heard. Not one woman spoke at the meeting. The following is from my fieldwork diary concerning the AGM:

> No women are involved in any capacity on the board of trustees or holding office. When it came to proposing and seconding matters it was only men who spoke, despite them being outnumbered 2:1. The women were, however, thanked for their tea making and baking skills and two young girls for cleaning skills. The chairman of the committee (an elder) said "we couldn't do that." (Fieldwork Diary, June 5th 2018).

Before analysing this data, I was minded of Jagger's writing that "my critique may not be their critique" (2019, p. 15). I needed to understand their analysis of the situation. L.'s critique, when I mentioned the AGM, was very different from my initial consideration.

> Women play a vital role in the church and have the room to nurture, whilst also being supported by office bearers. I do think some practices are outdated but I think humility is important to realise any service is service to God whether it is tea making, cleaning, or sorting finances and holding office.

L. also mentioned that she found some aspects of the Free Church of Scotland practices to be out of tune with present times, but then justified her compliance:

> With regards to holding office within the church I would say in a worldly sense that would be exactly what I would do and what would be expected. I do it for other organisations, so why wouldn't I do it for the church? However, I believe the Lord has created His church with a structure that is correct, but how it plays out day to day will vary from church to church.

This is an incongruence that Leamaster and Bautista examined during their research with Mormon women. They proposed that although the women acknowledged gender inequality, within the church community, they did not feel it was problematic as the parts /jobs men and women were tasked with were "complimentary and not complete without the other. The gendered expectations were different, but equally important" (2018, p. 9). Leamaster and Bautista (2018) further argue that:

> a woman who lives up to the gendered cultural expectations of her religion is using her agency because she is achieving a status that she desires (observant, religious woman), even if these actions seem to restrict her. (2018, p. 143)

From my time on Lewis, talking to the women and conducting interviews, I have been steadfast in my thinking that the women are not *doormats*, they have agency and own their own religious views. Could it be that those outside the religion are all too keen to see women in all conservative religions as being submissive or as locked in a constant battle with compliance and agency? Walby wrote of those who see it as a battle between subservience and freedom "they see the ideological constructs of the patriarchy as critical to women's subordination" (1990, p. 104) and fail to ponder the social and, I would add, religious constructs that surround actions and interactions.

As individuals in Western society, we have been exposed to, and shaped by, secular and religious norms, be that from our family, community or through our schooling. In my research I discovered that women were using their autonomy to join the church, L., an incomer, had come to the Free Church as an adult, not as a child. She holds a position of authority in her employment and can be viewed as inhabiting a religious space that bears no resemblance to her secular world with reference to gender equality. I am of the opinion that L. is using her agency to uphold religious norms that she views as valuable. Agency is not only situated in conducts that challenge the patriarchy of conservative religions but can also be achieved by upholding these religious norms. For L. the benefits of belonging to a patriarchal church community are greater than any struggles she may have with the finer details of the roles prescribed for her. She appears to compartmentalise the religious and social areas of her life by seeing her roles within the church as, not submissive, or inferior, but as a test. Society has placed her in a position of authority within the workplace, but religion is a test of her modesty and commitment to God. This is something she has freely consented to and not undertaken through allegiance to her cultural identity or through social coercion. This aligns with Mahmood's view that actions that may appear to be submissive and at odds with the secular construct of gender equality can be accepted "if it is determined that they are undertaken by a freely consenting individual who is acting of her own accord" (2012, p. 11).

However, I was left questioning what the women gained from their church roles as responsibility for refreshments and cleaning did not appear to be much of an advantage. One benefit, that I discerned from L.'s interview, may be that belonging to the Free Church of Scotland shields them from some of the stresses of the twenty-first century life. Following the birth of her eldest child, she felt isolated and overwhelmed by parenthood. The following quote offered me an explanation as to why she initially signed up for the Alpha course and the hopes she has for her children:

> I felt nowhere that there was really good in the world, but if there was really good, that had to be balanced out, you couldn't just say there was really good in the world, but there's no evil. There has to be both.... I know this is, right now, this is where we're meant to be, with our children, here, and this has given them a grounding, I think, that will prepare them for life.... you don't have to second guess people.

I was drawn once more to Brasher's 1998 work. She described the religious beliefs of those in her study as being "the sacred canopy that covers congregational life" (1998, p. 11). It is a canopy that shields all those who worship in the Presbyterian Churches. Under this sacred canopy, life reverts to an imagined idealised society. Brasher (1998), Furlong (1991) and Day (2017) all refer to religion as being a bastion of tradition. For the *Generation A* women in Abby Day's study the church "supports the sacred institutions of their day" (2017, p. 38). Brasher wrote that "religious communities generally function to conserve values within cultures, they tend to be harbours of tradition" (1998, p. 169). The sacred canopy may well serve to protect the women and their families from the more frightening parts of the modern world, providing "at least one refuge where everything remains the same" (Furlong, 1991, p. 8).

The world today can appear unsettled, and, for many people, this flux brings insecurity and, at times, fear. The remote communities of the Gàidhealtachd are not exempt from these changes nor these unpredictable times.[15] Karen McCarthy Brown argued that a conservative religion may be understood as "the religion of the stressed and the disorientated, of those for whom the world is overwhelming" (1994, p. 175). She proposes that rationalism promised by Enlightenment failed to give us the meaning of life through science and rational thought. Therefore, conservative religions may offer answers to those who feel disenfranchised by today's secularised societies. On analysing my transcripts, I suggest that what the participants are searching for is clarity and control over their lives and this is what belonging to this conservative denomination brings. I found McCarthy Brown's perspective interesting and one that, if my fieldwork had not been curtailed, I would have further investigated. What I did uncover was that for some of the participants change brings concern. The Church of Scotland's ordination of gay clergy four years ago had led to the founding of the new Free Church of Scotland congregation in Stornoway. Their sacred canopy appeared breached. As I mentioned, many of those who leave the island as young adults return when they have children of their own. All of those I spoke to did so to give their children the same freedoms growing up as they had themselves. They spoke of the safety of living in small communities, where everyone knows and looks out for each other. There is a perception of people searching for what Schudson (2020) refers to as an increase in life satisfaction through belonging. I must add that this applied to those who identified as religious as well as those who did not.

The women of Lewis can gain consistency and support for their values from religion, values such as heterosexual marriage, fidelity, and family. Ross adds a new dimension to the debate on the importance placed on family values and women's religious lives "[f]or the Protestant traditions, marriage was seen by the reformers, particularly Luther, as a real vocation in its own right." (2002, p. 228). In doing so, the tradition of entering a religious order was removed for Protestant women with their role being situated in the home. Yet, for various personal reasons, the women in my research are, or were, employed out with the home. Leamaster and Bautista discovered an anomaly in their findings when it came to women who hold positions of authority in their working lives. They noted that "women whose life status and occupations seemed to provide them with the resources and motivations to oppose gender

---

[15] Two of the victims of the Manchester Arena atrocity were from the Outer Hebridean Island of Barra.

traditionalism actually expressed strong support for gender traditionalism" (2018, p. 9). L. holds a job of status on the island, running a public organisation, yet she expressed strong support for traditional gender roles within the church. In this situation, L. is doing religion by utilising Avishai's first strategy of partial compliance. She also has a sense of belonging in a variety of settings (Chin, 2019), she belongs to her family group, her church group, and her work group. Each adding a dimension to her life.

There is research on women who belong to conservative religions yet do not undertake the idealised role of the stay-at-home mother. Leamaster and Bautista proposed that some of the women they interviewed worked because of financial need and expressed guilt and a desire to fulfil the role of a stay-at-home mother. This related to the Latter-Day Saints Church's traditional gender roles within the family structure where women are urged to "focus on motherhood and family duties above all else" (2018, p. 4). Benton (2014) explained the importance of motherhood from a different perspective "[s]o when motherhood is tellingly referred to as a 'career break', spot the lie. It would be closer to the truth to say that a mother's paid employment is a 'motherhood break'" (2014, p. 20). Burchill carried out research on a similar community to the communities on Lewis. Her research examined identity and religious observance in a rural community on the Northeast of Scotland. She discovered that for her participants, the women who continued to pursue their careers "did so on a part-time basis" (2008, p. 45) fitting work in around childcare.

Although L. and her husband A. spoke of their croft not providing financial stability and the need for them to have other income streams, this was not the sole reason for her being a working mother. She spoke of a loss of identity when she had her first child and her desire to restart her career. Leamaster and Bautista suggested that women, such as L, engaged in "ideological compensation" (2018, p.10). Although they may not conform to a traditional gender role in the home, they compensated by emphasising their commitment to gender inequality in the church. L, during both her interview and a later email exchange, spoke of her belief in the gender roles set out by church doctrine:

> I'm from a generation that understands that all opportunities are there for me as much as the next person.... I've got a job of responsibility, and this is how I manage my team. I also am chair of a board of trustees and again am used to being in a strategic role.... With regards to holding office within the church I would say in a worldly sense that would be exactly what I would do and what would be expected. I do it for other organisations, so why wouldn't I do it for the church? However, I believe

> the Lord has created His church with a structure that is correct, but how it plays out day to day will vary from church to church.

There is one interesting aspect that I noted in L. and A's interview. A. is a Sunday School teacher, a role that usually, as Ross noted "has traditionally been a preserve of women" (2002, p. 226). They also share childcare at home, as do many parents today. Irby raised the notion of men taking on a new form of conservative Protestant masculinity which "represents a domestication of men that creates 'soft patriarchs'" (2014, p. 1274). I suggest that as traditional gender roles at home are adapting with regards to childcare then the roles within the church such as being a Sunday School teacher, are viewed as being open to both men and women. However, what must be noted, is that although men may begin to take on such roles within the church, women cannot take on the men's roles. This research indicates that within the conservative churches, any change will be slow. Change may also be slower in rural communities, where Connell and Messerschmidt found "an increasing subtlety and fragmentation in the representation of hegemonic masculinity" (2005, p. 835). There are more nuanced changes within many domestic settings where social patriarchy is being rejected by both men and women, but this does not transmit into the religious domain of the Gàidhealtachd. The notion of family and heterosexual marriage lies at the heart of conservative churches, and this shapes the gendered lives of those who belong. The soft patriarchs may be more domesticated in the home, but they remain staunch patriarchs in the church.

One evening I attended a Fellowship meeting in the Fàilte Centre, in Stornoway. The minister asked a teenage boy, of around 15 years, to lead the prayer. The lady in front of me was a local doctor. The male/female differentiation was never more apparent, as this well-educated, accomplished woman was led in prayer by a schoolboy. The following afternoon I had the meeting with the young members of the congregation. The two girls and one boy were all in their last year of school. I used this event as a means of opening the conversation around the different roles in the church:

> **S:** "We do have our distinct roles."
>
> **F:** "Yeah. But I don't think it means that we are not valued as much."

Brasher suggested that young Christian women see the religious and secular spheres of their lives as different entities, "[t]o them religious congregations are special sites where different rules apply" (1998, p. 174). The rules within the church community come directly from God. The rules within the secular section of their lives are more ambiguous. The role of wife and mother, as caregiver, is lain down in the scriptures. However, the laws surrounding gender equality in society are man-made. Women who work may use religious compensation to offset a perceived neglect of their caregiver duties. Interestingly, S. took control of the conversation, with A. (the teenage boy) making little contribution unless directly asked. The boy may hold authority under the sacred canopy, but the girls directed the interview that afternoon in the An Lanntair café.

Shaming

One interview highlighted one way some women used their power to maintain social and religious customs on the island. M. had been a member of The Church of Scotland but had left the church as a young adult. She had been living and working on the mainland, before returning to the island in 2014. M. explained that the churches on Lewis were limiting her choices on how she wanted to live her life. This had not been the case on the mainland:

> There's a lot of things here that are, with the Churches here, you shouldn't do this, and you shouldn't do that.

She spoke of one incident that had particularly caused her offence. A friend was visiting from a town on the mainland, and M. put a post on a women's community social media platform asking for recommendations for family-friendly places that were open and served lunch on the Sabbath.[16] She received a lot of posts criticising her wish to eat out on the Sabbath.[17] It is notable that the criticism arose not from the men in the community, but from other women who were vocal in their disapproval. There is research into women being critical of other women within the workplace (Mavin, Grandyland and Williams, 2014; Sheppard and Aquino, 2017), however, I was unable to locate relevant literature specifically concerning women in a social / friendship setting. There are, however, similarities between workplace and social settings regarding prescribed behaviour can be discerned. Sheppard and Aquino's research pointed out that "there are consistent social penalties when women violate prescriptive stereotypes by behaving agentically" (2017, p. 696). M. violated the prescriptive stereotype of a conservative Presbyterian woman by openly challenging the rules surrounding Sabbatarianism. Her social penalty was a public dressing down by her female peers. This aligned

---

[16] I use *Sabbath* as to call the day *Sunday* is seen by those who belong to the conservative churches as demeaning this day of worship.

[17] Some hotel restaurants and cafes at tourist sites are open on the Sabbath. The majority of those who frequent these establishments on the Sabbath are tourists, not locals.

with Brasher's view of "the impressive amount of power that fundamentalist women can wield in their communities" (1998, p. 5). This cohort of women had the power to chastise and to do so on a public forum, using a form of informal social control.

On transcribing the interview tape, I was aware of the emotion in M.'s voice when speaking of the incident. The primary emotion was one of anger; anger at those who restricted her choice and anger with herself for compliance. Anger is an emotion which bears an affinity with shame with Scheff recognising that "one way of hiding shame is to become angry" (2003, p. 11). Shame threatens the social bond and can bring about feelings of rejection and conflict. As with anger, this conflict can be with the wider community, in this case, the women who were chastising M., but it can also be with oneself and self-reproachment (Scheff, 2003). The interaction between M. and the women was played out in a public forum bringing an unknown number of silent observers and possible participants. The threat to the social bond was, potentially, not just between M. and the women, but also between M. and the wider community. Lindores and Emejulu's wrote of "women policing women's behaviour in private space" (2019, p. 48) however social media blurs the lines between the public and the private. Burkell et al.'s research revealed that "online social spaces are indeed loci of public display rather than private revelation... it appears that participants view and treat online social networks as public venues." (2014, p. 974). The advice M. sought in a private social network group was taken public by those who believed she was taking inappropriate action. Her *crime* was exposed to a much wider community invoking maximum chastisement.

Mavin, Grandyland and Williams noted that "negative intra-gender relations between women are one way through which women's subordination and marginalization within gendered contexts is apparent." (2014, p. 441). M. decided against the lunch, so her choice over a social activity had been removed, not by men in authority, but by women using their power. Their power strategy of choice was shaming, a potent tool, which had the desired effect. Shaming was used to regulate behaviour. It stands, without authority, reinforcing behaviours over which formal law has no jurisdiction (Rosenblatt, 2013). To gain a measure of power over other women, Morris pointed out "[w]e [women] too often employ the historically white, Christian, male tactics of ostracism and shaming." (1992, p. 201). I was interested in the reasons behind the use of such a device and considered the views of the intellectual property professor, Betsy Rosenblatt:

> [s]haming may have many motivations, including a desire to impose norms on another, to trigger someone else's shame, or to inflict

> reputation-based punishment. Regardless of the motivation, shaming appeals to community norms and attempts to impose them on someone else. (2013, p. 8).

I offer that M.'s public dressing-down had the dual purpose of serving as a warning to others, and as a means of upholding the patriarchy of the Church. This especially potent threat of exclusion had the desired effect. Theology, doctrine, and cultural tradition bonded together to set community rules and the women were there to police them.

Conclusion

My research shows that women choose to belong to the Free Church of Scotland and in doing so, choose to uphold the patriarchy. Although female agency is limited within the Free Church of Scotland, it is not removed. Women are empowered in female-only spaces and in the roles, they believe God has specified for them. Doing the refreshments or the flowers may not seem to be as important as overseeing the spiritual health of the community, but the women interviewed believe that each role is essential in the maintenance and success of the church. Gender equality has different meanings for different people and in different situations. What was apparent was that the women gained autonomy and could navigate between the social and religious spheres of their lives by understanding religious gender equality as gender difference Women and men had distinctive yet compatible roles with each dependent on the other.

One way in which women validate their lack of religious authority is in their belief of the Bible as the ultimate authority. Through reading the Bible, attending Fellowship, and listening to sermons, people find structure. They are afforded guidance for lived religion with reference to the different gender roles allocated in church. Their critique of women holding no position of authority, their understanding of women being seen but not heard is not through male superiority, but because God has deemed it thus. Yet the Bible is not just relevant in religious belief and practice. As noted by some of the participants, the Bible gives assistance in problems experienced in their everyday lives. It is situated at the core of lived religion, becoming an extension of the sacred canopy of congregational life.

The women navigate between the religious and secular spheres of their lives by compartmentalising gender-specific roles. Conservative religions place an emphasis on the woman's idealised role as, foremost, a wife and mother. Yet many women are employed out with the family and some, like L. hold jobs with positions of authority. Throughout my interviews, there was no negativity concerning women working out with the home. All the women worked or had worked before retirement. There was, as mentioned, a degree of religious overcompensation in their gender-specific roles in the religious sphere as a way of offsetting employment which took them from their idealised role of a stay-at-home mother. Gender remains a dichotomy with identity resting within the male/female heterosexual family.

Within the island communities the conservative nature of the church appears to strengthen membership. The authority of the Bible being fundamental. For the majority of those who participated in this research, they did not see this as a church governed by men but as a church where belonging meant adhering to the edicts of the Bible. Membership reliant on observance.

Reference List

Aldredge-Clanton, J. (1990) *In Whose Image? God and Gender.* New York: The Crossroads Publishing Company.

Avishai, O. (2008) "'Doing Religion' in a Secular World: Women in Conservative Religions and the Question of Agency." *Gender & Society,* 22(4), pp. 409- 433.

Avishai, O. (2016) "Theorizing Gender from Religion Cases: Agency, Feminist Activism, and Masculinity." *Sociology of Religion: A Quarterly Review,* 77(3), pp. 261-279.

Barna Group (2015) *Transforming Scotland: The State of Christianity, Faith, and the Church in Scotland.* A Barna Report produced in partnership with the Maclellan Foundation, Barna Group, Ventura, CA: Barna Group.

Barton, J. (2019) *A History of the Bible: The Books and its Faiths.* London: Allen Lane.

Bartoszuk, K. and Deal, J. E. (2016) "Personality, Identity Styles, and Fundamentalism During Emerging Adulthood, Identity." *An International Journal of Theory and Research,* 16 (3). Benton, A. (2014) *Parenting Against the Tide: A Handbook for 21st Century Parenting.* Darlington: E.P. Books.

Berger, P. L. (1967) *The Sacred Canopy: Elements of a Sociological Theory of Religion.* New York: Anchor Books.

Brasher, B. E. (1998) *Godly Women: Fundamentalism and Female Power.* London: Rutgers University Press.

Burchill, C. (2008) *Fishing for Souls, Faith and Community in a Moray Fishing Village,* PhD Thesis. The University of Aberdeen.

Burkell, J., Fortier, A., Wong, L. Y. C. and Simpson, J. L. (2014) "Facebook: public or private space?" *Information, Communication and Society,* 17(8).

Chin, C. (2019) "The concept of belonging: Critical, normative and multicultural." *Ethnicities,* 19(5), pp. 715-739.

Connell, R. W. and Messerschmidt, J. W. (2005) "Hegemonic Masculinity: Rethinking the Concept." *Gender and Society,* 19(6), pp. 829-859.

Croatto, J. S. (1987) *Biblical Hermeneutics: Toward a Theory of Reading as the Production of Meaning.* Translated from the Spanish by Barr, R. R. New York: Orbis Books.

Day, A. (2017) *The Religious Lives of Older Laywomen.* Oxford: Oxford University Press.

Etherington, K. (2004) *Becoming a Reflexive Researcher: Using Our Selves in Research.* London: Jessica Kingsley.

Furlong, M. (1991) *A Dangerous Delight: Women and Power in the Church.* London: SPCK.

Gilfillan Upton, B. (2002) "Feminist theology as biblical hermeneutics." In Parsons. S. F. (ed.) *The Cambridge Companion to Feminist Theology.* Cambridge: Cambridge University Press, pp. 97-113.

Iannaccone, L. R. (1994) "Why Strict Churches Are Strong." *American Journal of Sociology,* 99(5), pp. 1180-1211.

Irby, C. A. (2014) "Moving Beyond Agency: A Review of Gender and Intimate Relationships in Conservative Religions." *Sociology Compass,* 8(11) pp. 1269-1280.

Jagger, S. (2019) *The Dialectic of Belonging: Resistances and Subversions of Women Priests in the Church of England.* PhD Thesis, The University of York.

Johnson, A. G. (2005) *The Gender Knot: Unravelling our Patriarchal Legacy.* Philadelphia: Temple University Press.

Leamaster, R. and Bautista, A. (2018) "Understanding Compliance in Patriarchal Religions: Mormon Women and the Latter-Day saints Church as a Case Study." *Religions* 9(5) 143, pp. 1-18. Available at: https://www.mdpi.com/2077-1444/9/5/143 Accessed: 16/6/2022.

Lindores, S. and Emejulu A. (2019) "Women as Sectarian Agents: Looking Beyond the Football Cliché in Scotland." *European Journal of Women's Studies,* Vol. 26(1), pp. 39-53.

McCarthy Brown, K. (1994) "Fundamentalism and the Control of Women." In Stratton Hawley J. (ed.) *Fundamentalism and Gender.* Oxford: Oxford University Press, pp. 175-202.

McDowell, J. (2004) *Evidence that Demands a Verdict.* Milton Keynes: Authentic Media.

Mahmood, S. (2012) *Politics of Piety.* Princeton: Princeton University Press.

Mavin, S., Grandyland, G. and Williams, J. (2014) "Experiences of Women Elite Leaders Doing Gender: Intra-gender Micro-violence between Women." *British Journal of Management,* 25, pp. 439–455.

Morris, B. (1992) "A Separate Violence: The Politics of Shaming." *NWSA Journal,* 4(2), pp. 200-204.

Nyhagen, L. (2019) "Mosques as Gendered Spaces: The Complexity of Women's Compliance with, And Resistance to Dominant Gender Norms, And the Importance of Male Allies." *Religions* 10(5), 321, pp. 1-15. Available at: https://doi.org/10.3390/rel10050321. Accessed: 16/6/2022.

Radford Ruether, R. (2002) "The emergence of Christian feminist theology." In Parsons. S. F. (ed.) *The Cambridge Companion to Feminist Theology.* Cambridge: Cambridge University Press, pp. 3-22.

Rose, J. (2009) *Church on Trial.* London: Darton, Longman and Todd.

Rosenblatt, E. L. (2013) "Fear and Loathing: Shame, Shaming, and Intellectual Property." *DePaul Law Review,* 63(1), pp. 1-48.

Ross, S. A. (2002) "Church and sacrament – community and worship." In Parsons. S. F. (ed.) *The Cambridge Companion to Feminist Theology.* Cambridge: Cambridge University Press, pp. 224-242.

Scheff, T. J. (2003) "Shame in Self and Society." *Symbolic Interaction* Volume 26(2), pp. 239-262. Available at: https://doi.org/10.1525/si.2003.26.2.239. Accessed: 12/6/2022.

Schudson, Z. C. Beischel, W. J. and van Anders, S. M. (2019) "Individual variation in gender/sex category definitions." Psychology of Sexual Orientation and Gender Diversity, 6(4), pp. 448-460. Available at: *https://psycnet.apa.org/record/2019-42958-001* Accessed: 12/6/2022.

Schüssler Fiorenza, E. (2006) "A Critical Feminist Emancipation Reading: Invitation to "Dance" in the Open House of Wisdom." In An, C. H., and Darr, K. P. (eds.) *Engaging the Bible: Critical Readings from Contemporary Women.* Minneapolis: Fortress Press, pp. 81-104

Schüssler Fiorenza, E. (2001) *Wisdom Ways. Introducing Feminist Biblical Interpretation.* Maryknoll: Orbis Books.

Sheppard, L. D. and Aquino, K. (2017) "Sisters at Arms: A Theory of Female Same-Sex Conflict and It's Problematization in Organizations." *Journal of Management,* 43(3), pp. 691-715.

Stacey, J. and Gerard, S. E. (1990) "We are not doormats: The influence of feminism on contemporary Evangelicals in the United States." In Ginsberg, F. and Tsing, A. L. (eds.) *Uncertain terms: Negotiating gender in American culture.* Boston: Beacon Press, pp. 98-117.

Walby, S. (1990) *Theorizing Patriarchy.* Oxford: Basil Blackwell.

Ward, K. (1999) *Religion and Community.* London: Clarendon Press.

Chapter 4

Muslim women in Britain: Adherence to Islamic Marriage Laws

Nazia Yaqub

Leeds Becket University

Abstract: In the context of marriage laws, parallel legal systems exist in Britain under which different religious groups adhere to their own religious practices. The focus of Nazia Yaqub's chapter is on Muslim women living in Britain and the demonstrable sense of belongingness to their faith. Irrespective of religiosity, the six studies examined by the author illustrate that Muslim women living in Britain adhere to Islamic personal laws on marriage, even though Islamic law is unenforceable in the UK and so cannot provide Muslim women with the legal protections they would otherwise enjoy living in an Islamic law country. The chapter reflects upon the perspectives of Muslim women living in Britain who explain the reasons why they elect to undergo a religious marriage, over the option of a civil law marriage – particularly as the civil law marriage is legally recognised in Britain and would consequently afford Muslim women matrimonial rights. Building upon existing research in this area, Dr Yaqub's chapter offers a fresh perspective to this ongoing debate and examines the choices Muslim women make through the conceptual framework of Belongingness.

Keywords: belonging, choice, civil law, community, cultural factors, identity, Islamophobia, Islamic, marriage contracts, Muslim, Qur'an, relational factors, religiosity, Shariah Councils, shariah law, spiritual, tradition.

***

Introduction

Whilst Muslims have been present in Britain from as early as the seventeenth century (Ballard, 1994) the migration and settlement we observe as part of multicultural Britain today occurred in the latter half of the last century (Saifullah-Khan, 1977; Werbner, 1991). This period saw the settlement of

Muslims in Britain, particularly South Asians recruited in response to labour shortages (Anwar, 1979; Ballard, 1994) and Muslim women migrated with their families (Anthias and Yuval-Davis, 1992). Migration and settlement of Muslims from other parts of the world has also occurred in response to global events such as war and according to the most recent census figures, more than 3 million Muslims are living in the UK and Muslims comprise 4.8% of the total British population.[1] Despite their minority status, the presence of Muslim women in Britain has resulted in significant academic interest, documenting their arrival (Werbner, 2000), their reasons for remaining in Britain (Werbner, 1996), their integration into British society (Ballard, 1994), and the fragmented identities within the Muslim community in Britain (Modood, 2003, 2005).

The analysis undertaken in this chapter builds upon these earlier works and reflects upon the religious lives of Muslim women in Britain today. Religiosity, as was explained in the introductory chapter, is not easy to define and capturing a community's religiosity can be an impossible task, since religiosity can encapsulate religiousness, belief, and faith (Holdcroft, 2006; Bergan and McContha, 2000). Religiosity is defined in this text as incorporating faith, knowledge, belief, and practise and since this text seeks to examine religion as a lived experience - a reflection on the lives of Muslim women in Britain is possible through examining their observance of Muslim marriage laws.

Saroglou et al.'s (2011, 2020) theoretical perspective on religiousness is an effective framework through which to undertake the analysis. Saroglou et al. identify that religiousness comprises four basic dimensions:

- Believing
- Bonding
- Behaving
- Belonging

and contend that each of the four dimensions corresponds to a specific aspect of religion, such as different ways to express religiousness and specific motives within religion (for example, to become, continue, or stop being religious). On belonging, which is the theme of this text, they identify that this dimension refers to the social aspects of religion, insertion into a community,

[1] 2021 Census data is not yet available. For full breakdown of the Census data visit The Office for National Statistics website at http://www.ons.gov.uk; Statistical analysis is undertaken in February 2020 by the ONS: See [Online] https://www.ons.gov.uk/peoplepopulationandcommunity/culturalidentity/religion/articles/exploringreligioninenglandandwales/february2020 (last accessed 28.07.21)

continuity with a tradition, and the search for collective identity and social self-esteem by belonging to a group with a glorious past and an eternal future. This definition of belonging will underpin the analysis in this chapter to help in understanding the religiosity of Muslim women in Britain.

As the religion of Islam is the majority religion across a large part of the globe, the term *Muslim women* will encompass a diverse group of individuals, deriving from different racial, cultural, and geographical backgrounds and so understandably, not all Muslim women in Britain can be understood in a uniform way (Sayyid, 2000). What is more, as with other world religions, not all Muslims hold the same beliefs and there is no systematic or unified account of what Islamic (sharia) law is or what it should look like in modern times (Hallaq, 2006).[2] The analysis in this chapter builds upon the work undertaken in six earlier studies in which Muslim women in Britain are interviewed (Akhtar,2018; Bano, 2004; Bibi, 2018; Parveen, 2017; Phoenix, 2019; Uddin, 2018) and notably, the majority of participants in those studies are Muslim women of South Asian heritage, and so it is this group of Muslim women who will form the focus of this analysis. It is also worth noting here that the participants in these studies vary in their social identity (not always stated in the studies) and so the author is mindful that as Isakjee expresses: "the politics of belonging does not act evenly on members of a group" (2016, p. 1339) so a professional Muslim woman living in a wealthy suburb may have different experiences and perspectives compared to a Muslim woman from a deprived inner-city neighbourhood (see the work of Nash, 2008; Yuval-Davis, 2007).

With this in mind, this chapter will reflect upon the adherence of Muslim women living in Britain to Muslim marriage laws. The following section provides some context on Muslim marriage laws and their positionality in the English legal system, whilst the second section examines the relationship between religiosity and Muslim marriage laws. Section three considers the situation of Muslim women in Britain within the contextual framework of belonging. And the fourth section will develop this discussion to reflect upon whether the need to belong could be one of the reasons why Muslim women in Britain elect religious-only marriage.

I, the author, as a Muslim woman born and raised in Britain, reflect on these issues from my perspective as a lawyer, academic and researcher interested in gender justice and women's rights. Whilst reading this chapter, I ask you, the reader, to reflect on your assumptions on the issue of Muslim marriage and why

[2] Different jurisprudential "schools of thought" exist within the Muslim community. For a detailed discussion on the historical development and differences between each, see Kamali (1999); Hamdeh (2017).

many Muslims in Britain actively choose not to undergo a civil ceremony or marry aboard, which would legally recognise the marriage under English law.

Marriage laws for Muslim women

Marriage rites and traditions exist across all faiths, and this is no different for Muslim marriages. The formalities that exist for Muslim marriage ceremonies are fairly straightforward, the parties must both provide full and free consent, be regarded as having the legal capacity (of age and sound mind), the ceremony must be undertaken in the presence of witnesses and the agreement must include details of the wedding gift (also referred to as dower or mahr) from the husband to the wife. In Islamic law countries, the parties to a marriage can register their union with the State, which then legally validates that marriage and in turn provides individuals with the relevant rights and protections on the breakdown of that marriage (Akhtar et al., 2020; Uddin, 2018; Sona, 2014).

When Muslims conduct the same marriage ceremony in Britain, the marriage is not recognised in law. This is because English law, namely sections 41-44 *Marriage Act 1949* (as amended) require marriages to be conducted in premises registered for the purposes of marriage by a Registrar of marriages or an authorised person. As there is no requirement for the Muslim marriage ceremony to be conducted by an authority figure such as a religious cleric or be conducted in any particular location such as a religious or registered building, the Islamic marriages conducted in Britain rarely comply with the requirements of the Marriage Act 1949. Whilst the differences appear trivial, the consequence of the *unrecognised marriage* is that women in Muslim-only marriages are not treated as a spouse in law. Women in Muslim marriages are treated in English law as cohabitees, which affects their financial entitlement to the couple's assets in the event the marriage comes to an end. The consequences of a religious-only marriage are that the English law courts are unable to intervene and assist Muslim women in this situation on the breakdown of that relationship and award maintenance payments or financial remedy. Muslim women in this situation have no automatic entitlement to spousal maintenance and matrimonial assets, including the family home, family savings and pensions. Even after very long marriages, Muslim women can be left in a precarious situation if they do not jointly own the matrimonial home or have their own income.

Non-recognition of the Muslim marriage also affects Muslim women on the death of their spouse, as they will not be considered a spouse for the purpose of succession laws. Muslim women in this situation do not benefit from the automatic entitlement from an intestate estate (pursuant to s.46 of the *Administration of Estates Act 1925*). Whilst Muslim women in Islamic-only marriages could apply for some "reasonable financial provision" reserved for dependents (under the *Inheritance (Provision for Family and Dependants) Act 1975*), they are not automatically entitled and so are in a weaker position to a spouse. Muslim women who enter a religious-only marriage in Britain are left with little security and rights which some commentators argue could leave them vulnerable to exploitation within the marriage (Jaan, 2014; Ramadan, 2004).

The legal quandary could be remedied by Muslim women undergoing a second ceremony at a Register Office. Though it appears this does not routinely occur as a study undertaken of 923 Muslim women across 14 cities in Britain suggests that whilst all Muslim women who marry will undergo the religious marriage ceremony, only 40% of Muslim women in Britain have had a separate civil ceremony to make their marriage valid under English law (Sherwood, 2017). Other data estimates the number of Muslim women in Britain who do not undergo a legally recognised marriage ceremony could be between 50- 90% (Douglas et al., 2012; Grillo, 2015; Jaan, 2014).

The available data illustrates that Muslim women prioritise religious marriage over and above the legally recognised marriage. A substantive review was undertaken at the request of the British government on the application of Islamic (shariah) law in England and published in 2018. One of the purposes of that review was to consider the reasons why Muslim couples choose not to enter civil marriages and the report suggests that the reasons include:

> [a] lack of awareness that Islamic marriages need to be registered separately to be legal; failure to register the marriage for financial reasons, the belief that should the couple divorce one partner may lose out financially in civil divorce proceedings; couples wishing to co-habit who see Islamic marriage as a way of appeasing family but are not "ready" to marry legally; couples who intend to register their marriage after the Islamic ceremony but never get round to doing it; possible confusion caused by the recognition of Islamic marriages conducted overseas as valid, when the same ceremony conducted in England or Wales would not be recognised; individuals who for religious or cultural reasons do not wish to engage with secular marriage at all and so choose to opt out of the civil society process and the rare practice of polygamy in some Muslim communities which would be illegal in England and Wales. (Siddiqui Report, 2018, p14).

The report highlights the vast range of reasons why Muslim women in Britain are not in legally recognised marriages. Many of the reasons cited have been explored by other commentators (Shah-Kazemi, 2001; Saleem and Probert, 2018; Fisher, Saleem and Vora, 2018; Manea, 2016; Vora, 2015) and so will not be repeated here. One factor listed in the report which has been given less attention is the category of Muslim women who, for religious reasons, do not wish to engage with secular marriage. The contribution this chapter makes is to expand on this topic and explore the idea that some Muslim women may choose to undergo a religious marriage because of their religiosity and sense of belongingness to their faith. The analysis will be undertaken by applying the conceptual framework of belongingness espoused by Saroglou et al. (2020).

Marriage and religiosity

Great significance is placed upon marriage in Islamic (shariah) law, and this emphasis is visible in a number of sources. The holy book the Qur'an refers to marriage as a relationship of tranquillity compassion love and mercy (Qur'an 30.21). In another important source of Islamic law, the teachings of the Prophet Mohammed, marriage is understood as comprising half of one's faith (At-Tirmidi Hadith: 3096). Muslims adhere to their religious values to ensure they enter Heaven and avoid Hell. They believe that any struggle or concessions they make in this temporary life will be rewarded in the afterlife through the safe passage to Heaven (Qur'an 18: 108 and 57:20, Haleem, 2014; Cornell, 1999). Data from the six studies examined illustrates the importance the Muslim women interviewed place upon marriage as a part of their religious faith, belief, and practice, regarded by some as a rite of passage. Participants were asked in the six studies examined why they chose to undergo a religious-only marriage (sometimes referred to as "niqaah") whilst living in Britain:

> it's easier just to have a nikaah.... that's the most important [one] in front of Allah (Halima). (Parveen study, 2017, p. 238).

> I've never questioned it, it's all part of being a Muslim. If you're a Muslim, you would have one [Muslim marriage] .... it doesn't even have to be that you're really religious. Getting married in God's eyes is more important than getting married for English law (Raheela, London). (Bano study, 2004, p. 207).

> I think the main thing is the Islamic nikaah.... in our religion we have to be married, it's very important and the English one, I don't see that as very important to be honest with you (Noorie). (Parveen study, 2017, p. 234)

> Well, the Islamic marriage is very important for me. I could get married in a civil registry office and not regard myself as married, I might be

> legally married, but I wouldn't be married in my heart and in my mind (Fauzia, London). (Bano study, 2004, p. 208)

> I would just do a nikaah.... for me civil marriage doesn't really matter.... I have to answer Allah, I don't have to answer this world (Layla). (Parveen study, 2017, p. 238)

> I didn't have a civil marriage as I didn't feel it was necessary.... the most important thing was to be married in the eyes of Allah... (Kulsoom). (Parveen study, 2017, p. 234)

The views demonstrate that for these participants, Muslim marriage is very much a part of their religious lives as Muslim women in Britain. This is even though the Muslim marriage ceremony is in fact not spiritual or sacred in nature. Indeed, the Muslim marriage is regarded as being a "contractual arrangement" (al Faruqi, 1985, in Scott and Warren, 2007, p. 466). A view similar to one taken in Britain in the seventeenth century according to John Sedden (1584–1654), who wrote then that "marriage is nothing but a civil contract" (cited in Todd, 2006, p. 540). As explained above in section two, there is no requirement for the Muslim marriage to be conducted in a religious building or by a religious cleric. All that is required is an agreement (consent) between a man and woman, who are of sufficient age and sound mind to have the capacity to enter into an agreement and the agreement must be declared in public in the presence of witnesses. The wedding gift from the husband to the wife is also stipulated at the time. The wedding gift has been discussed elsewhere in literature (Welchman, 2004) and so will not be repeated here, but for the purpose of the analysis in this chapter, it can be understood as a gift or sum of money that is promised to the wife which she can request from the husband at the outset of the marriage, at any time during the marriage, upon divorce, or from the husband's estate after his death.

The marriage agreement established the rights and duties of the husband and the wife, and the couple are able to regulate the terms of their relationship from the outset. The husband and wife can also refer to other matters, or "special conditions" in the agreement (The Muslim Institute, 2008, p. 5). A wife can, for example, stipulate in the event of separation, any children remain in her custody until they reach adulthood. One of the parties can ask for maintenance during and after the marriage or can specify where they wish to set up home. At this early negotiation stage, the terms of the relationship are formed and if either party is not happy, each is free to decline and not marry. Once agreed and the marriage is entered, breach of the agreement allows the other party to have the marriage dissolved. Muslim women in Britain do not have access to the Islamic courts that are accessible to Muslim women living in Islamic law countries and so enforcement of the marital agreement can be more complex for women in Britain. These women must seek the support of *Shariah Councils* which have been established to assist Muslim women in Britain seeking to end the religious marriage (Ali, 2013; Parveen, 2018). There is insufficient scope within this chapter to explore the enforceability of marriage contracts, but this is addressed in the body of work that captures the purpose, effect, and legitimacy of the Shariah Councils in Britain (Hallaq, 2006; Ali, 2013; Bano, 2012). The literature recognises the complexities of legal pluralism and navigating between the two legal systems in operation, with Muslims adhering to Islamic (sharia) law for matters relating to marriage and divorce. Significant critique of whether and to what extent English law should accommodate other *unofficial law* has also been undertaken (Nielsen, 1991; Nasir, 1986; Anthias and Yuval-Davis, 1992; Menski, 1993). These debates continue without any conclusive resolve (Siddiqui Report, 2018) and so Muslim women in Britain who marry must still choose whether they undergo a Muslim marriage, a civil marriage or both.

The religious nature of the Muslim marriage might be assumed because in Islamic law countries, this is the only form of marriage and so all Muslims originating from Islamic law countries are accustomed to the rules as prescribed in their homelands. The idea that the civil ceremony recognized in English law could be an alternative to the Islamic marriage ceremony is worthy of further exploration since the requirements of capacity, consent and witnesses are catered for as part of the civil ceremony. Despite this contention, Uddin (2018) observes that experts he interviewed as part of his study, including imams and Shariah Council judges, stipulate the civil law ceremony does not establish the Muslim marriage, and as such civil marriages are seen as a secondary issue compared to the religious marriage. Whether or not the Muslim marriage ceremony itself is spiritual, the data illustrates that it is clearly regarded by the Muslim community as a religious marriage and one that the Muslim community value as part of their religious observance and religiosity. Indeed, for devout Muslims, marriage is significant enough to comprise half of their faith. The participants in the studies expressed that to them, the Muslim marriage ceremony has spiritual and religious meaning, as a: “covenant” and “something that is huge” ... “it is spiritual and meaningful” (Participant 2:3) (Akhtar Study, 2018, p. 443). It is understandable why they might interpret the marriage in this way, since Muslim clerics in Britain who were also interviewed as part of some of the studies clearly held this view, with one Shariah Council judge stating:

> Civil registration is for legal convenience i.e., benefits and taxes. For Muslims civil registry is not getting married but a pre-party to the

> nikah [Muslim marriage], it carries no weight. The nikah has weight in the eyes of God, faith, and the community. The couple would not live together after a civil registration. (Participant SC Judge #1) (Uddin study, 2018, p. 83).

Muslim women in Britain and the desire to belong

The sense of belongingness Muslim women perceive in their religion is identified in a range of literature (Nasir, 1986; Wadud, 2006; Cooke, 2008; Engineer, 2008; Welchman, 2010; Yuval-Davis, 2011). This sense of belongingness Muslim women in Britain accomplish through religion also appears to fulfil the concept of belongingness espoused by MacMillan and Chavis (1986) as involving the belief that one belongs in and has a place in a group which is identified as a feeling of acceptance in the group. The shared beliefs Muslims hold can also influence the development of a sense of belonging (Winter-Collins and McDaniel, 2000). The narratives in the descriptions of Muslim women provided illustrate their greater affiliation and sense of belonging to their religious group, compared with other social and cultural communities and groups referred to in the women's accounts. One of the possible reasons is found in the references women make that their religion made them outsiders in Britain. Meer and Madood (2009) argue that it is not possible to understand the lives of Muslim women in Britain without an understanding of Islamophobia. Indeed, the centrality of Islamophobia is reflected in the comments of the participants in the six studies. These comments provide some insight into which Islamophobia is experienced by Muslim women in Britain. Islamophobia is described as the perceived differences between Muslims and others which will, in turn, affect how Muslim women are able to openly practise their religion (Werbner, 2000, p. 13), whether through their attire or other forms of religious observance. In a report on Islamophobia for the Human Rights Council, Awan and Zempi develop a new definition for Islamophobia:

> [a] fear, prejudice and hatred of Muslims or non-Muslim individuals that leads to provocation, hostility, and intolerance by means of threatening, harassment, abuse, incitement and intimidation of Muslims and non-Muslims, both in the online and offline world. Motivated by institutional, ideological, political, and religious hostility that transcends into structural and cultural racism which targets the symbols and markers of being Muslim. (2018, p. 2)

These types of Islamophobic behaviours, covered within the definition, are likely to affect Muslim women and the choices they make. And as Yuval-Davis argues, "the emotional components of people's constructions of themselves and their identities become more central the more threatened and the less secure they become." (2011, p. 15).

Islamophobic attitudes resulted in some of the Muslim women participating in the studies stating that they do not feel they "belong" in Britain. As one participant shares:

> there's still a sense of not belonging, but I think for me it's based in more substance, it's based in more thought and reflection, rather than, "This is scary, where do I go?" Now I'm thinking, I belong somewhere, I belong in the universe, I belong with God, but where is my physical space, my practical space? (Yasmin) (Phoenix study, 2019, p. 1640)

This relationship of belonging, religion and physical space is also identified in the discourse around the identity of Muslims in Britain, and it is suggested the identity of Muslim women in Britain is interrelated with their sense of belonging. Isakjee proposes that belonging is about "feeling safe and at home" (2016, p. 1338) and that home is not necessarily a physical space but that the sense of being *at home* in the context of belonging to a place is to be understood as a psychological attachment, imagined, and felt.[3] He argues that the conceptual value of belonging over place-attachment is its ability to incorporate both the emotional and political dimensions of place-identity. Similarly, Antonsich (2010) identifies several factors which contribute to the emotional feeling of belonging. These include the social and personal connections individuals have with others that connect them to given places (he refers to as *relational factors*). As well as (*cultural factors*) familiar languages, cultural traditions, and expressions which Antonsich asserts can invoke the feeling of individuals belonging to their surroundings.

Psychological attachment and belonging to Britain will vary for Muslim women depending upon their relational and cultural experiences and circumstances. Recognising they do not belong to the country they were born and grew up in is problematic for those Muslim women who are the second and third generations of migrants to Britain, who neither feel they belong in Britain nor have any attachment to their original homelands. The sense of belonging younger Muslim women in Britain perceive is therefore likely to differ from that sense of belongingness Muslim women in Britain in previous generations experienced – those with memories and connections to their homelands. The inter-generational differences of Muslim women in Britain

---

[3] See also the works of Hedetoft and Hjort, (2002); Ignatieff, (1994).

are captured in research (Brah, 1996; Dwyer, 2000; Ahmad, 2003). Studies illustrate that Muslim women in Britain can be marginalised in British society due to their religious and cultural heritage but also made to feel like outsiders in their own communities because they are perceived as Western. Hoque (2018) suggests this identity vacuum has created a *transcultural* and *transnational* British-Islamic identity with young people identifying as *British Muslims* (see also the work of Mythen, Walklate and Khan, 2009). The second and third generation of Muslim women interviewed in the six studies also identify as an *in-between* generation which Haw refers to as:

> an active re-construction and re-evaluation of the relationship between the traditions they inherited from their parents, the role of religion within that and the relationship of those traditions and religious beliefs with British culture and identity. This generation are in the process of re-constructing and re-integrating both their parents' traditional and cultural notions of being Muslim, and their idealisation of British identity with the re-assertion of their religious values. In doing so they are being socially constructed as becoming "more Muslim." (2010, p. 358)

Differing aspirations, opportunities, expectations and lived experiences of the second and third generation of Muslim women in Britain, have a distinct impact on identity and belonging. Children and grandchildren of Muslim migrants to Britain appear to feel more affiliated with their religion than any cultural heritage and fulfil their desire to belong through identification with a global Muslim community (Castells, 1997). As one participant reflects:

> Culturally, am I in the culture group, am I in the religion group? Or am I in the religion and culture group, or am I in the British group? Or am I in the Bangladeshi group or am I in the working-class group? It's a bit confusing. I don't want to be in any group other than being a Muslim cos everything else is not fixed, everything else it changes. Being a Muslim is kinda something fixed and it's something secure and it feels right. (Aaminah) (Phoenix study, 2019, p. 1640)

We understand from studies that the need to belong is an essential physiological human need and Baumeister and Leary observe that the need to belong is a need that subsumes the need for social inclusion, secure attachment, love relationships, and social support and go as far as to say, "belongingness can be almost as compelling a need as food." (1995, p. 498). If the sense of belongingness for Muslim women who experience Islamophobic behaviours is not fulfilled through connection to their surroundings or their homelands, then it is suggested that such women are likely to seek to fulfil that desire to belong elsewhere. It is also understood that the universal need to form interpersonal relationships is found across all cultures and different types of people (Baumeister and Leary, 1995) and the data examined suggests that Muslim women in Britain feel a greater sense of belonging to their religion – because religion is a universal connection that transcends geography, race, and heritage. Muslim women accomplish the sense of belongingness in religion that they lose through departing their homelands and settling in Britain (Isakjee, 2016; Lewicka, 2011).

This attachment to religion might seem logical, as the need to belong can motivate belief in God (Gebauer and Maio, 2012). Ritual and congregational religious prayer can also fulfil the need for belonging, which is something Muslims are expected to perform daily. The lack of connection with their original homelands and the implication of Islamophobia appears to have resulted in Muslim women seeking the fulfilment of belonging elsewhere and has contributed to the renewed Muslim religious identity. This is observed by Phoenix (2019), who explains the political discourse around Muslims in Britain and their portrayal in the media has impacted the way in which the identities of Muslim women in Britain have developed. The hostility towards Muslims has strengthened their religious identities and the exclusionary discourses push young Muslim women to prioritize their religious identities above their ethno-cultural, class and other identifications (Dwyer, 2000). As one participant comments:

> I feel like if you want to accept me, accept me. If you don't, that's okay. It's like, "what do I have to do to be accepted?" It's my religion that's a problem, right? It's not my colour. It's not that I eat rice and curry, it's my religion. So, if you can't accept my religion then it's fine. I don't wanna be in your society if you can't accept my religion. (Aaminah) (Phoenix study, 2019, p. 1641-2).

Mohammad's (2013) study also recognises that the growth of Islamophobia, and the intensification of racial exclusion have supported Muslim women's identifications with Islam. She focuses on the positive aspects of this situation and observes that this form of attachment enables young Muslim women to mobilise Islam as a resource in their everyday lives to advance their own gendered interests within the community. She argues that for the second and third generations of Muslim migrants, religious belonging is more than just a resource; however, it is also an identity for which they demand public recognition and validation (See also Mirza, 2009). The data suggests that Muslim women empowered through their faith, fulfilled with the sense of belongingness have the confidence to adhere to their religious rules – more so than the previous generations of Muslim women in Britain who are characterised by their cultural origins more so than religion. The Muslim women who originally migrated to Britain who married in their homelands were not compelled to choose whether to marry according to religious Islamic law or English law, as their overseas marriage is legally recognised in Britain. The issue of recognition and choice affects second and third generations of Muslim women who marry in Britain, and it is these women who are the focus of this analysis.

The discussion thus far has provided some context on how Muslim women came to be situated in Britain, and why later generations of Muslim women in Britain appear to attach greater significance to their religious identity than previous generations. The analysis now turns to a more specific aspect of the lives of Muslim women in Britain - their adherence to Muslim marriage laws.

Muslim Women in Britain and the choice of religious only marriage: is it all about religious belonging?

The discussion above reaffirms from the six studies examined that religion caters to the essential psychological desire Muslim women -like all individuals have- to belong to a group or a community (Hurtado and Carter, 1997). Religion allows Muslim women in Britain to feel an integral part of a system of environment which is the essence of belonging (Hagerty et al., 1992). The discussion so far has also illustrated how the younger generation of Muslim women in Britain straddle the boundaries of religion, culture, and nationality to a greater extent than their mothers and grandmothers who originally migrated to Britain from Muslim countries. These Muslim women in Britain articulate a greater sense of belonging to their religion and religious identities – and are thus regarded as more religious (Phoenix, 2019; Isakjee, 2016; Mohammad, 2013). Religiosity encompasses this religious identity (Holdcroft, 2006) and will positively affect the decisions Muslim women make when deciding to marry.

Muslim women in Britain have a choice on whether they undergo a religious marriage, a civil marriage or both. This is not the case in Islamic law countries, where there is little demarcation between religion and law (Akhtar, 2018; Nisa, 2018; Kolman, 2018) and so in Islamic law countries, couples do not need to elect the form of marriage ceremony. All marriage ceremonies conducted in Islamic law countries that comply with the requirements discussed above, of capacity, consent and witnesses will be registered as a legally binding marriage. The choice, or issue only transpires where Muslims marry in a non-Islamic law country such as Britain – where the Muslim marriage is not recognised in law as a valid marriage.

Reflecting on the choice of Muslim women in Britain who undergo a Muslim wedding ceremony could be indicative of the religiosity of Muslim women in

Britain -since the data confirms all Muslim women undergo a Muslim marriage ceremony, rather than a civil ceremony. Religiosity comprises the components of faith, knowledge, belief and practise and the Muslim marriage ceremony appears from the data to attach meaning to each of these components for Muslim women. The Muslim marriage ceremony is a social construct that holds religious significance for the participants in the studies examined. It enables Muslim women to adhere to the traditions and tenants of their faith. Religion for Muslim women prescribes that the marital relationship is intended to create tranquillity compassion love and mercy between spouses (Quran 30.21). And those entering a marital union for the sake of their religion are promised that by doing so, they have completed half of their faith (At-Tirmidi Hadith: 3096) which will secure passage to Heaven (Qur'an 18:108 and 57:20; Cornell, 1999).

Electing a religious-only marriage fulfils many aspects of religiousness for Muslim women in Britain. The motives for doing so are also assessable through the four dimensions of religiousness identified by Saroglou et al. (2020) believing, bonding, behaving, and belonging. These are visible in the narratives of the Muslim women in the six studies examined. In the context of Muslim marriage laws, the believing dimension is visible when Muslim women discuss the cognitive aspects of religion, Islamic beliefs related to the transcendence, and functions such as the search for meaning and epistemic certainty. The bonding dimension incorporates the emotional aspects involved when connecting with the group through religious rituals and functions, such as the marriage ceremony which Saroglou (2011) identifies as emotional regulation and attachment security. The behaving dimension recognises the moral aspect of religion the women discuss, the norms of moral rules and order, such as seeking God's approval to commence the union.

The belonging dimension of religiousness highlights the social aspects of religion and continuity with a tradition – factors that are central to the Islamic marriage question under consideration here. Saroglou et al. (2020) also observe that the belongingness dimension encompasses the search for collective identity and social self-esteem by belonging to a group with a glorious past and an eternal future. The discussion above in section three indicates that the desire to belong by Muslim women in Britain is fulfilled by their association with their religion. It is suggested here that the choice to undergo a religious only marriage despite this leaving Muslim women in Britain economically vulnerable fulfils the desire to belong. This is through adhering to the collective group practice of the Muslim marriage ceremony, which continues with a tradition and secures the approval of that community. As one participant explains:

> It's the nikah that's binding in the Islamic setting and it's at that point, whether you have the registry marriage or not, that you're considered to be married by people in the family, the community you know people who know your family. Were all Muslims and we know what's important to us. (Sameena, Birmingham). (Bano study. 2004, p. 208).

This viewpoint illustrates that for these participants, adherence to their religious practices and traditions which the Muslim community recognise, is of greater significance than any legal recognition of that union. Their religiosity requires them to submit to religious norms and they do not attach the same significance to the non-religious registration process.

It is interesting to observe that the participants regard the Islamic marriage ceremony as necessary approval to enter an intimate relationship that requires approval by God. And so, as Akhtar (2018, p. 430) explains, religious marriages can be inspired by a desire on the part of observant Muslims to adhere to normative religious principles in entering a physically intimate relationship. She explains the ability to enter a religious-only marriage is synonymous with the right to enter a sexual relationship and the absence of the Muslim marriage ceremony results in such a relationship being considered sinful. This correlates with the symbiotic association the Muslim women interviewed held with respect to Muslim marriage and religion (Siddiqui, 1996). We can see from the accounts above, for these Muslim women, there is a clear connection between the Muslim marriage and their relationship with God. Commentators have suggested this is because Muslim marriage is central to the construction of Muslim family life, procreation, and paternity of children (See Ali, 2000) and so, as Bano identifies, religion and marriage are viewed as a "symbiotic relationship" holding "symbolic power" (2004, p. 37).

According to Saroglou et al. (2020), cognitive, emotional, moral, and social factors play a part in individuals being religious—or irreligious and this could explain why Muslim women, many of whom indicated they were aware of the resulting lack of legal protection, choose a religious only marriage. The decisions on religiosity are all affected by psychological human behaviours and dimensions of human development, such as cognitive, emotional, moral, and social factors (Fiske, 2014). Difficulty in understanding religiosity and spirituality across different cultures can arise from the fact that religion is malleable and can be more convictional, affective, moralistic, or communitarian across different cultures (Saroglou et al., 2020) and so other women in Britain, religious or otherwise, may not be able to comprehend the decision of these Muslim women to make choices that might disadvantage their future economic position as a form of religiosity. It was explained in the introduction to this text, that belonging is an important social motive and the need for acceptance and belonging is a fundamental concept as it helps explain behaviours. It grants an understanding of how choices are made, both by the individual and by the group. Uddin's (2020) exploration of the practices of marriages and divorce among British Muslims reveal the strong influence of religion and culture in establishing social norms, dictating the importance of Muslim marriage and divorce laws. MacMillan and Chavis (1986) recognize belongingness as the feeling of acceptance in the group and a willingness to sacrifice for the group. The accounts provided by Muslim women in the studies examined are suggestive of the need to belong and would conform with the defined understanding of belongingness theory. Though Muslim women may be perceived as sacrificing their rights through electing not to undergo the civil marriage ceremony, the discourse of sacrifice is not observed in any of the six studies examined. Rather the Muslim women discuss that the civil marriage ceremony does not add any additional legitimacy to their marriage.

Hearing the voices of Muslim women provides some insight as to the reasons why Muslim women in Britain place greater emphasis on the religious marriage ceremony and why they regard the religious marriage ceremony as a priority and a large part of how they adhere to the religious tradition whilst in Britain. The premise upon which this analysis is based is that Muslim women do so as a "social aspect of their religion", and "continuity with a tradition" which is, as Saroglou et al. (2020, p. 553) assert, underpinned by emotional, social, cognitive, and moral factors. Religiosity and a sense of belonging to their religion results in a feeling of contentment which overrides any fear of economic disadvantage, which the participants say would prompt them to seek protection in English law, encouraged instead that their faith will suffice, and God will protect them if they later divorce. The Quran instructs Muslims to believe that this life is a test after which their actions and intentions will be judged to determine whether they spend their eternity in Heaven or Hell (Quran 18:108 and 57:20). For those devout individuals having greater faith in God's laws is a form of religiosity. Muslims are not prohibited from undergoing a civil marriage that is recognised in English law – but it is understandable why Muslim women may not prioritise this, and for the very devout, strict adherence purely to religious laws could be appealing and regarded as a form of religiosity, benefitting in the *afterlife*. It is argued here that the emotional, social, cognitive, and moral factors at play in decisions made by Muslim women in Britain support the assertion that some Muslim women undergo a religious-only marriage as a form of religiosity. Data from the six studies examined illustrates that religion and adherence to religious traditions are important to the Muslim women interviewed. The accounts provided suggest the women focus on the positive aspects of their religion going about their daily lives, conforming to the norms and traditions of their religious group. They did not dwell on the economic consequences of separation unless and until they actually divorced. The devout Muslim women who did divorce did not appear persuaded that a legally recognised marriage would assist their position in this life, or the next.

The choices Muslim women in Britain make to elect a religious-only marriage is not regarded as a real choice for many concerned about the fact that Muslim women are left economically vulnerable on divorce. There exists a great deal of debate on whether the Muslim marriage should be automatically recognised in English law, so that Muslim women in Britain do not need to choose between the Muslim marriage and legal protection. The English courts attempted to provide Muslim women with the safeguard of legal protection in a religious only marriage in 2018, but the appeal courts overturned the decision in February 2020 and affirmed the law requires that marriages must comply with all the formalities stipulated in the Marriages Act 1949.[4] One of the recommendations to the Government in the review of the use of sharia (Islamic) law in Britain (2018) is for a change in the law to require a Muslim couple to undergo a civil marriage ceremony before or at the same time as the Muslim marriage ceremony. This view is echoed by the Parliamentary Assembly of the Council of Europe which passed a resolution in 2019, calling for the UK to require Muslim couples to register their marriage according to English law.[5] Whilst these recommendations aim to provide greater legal protections for divorcing Muslim women in Britain, not all Muslim women interviewed agreed with compulsory registration of their marriage and some participants expressed the importance of "choice", "independent decision", "informed decision", expressing individuals "shouldn't be forced to do it" [register your marriage]. (Akhtar's study, 2018, p. 438).

Conclusion

At the outset of this chapter, the author asks the reader to reflect on their assumptions on the issue of Muslim marriage and why many Muslims in Britain actively choose not to undergo a civil ceremony or marry aboard, which would legally recognise the marriage under English law. The discussion has intended to highlight to the reader that the migration of Muslim women to Britain has resulted in later generations of Muslim women losing their

---

[4] Nasreen Akhtar v Mohammad Shabaz Khan [2020] EWCA Civ 122Case No: B6/2018/2656

[5] Parliamentary Assembly of the Council of Europe, Resolution 2253 (2019), Sharia,the Cairo Declaration and the European Convention on Human Rights.

affiliation with their cultural heritage and have instead grown a greater and deeper connection to their religion. This connection fulfils the innate need to belong. Their journey appears to map well with the components of religious belonging identified by Saroglou (2011, 2020) and the desire to elect a religious-only marriage makes sense when understood through this definition, where Muslim women in Britain search for collective identity and social self-esteem by belonging to a group, the marriage comprising the social aspects of their religion, allowing insertion into a community, and displaying continuity with a tradition. The decision of Muslim women in Britain to engage in religious-only marriage when viewed through wider theoretical constructions of belongingness can also demonstrate the need to belong and conform, to allow Muslim women to feel an integral part of a system of environment (Hagerty et al., 1992), which they have lost through migrating and settling in Britain. This, as well as reactions to Islamophobia, have created in some Muslim women a greater sense of religiosity than is seen in earlier generations of Muslim women in Britain. Complying with religious norms and traditions allows Muslim women in Britain to experience a much-needed psychological feeling of belonging to a group or a community (Hurtado and Carter, 1997). Whilst Muslim women in Britain need not sacrifice their legal rights when electing a religious marriage (as they can undergo a civil ceremony also) the voices of Muslim women in the studies suggest that for some, the feeling of acceptance and a willingness to sacrifice (MacMillan and Chavis, 1986) may fulfil the need to belong as the shared belief that the Muslim marriage is religious in nature (rather than contractual) influences the development of a sense of belonging (Winter-Collins and McDaniel, 2000).

The aim of this analysis is to examine whether Muslim women in Britain choose a religious-only marriage purely for the purpose of religiosity and motive of belongingness to their religious group. The analysis has demonstrated that Muslim women are permitted to undergo both a religious and a civil ceremony in compliance with their religion. But many still do not - and the voices of women who participated in the studies examined demonstrates that some Muslim women choose a religious-only marriage as a form of religiosity and to affirm belongingness to their faith. The views, whilst not representative of the entire sample, reflect the lived experiences of Muslim women in Britain and demonstrate a strong influence of religion in establishing norms and dictating the importance of the Muslim marriage in establishing the "real marriage" (Uddin, 2020, p. 6) whereas civil marriage and legal recognition of the union is not accorded significant weight.

Muslim women are not a homogenous group and whilst the Muslim women in Britain who were interviewed as part of the six studies examined derive from different social and community backgrounds, they can still not possibly reflect the voice of all Muslim women. What the studies have illustrated is that adherence to Islamic personal laws is very much a part of the religious lives of Muslim women in Britain today. The use of the conceptual framework of belongingness has provided a helpful context through which to reflect upon the religious lives of Muslim women in Britain, through examining their adherence to Islamic marriage laws. The analysis has illustrated that the significance of belonging, to a group, a community, a religion, can play a part in the decision by some women to elect a religious-only marriage despite the widespread concerns that this could leave Muslim women economically vulnerable upon divorce.

Reference List

Ahmad, F. (2003) "'Still in Progress?' Methodological dilemmas, tensions, and contradictions in theorising South Asian Muslim women." In Puwar, N. and Baghurum, P. (eds.) *South Asian Women in the Diaspora.* Oxford: Berg, pp. 43-65.

Akhtar, R. C. (2018) "Modern Traditions in Muslim Marriage Practices, Exploring English Narratives." *Oxford Journal of Law, and Religion*, 7, pp. 427-454.

Akhtar, R. C., Nash, P. and Probert, R. (2020) *Cohabitation and Religious Marriage: Status, Similarities and Solutions.* Bristol: Bristol University Press.

Ali, S. S. (2000) *Gender and Human Rights in Islam and International law: Equal Before Allah? Equal Before Man?* London: Kluwer Law International.

Ali, S. S. (2013) "Authority and Authenticity: Sharia councils, Muslim women's rights and the English courts." *Child and Family Law Quarterly*, 25(2), pp. 113-137.

Anthias, F. and Yuval-Davis, N. (1992), *Racialized Boundaries: Race, Nation, Gender, Colour and Class and the Anti-Racist Struggle.* London: Routledge.

Antonsich, M. (2010) "Searching for belonging – An analytical framework." *Geography Compass*, 2(6), pp. 644–659.

Anwar, M. (1979) *The myth of return: Pakistanis in Britain.* London: Heinemann Educational.

Awan, I., and Zempi, I. (2018) *A Working Definition of Islamophobia: Written Evidence Submission prepared for the United Nations Special Rapporteur on contemporary forms of racism, racial discrimination, xenophobia, and related intolerance.* Available at: http://irep.ntu.ac.uk/id/eprint/45215/1/1505050_Zempi.pdf. Accessed: 28/6/2022.

Ballard, R. (1994) "The Emergence of Desh Pardesh." In Ballard, R. and Banks, M. (eds.) *Desh Pardesh: The South Asian Presence in Britain,* London: C. Hurst and Co., pp. 1-34.

Bano, S. (2004). *Complexity, Difference and Muslim Personal Law: Rethinking Relationships between Shari'ah Councils and South Asian Muslim Women in Britain.* PhD Thesis, Warwick University.

Bano, S. (2012) *Exploratory Survey of Shariah Councils in England with respect to family law.* [Research paper for the Ministry of Justice] University of Reading.

Available: https://eprints.soas.ac.uk/22075/1/An_exploratory_study_of_Shariah_councils_in_England_with_respect_to_family_law_.pdf. Accessed: 10/6/2022.

Baumeister, R. F. and Leary, M. R. (1995). "The Need to Belong: Desire for Interpersonal Attachments as a Fundamental Human Motivation." *Psychological Bulletin*, 117(3), pp. 497-529.

Bergan, A. and McContha J. T. (2000) "Religiosity and Life Satisfaction." *Activities, Adaptation and Aging*, 24(3), pp. 23-34.

Bibi, R. (2018) *Challenging discourses on BSA Muslim women through an intersectional analysis of everyday experiences across spaces of home, work, and public space.* PhD Thesis, University of Manchester.

Brah, A. (1996) *Cartogrophies of Diaspora.* London: Routledge.

Castells, M. (1997) *The Rise of the Network Society.* Oxford: Basil Blackwell.

Cooke, M. (2008), "Deploying the Muslim woman." *Journal of Feminist Studies in Religion* 24(1), pp. 91–99.

Cornell, V. J. (1999) "Fruit of the Tree of Knowledge: The Relationship Between Faith and Practice." In Esposito, J. L. (ed.), *The Oxford History of Islam.* Oxford: Oxford University Press, pp. 63-105.

Douglas, G., Doe, N., Gilliat-Ray, S., Sandberg, R. and Khan, A. (2012) "The Role of Religious Tribunals in Regulating Marriage and Divorce." *Child and Family Law Quarterly*, 24(2), pp. 139-157.

Dwyer, C. (2000) "Negotiating diasporic identities: Young British South Asian Muslim women." *Women's Studies International Forum*, 23(4), pp. 475-486.

Engineer, A. (2008) *The Rights of Women in Islam.* New Delhi: Sterling.

Fisher, M., Saleem, S. and Vora, V. (2018) "Islamic Marriages: Given the independent review into the application of Sharia Law in England and Wales, what is the way forward?" *Family Law Review*, (May), pp. 552-557.

Fiske, S. T. (2014) *Social beings: Core motives in social psychology, 3rd Edition.* Oxford: Wiley.

Gebauer, J. E. and Maio, G. R. (2012) "The need to belong can motivate belief in God." *Journal of Personality*, Apr, 80(2), pp. 465-501.

Grillo, R. (2015) *Muslim Families, Politics, and the Law.* Farnham: Ashgate Publishing.

Hagerty, B. M. K., Lynch-Sauer, J., Patusky, K., Bouwsema, M. and Collier, P. (1992) "Sense of belonging: A vital mental health concept." *Archives of Psychiatric Nursing*, 6, pp. 172–177.

Haleem, M. A. (2014) *Understanding the Qu'ran Themes and Styles* London: I. B. Tauras.

Hallaq, W. B. (2006) "What is Shari'a?" *Yearbook of Islamic and Middle Eastern Law (2005-2006).* Leiden, Netherlands: Brill, pp. 151-176.

Hamdeh, E. (2017) "Qurʾān and Sunna or the Madhhabs? A Salafi Polemic Against Islamic Legal Tradition." *Islamic Law and Society, 24*(3), pp. 211-253.

Haw, K. (2010) "Being, Becoming and Belonging: Young Muslim Women in Contemporary Britain." *Journal of Intercultural Studies*, 31(4), pp. 345-361.

Hedetoft, U. and Hjort, M. (2002) "Introduction." In: Hedetoft, U. and Hjort, M. (eds.) *The Postnational Self: Belonging and Identity.* Minnesota: University of Minnesota Press, p. 1.

Holdcroft, B. (2006) "What is Religiosity?" *Catholic Education: A Journal of Inquiry and Practice,* 10(1), September, pp. 89-103.

Hoque, A. (2018) "Third-generation British-Bangladeshis from East London: Complex Identities and a Culturally Responsive Pedagogy." *British Journal of Sociology of Education* 39(2), pp. 182–196.

Hurtado, S. and Carter, D. F. (1997) "Effects of college transition and perceptions of the campus racial climate on Latino College students' sense of belonging." *Sociology of Education,* 70, pp. 324–345.

Ignatieff, M. (1994) *Blood and Belonging: Journeys into the New Nationalism.* New York: Farrar, Straus, and Giroux.

Isakjee, A. (2016) "Dissonant belongings: The evolving spatial identities of young Muslim men in the UK." *Environment and Planning A,* 48(7), pp. 1337–1353.

Jaan, H. (2014) *Equal and Free? 50 Muslim Women's Experiences of Marriage in Britain Today.* Open Library: Aurat.

Kamali, M. H. (1999) "Maqāsid al-sharī'ah': The Objectives of Islamic Law." *Islamic Studies, 38*(2), pp. 193–208.

Kolman, I. (2018) "Beyond registration: Women opting for cohabitation in Tunis." *Sociology of Islam,* 6(3), pp. 381 400.

Lewicka, M. (2012) "Place attachment: How far have we come in the last 40 years?" *Journal of Environmental Psychology,* 31, pp. 207–230.

Macmillan, D. W. and Chavis, D. M. (1986) "Sense of community: A definition and theory." *Journal of Community Psychology,* 14, pp. 6–23.

Manea, E. (2016) *Women and Shari'a Law: The Impact of Legal Pluralism in the UK.* London: I. B. Tauris.

Meer, N. and Modood, T. (2009) "Refutations of racism in the 'Muslim question.'" *Patterns of Prejudice,* 43(3-4), pp. 335-354.

Menski, W. (1993) "Asians in Britain and the Question of Adaptation to a New Legal Order: Asian Laws in Britain?" In Milton, I., and Wagle, N. (eds.) *Ethnicity, identity, migration: The South Asian Context.* Toronto: University of Toronto Press, pp. 238-269.

Mirza, M. (2009) "Multiculturalism, religion, and identity." In Kalra, V. (ed.) *Pakistani Diaspora Culture, Conflict, and Change.* Oxford: Oxford University Press, pp. 273–284.

Modood, T. (2003) "British Muslims and the Politics of Mutliculturalism." In Modood, T., Triandafyllidon, A. and Zapta-Barrero, R. (eds.) *Mulitculturalism, Muslims, and Citizenship: A European Approach.* London, Routledge, pp. 37-56.

Modood, T. (2005) *Multicultural Politics, Racism, Ethnicity and Muslims in Britain.* Edinburgh: Edinburgh University Press.

Mohammad, R. (2013) "Making gender ma(r)king place: Youthful British Pakistani Muslim Women's Narratives of Urban Space." *Environment and Planning A,* 45, pp. 1802-1822.

Muslim Institute, (2008) *Muslim Marriage Contract.* London: The Muslim Institute.

Mythen, G., Walklate, S. and Khan, F. (2009) "'I'm a Muslim, but I'm not a Terrorist': Victimization, Risky Identities and the Performance of Safety." *British Journal of Criminology* 49, pp. 736–754.

Nash, J. C. (2008) "Re-thinking intersectionality." *Feminist Review* 89(1), pp. 1-15.

Nasir, J. (1986) *The Islamic Law of Personal Status.* London: Graham and Trotman.

Nielsen, J. S. (1991) "A Muslim Agenda for Britain: Some Reflections." *New Community,* 17:3, pp. 467-75.

Nisa, E. (2018) "Unregistered Marriages of Indonesian Migrant Workers in Malaysia: Contrasting Positions of State Agents." *Sociology of Islam,* 6(3), pp. 338-358

Parveen, R. (2017) *Do Shari's Councils meet the needs of women?* PhD Thesis, University of Birmingham.

Parveen, R. (2018) "Religious-only marriages in the UK: Legal positionings and women's experiences." *Sociology of Islam,* 6(3), pp. 316-337.

Phoenix, A. (2019) "Negotiating British Muslim belonging: a qualitative longitudinal study." *Ethnic and Racial Studies,* 42(10), pp. 1632-1650.

Ramadan, T. (2004) *Western Muslims and the Future of Islam.* Oxford: Oxford University Press.

Saifullah-Khan, V. J. (1977) "The Pakistanis: Mirpuri villagers at home and in Bradford." In Watson, J. L. (ed.) *Between two cultures.* Oxford: Blackwell, pp. 57-89.

Saleem, S. and Probert, R. (2018) "The Legal Treatment of Islamic Marriage Ceremonies." Oxford Journal of Law and Religion, 7(3), pp.376-400.

Saroglou, V. (2011) "Believing, bonding, behaving, and belonging: The big four religious dimensions and cultural variation." *Journal of Cross-Cultural Psychology, 42*(8), pp. 1320–1340

Saroglou, V., Clobert, M., Cohen, A. B., Johnson, K. A., Ladd, K. L., van Pachterbeke, M., Adamovova, L., Blogowska, J., Brandt, P-Y., Çukur, C. S., Hwang, K-K., Miglietta, A., Motti-Stefanidi, F., Mufioz-Garcia, A., Murken, S. and Roussiau, N. (2020) "Believing, Bonding, Behaving, and Belonging: The Cognitive, Emotional, Moral, and Social Dimensions of Religiousness across Cultures." *Journal of Cross-Cultural Psychology,* 51(7-8), pp. 551-575.

Sayyid, S. (2000), "Beyond Westphalia: Nations and Diasporas- the Case of the Muslim Umma." In Hesse, B. (ed.) *Unsettled Multiculturalisms: Diasporas, Entanglements, Transruptions.* London: Zed Books, pp. 33-50.

Scott, K. and Warren, M. (2007). *Perspectives on Marriage, 3rd Edition.* Oxford: Oxford University Press.

Shah-Kazemi, S. N. (2001) *Untying the Knot Muslim Women, Divorce and the Shariah.* Mumbai: The Signal Press.

Sherwood, H. (2017) "Most women in UK who have Islamic wedding miss out on legal rights." Guardian [online]Available at: https://www.theguardian.com/world/2017/nov/20/women-uk-islamic-wedding-legal-rights-civil-ceremony-marriage. Accessed 14th June 2022. Accessed: 10/6/2022.

Siddiqui, M. (1996) "Law and the desire for Social Control: An Insight into the concept of kafa'ah (equality) in Islamic Law." In Yamani, M. (ed.) *Feminism and Islam.* New York: Ithaca Press, pp. 49-68.

Siddiqui Report (2018) *The Independent Review into the Application of Sharia Law in England and Wales.* Cm 9560. London: Home Office.

Sona, F. (2014) "Defending the Family Treasure Chest: Navigating Muslim Families and Secured Positivistic Islands of European Legal Systems." In Shah, P., Foblets, M. C. and Rohe, M. (eds.) *Family, Religion and Law: Cultural Encounters in Europe.* Farnham: Ashgate Publishing, pp. 115-142.

Todd, R. (2006) "The Inevitable Triumph of the Ante–Nuptial Contract." *Family Law Journal,* 50, p. 539.

Uddin, I. (2018) "Nikah-Only Marriages: Causes, Motivations and its Impact on Dispute Resolution and Islamic Divorce Proceedings in England and Wales. *Oxford Journal of Law and Religion,* 7(3), pp. 401– 426.

Uddin, I. (2020) "Reformulation of Islamic Matrimonial Law: British Muslims, Contemporary Understandings and Normative Practices." *Journal of Muslim Minority Affairs,* 40(1), pp. 6-25.

Vora, V. (2015) "Unregistered Muslim Marriages in England and Wales: The Issue of Discrimination Through 'Non-Marriage' Declarations." In Suleiman, Y., and Anderson, P. (eds.) *Muslims in the UK and Europe II.* Cambridge: Centre of Islamic Studies, pp. 129-141.

Wadud, A. (2006) *Inside the Gender Jihad: Women's Reform in Islam.* Oxford: Oneworld Publications.

Welchman, L. (2004) *Women's Rights and Islamic Family Law: Perspectives on Reform.* London: Zed Press.

Welchman, L. (2010) "Women, Family and the Law: The Muslim Personal Status Debate in Arab States." In: Hefner, R. W. (ed.) *New Cambridge History of Islam, Vol.6.* Cambridge: Cambridge University Press, pp. 411-437.

Werbner, P. (1991) "The fiction of unity in ethnic politics." In Werbner, P. and Anwar, M. (eds.) *Black and Ethnic Leadership in Britain.* London: Zed Books, pp. 77-100.

Werbner, P. (1996) "Public Spaces, Political Voices: Gender, Feminism and Aspects of British Muslim Participation in the Public Sphere", in Shadid, W. and Konindsveld, V. (eds.) *Political Participation and Identities of Muslims in Non- Muslim States.* Kampen, Netherlands: Kok Pharos, pp. 206-228.

Werbner, P, (2000), "Divided Loyalties, Empowered Citizenship? Muslims in Britain." *Citizenship Studies,* 4(3), pp. 307-324.

Winter-Collins, A. and McDaniel, A. (2000) "Sense of belonging and new graduate job satisfaction." *Journal for Nurses in Staff Development,* 16, pp. 103–111.

Yuval-Davis, N. (2007) "Intersectionality, citizenship, and contemporary politics of belonging." In: Bennett, J. (ed.) *Scratching the Surface: Democracy, Traditions, Gender.* Lahore: Heinrich Boll Foundation, pp. 7–22.

Yuval-Davis, N. (2011) *The Politics of Belonging: Intersectional Contestations.* London: Sage.

Chapter 5

Humanism and Motherhood

Amanda Norman
University of Winchester

Abstract: Chapter 5 moves from the path of organised institutional religion to that of Humanism, a non-religious belief system. Amanda Norman considers the Humanistic ethos women use to seek and gain a positive attitude to their world, proposing that this is enabled by Humanism being that it is centred on human experience, connection, thought and hope. Spirituality and Humanism, choice and belonging are explored from women's perspectives with specific reference to pregnancy and childbirth. Humanism, Dr Norman argues, can give meaning and shape to women's lives during both during pregnancy and when celebrating the birth of their babies as a family member. Dr Norman provides a personal narrative which adds depth to the subject of women belonging to a group which is both spiritual and informal.

The latter part of the chapter discusses selected welcoming ceremonies aligned to Humanism. The Mother Blessing and Naming Celebrations are viewed as a way of recognising the belonging of both the mother and the baby to the group. Using a reflexive model, a deeper appreciation of connection and belonging as a mother within Humanism is explored. The transition of birth and motherhood is reflected upon in relation to spiritual questions regarding the commitment to moral values, human experience, happiness, pro-life choices, and lack of faith. This chapter examines what is gained from being a humanist as a new mother in her sense of self and relation to others.

Keywords: artefacts, auto-ethnography, belief system, childbirth, choice, ethical, faith, family, Humanism, individuality, mentors, Mother Blessing, motherhood, Naming Ceremony, (non)religious, pregnancy, proverbs, ritual, spirituality, scientific, values.

***

Introduction

In twenty-first century Britain, there are communities, subgroups and individuals who construct their belief systems, ethical decisions, and a sense of purpose, independent of institutional religious teachings (Norman, 2012). This chapter will explore Humanism and its multi-faceted and multi-stranded active philosophical life stance. It will specifically focus on women transitioning to motherhood today. An understanding of Humanism and the appeal for women, especially in their transition to motherhood will initiate the discussion. Whilst the transition to motherhood takes many forms, this chapter will focus on biological childbirth experiences. It will then discuss family rituals, including mother blessings and naming ceremonies. Spiritual Humanism will be critically explored in relation to the birth experience, the prior and subsequent rituals during this transitional life stage. It aligns closely with my personal humanist beliefs and invites the reader to make connections with how some women navigate their lives through pregnancy and motherhood in Britain today.

From its beginning in 1896, Humanists UK now has around 100 000 members and whilst this remains proportionally low, in comparison with affiliation to institutional religions, it denotes the increasing numbers in recent years (Thompson, 2021). Historically and traditionally, religion includes the practising, believing, and making of ethical decisions based on their religious teachings:

> One life is all we have, and we live it as we believe in living it. But to sacrifice what you are and to live without belief, that is a fate more terrible than dying. (Joan of Arc, c. 1412 – 30 May 1431).

Living as a Humanist: My Positionality

Humanism was a belief system introduced to me from my university days, having studied world religions as part of my degree. As a child, I had been brought up in a Christian household with a parent who had attended Catholic boarding school. Whilst my household did not include numerous prayers or reference to Jesus, we were expected to attend church every Sunday and having been baptised I took my confirmation at 12 years of age.

I recall trying to make sense of my family's religion although my personal view was one where Christianity often depicted a helpless female being saved by the hero. This was often the male breadwinner even when the reality presented was often in discord with this idea. I became conscious of how women were portrayed in the past and their continuing position within religious circles throughout Britain. As a young adult at university, approaching religion through an academic lens, I developed a questioning mind and began to align with the value placed on the here and now. I began to consider the potential contributions I, as a woman, could offer in creating a good life not just for me but for my community, for those around me.

Humanism moves beyond a psychological perspective to an inclusive philosophical stance. It emphasises the value and agency of human beings, individually and as a collective. The meaning of the term Humanism itself has also fluctuated, according to the successive intellectual movements who have identified with its beliefs and rejected religious associations, alongside the historical changing cultural landscapes. In the twenty-first century, Humanism refers to a perspective that affirms some notion of human freedom and progress. Fowler (1999) in Humanism: Beliefs and Practices, draws attention to and reminds us about what Humanism essentially is:

- *Hum* in human and Humanism stems from the Latin *humus* meaning earth or soil.
- *Homo* (as in homo sapiens) meaning earth-being.

In this definition, we are therefore made from matter, humans are from their present world and no other realm exists. Subsequently, when a human dies, our body, the physical matter, dies and there is the acceptance that our bodies or soul do not continue to exist in some other realm or reincarnate as a human or another life form (Bruce, 2002). As Humanists do not accept life after death value is placed on their current life of the present. Death is final and through this acceptance, it enriches life as being more precious. Life is therefore lived and experienced through a new perspective with the beauty of the environment and those around. This position about life and death culminates in the understanding that humans were not created as the result of a higher power, but natural, purposeless, physical, and biological evolutionary processes (Rosen and Young, 2015). Another key concept is that during life an individual is also thought to develop from being nurtured in nature (Barlow, 2018). We are therefore the result of genetic inheritance, but those genetic predispositions are not fixed and influenced by the environment in which we live and experience (Norman, 2019). Our personalities and behaviour are dependent on our physical brains, rather than anything immaterial or Godly (Koenig, McCullough and Larson, 2001). The development of neuroscience and science more broadly has enriched a deeper understanding of the science of life and, subsequently, how our emotions and moral compass are influenced by our lived experiences.

Humanism advocates equality and dignity for all human beings, emphasising a concern for humans and living things in relation to the world, referring to a life stance, centred on human agency. As human beings, we are guided by the knowledge of science rather than revelations from a supernatural source in understanding the world (Fowler, 1999; Norman, 2012). As a way of introducing Humanism, I will initially examine it from a female perspective. Discourses about belonging will be framed around the transition to motherhood, including childbirth. In exploring this further and arguing towards a humanistic, whist retaining a spiritual outlook I will be drawing on an auto-ethnographical approach by capturing my lived experience, transitioning to motherhood. In developing a sense of belonging connections are also sought and therefore two-fold. These are connecting and belonging as a new mother and secondly making connections and belonging with those of a similar belief and meaning about life. Further studies and autobiographies, including Wilson (1997) will compliment my narrative about exploring life as a Spiritual Humanist. Subsequently, rituals will then be explored and will include mother blessings and naming ceremonies with an evaluation of their symbolic representations. Parenting will conclude the chapter in its evaluation about upbringing within a Humanistic family with further invitations to reflect on some of the topics through an auto- ethnographical approach.

Humanism assumes a proactive and positive attitude to the world (Sherwood, 2020) as it centres on the human experience through thought, individual hope, and the moral code to live by within the one life given (Vernon, 2010). Within this frame of morality and developing an understanding of morality and how individuals would like to lead their lives ethically, like-minded individuals come together and celebrate life within The British Humanist Association and The International Humanist and Ethical Union (Joas and Wiegandt, 2009; Sherwood, 2020). They connect and share similar philosophies whist retaining their own individuality in how to live a good life. By seeking to live good lives without religious or superstitious beliefs a humanist believes moral values follow on from human nature and experiences. In creating a community, individuals proactively work together to improve the quality of life for all, imparting a fair and equitable society. Whilst membership is not a driver to being a Humanist the opportunity to gather creates a space to collectively share feelings, ask questions and engage in alternative views about the world and discussions about the ways to live a good life (Humanists UK, 2021).

Organisations such as Humanists UK, which began in 1896, were a movement with views about social change being one of their primary aims within society. Today there are currently over 100,000 members and supporters (Brierley, 2006; Thompson, 2021). There are also 70 local and special interest affiliates promoting Humanism. Campaigning is part of the mission, with the purpose of leading happier, fulfilling lives. Humanist groups also share informed thinking, with the support of prominent philosophers, scientists, and other experts (Humanists UK). Activities discussed in groups include rituals, including non-religious funerals, weddings, and baby-naming ceremonies. These have been delivered for a hundred and twenty years (Adams, 1996). Humanism is therefore recognised as a philosophy and worldview encouraging individuals to reach their full potential, symbolized by the society's emblem (Humanists UK). Humanism is also referred to as a democratic and ethical life stance. This includes accepting the rights and responsibilities that give meaning and shape to their own lives. In wider society Humanism aims to develop a more humane society ethically framed around reason and free inquiry and embracing successes and failure as part of self-growth (Cave, 2009). It is concerned with valuing and self-development and experience. A key organiser of the World Union of Freethinkers' conference in London in 1938, and, after World War II, a founding member of the International Humanist and Ethical Union (IHEU) was Harold Blackham (1987) viewing

> life as important and a privilege within Humanism (Blackham, 1987; Norman, 2012). This involves allowing everyone equal opportunities and choices in the worlds of education, employment, and the home. It does not assert a higher ground to that of other beliefs and religions but acknowledges there are differing views about life. It not for a Humanist to critically challenge other beliefs, rather accept it is their freedom to choose (Cave, 2009).

Women, Feminism, and Humanism

In many patriarchal societies, evidence suggests a male-dominant culture, denying women of their equal rights. Furthermore, the social construction of the family in these societies has been used to strictly define roles, and to control women (Aune, 2008). Social stereotyping and *tradition* have been argued to discriminate against women, with assumed roles such as childcare and domestic work assigned to women. Within Humanism there is an agreement that women should resist restricted roles imposed on them. Humanism emphasises democracy and the father's role should be equitable regarding choices made about their children and childcare (Law, 2011; McGuire, 2008). Decisions about the division of labour for the parenting couple should be as an equal status in a relationship and a cooperative venture. This can often be contrary to historical, cultural, and social division found in communities where Humanists live.

In gaining perspectives of individuals views and a life stance, it would be customary to approach the organisations aligned to the faith. However, women may choose not to associate themselves with a national organisation, resisting the collective approach and membership. In comparing Humanists from the twenty-first century to Campbell 1964 survey, Longden (2015) evaluated 1,097 British Humanist Association members from a survey conducted in 2014. In his comparisons to the mid-twentieth century British survey, he found members in 2014 continued to be predominately male, well educated, work in professional jobs, and live in urban areas. They were typically older and consequently more likely to be retired. However, in reflection on these findings, I would argue they were taken from a very small sample. Many women may also turn to secular belief systems as a subsequent disengagement to their families' religious beliefs but would not necessarily apply for membership in a society, so the numbers may be skewed. The evidence researched does suggest many children are growing up in non-religious households, and therefore associating themselves as non-religious (Voas and Crockett, 2005), including identifying as a Humanist, at a younger age than in previous generations. Moreover, representation regarding the lack of women's involvement from Campbell (1964) and Longden (2005) seems to be contrary to the involvement of women in developing ethical societies and Humanism.

The Humanist Heritage Project developed by Madeleine Goodall (2020) evaluated key female pioneers within Humanism, highlighting their vision for democracy, equal acknowledgement, and rights, prior to Humanist organisations familiar with today. These included Mary Wollstonecraft (1759-1797) and Frances Wright (1795-1852) who combined feminism and freethought in writing and lecturing for social reform. Whilst following Robert Owen, who lectured widely in the name of socialism and secularism, Margaret Chappellsmith (1806-1883), Ernestine Rose (1810-1892), and Emma Martin (1812-1851) were all women considered outspoken and godless women of the time (Goodall, 2020). Wollstonecraft (1759 – 1797), was often criticised by the conservative press for blasphemy, and for having a child outside marriage. In her novels, she was condemned for her views about the patriarchal institution of marriage. She often featured women as passionate, having romantic friendships outside of marriage with both sexes (Goodall, 2020). Her overarching belief was that women should have the same fundamental rights as men, including the right to be educated, benefiting from the same opportunities. She did not claim women should supersede men but for women to aspire as an equal, alongside men.

During the mid-twentieth century, Brown (2001) evaluated a renewed tension regarding the feminist, sexual liberationist discourses and the Christian discourses that assumed to regard femininity as a form of submission to their husbands. This was recognised through the teachings and service of religious life, with obedience advocated. This included the act of procreation and how sexual relationships were observed. Within Humanism, an alternative view is applied. For humanists, the birth of a baby is not a gift of God or a sexual relationship just for the procreation of children. Contraception has been made possible for sex to be enjoyed in its own right. In past generations, women struggled to bring up large and often ailing families. Their only respite from childbirth was when their husband was considerate by either abstaining from sex or by going elsewhere for sexual gratification. These women frequently died young leaving the eldest daughter often no more than a child herself to run the home. Religions, such as Roman Catholicism, teaches that artificial methods of contraception are wrong. We sometimes forget the debt we owe the pioneers of birth control and those who have fought, and are still fighting, against prejudice to make it available worldwide to all who wish to use it (Wilson, 1997).

It was thought, in part, that organised religion had lost some of its authority as women declined to attend formal worship on a regular basis. Women were argued to have fewer children than previous generations and therefore needing less religious guidance. Historically many families often returned to organised faith as a way of framing their everyday family life (Voas and Crockett, 2005). A further factor was increased paid employment, whereby women were spending less time in their domestic space and therefore having less time for religious activities (Aune, 2011).

Although Feminism and Humanism have been aligned in outlook, many women identifying as a Humanist in the twenty-first century may distinguish themselves from feminism. Feminism for some may be broadly considered as the promotion of women's rights on the ground of the equality of the sexes, whereas a Humanist believes in the authority of the scientific method in understanding the world. Humanists may also reject the supernatural and a higher God, seeking to live an ethically fulfilling life based on reason and humanity. However, there are connections to both feminism and Humanism (Vernon, 2010). The British Humanist Association (BHA) as well as Feminism retains an emphatically pro-choice position on the issue of abortion, with Munday, the feminist campaigner who lobbied successfully for the passing of the Abortion Act (1967), as a patron. Humanism considers the legalisation of abortion a moral right, because it respects and supports non-religious beliefs, alongside respecting women's rights, and autonomy (O'Sullivan, 2015). BHA also actively campaigns for the reproductive rights for all women, such as using assisted fertility treatment (ART).

The BHA and other Humanist organisations and societies actively campaign for the provision of human rights to all and support progress in the direction of women's substantive emancipation worldwide. These are both issues Feminists typically also support. Humanism seeks moral guidance based on common reason and humanity, including autonomy as central to morality, and living a good human life, personal to the individual (Aune, 2008). Feminism could therefore be considered, closely associated with, and supporting Humanism, but having distinguishable features. Feminism is the action of the principles relating to women. Humanism believes all humans are the measure of things, whilst feminism differs because they view women as a priority.

Through life events such as marriage, I chose a non-religious ceremony. Childbirth evoked further questions about my spiritual self and my faith. I have joined online humanism groups and feel a sense of belonging with like-minded individuals, both men and women, although I do feel a draw to the way women belong. I do not however simply define myself as a humanist but include a spiritual sense of being within my faith since having children. Therefore, I do believe I can reshape and identify myself a humanist with a sense of spirituality as a woman. This shift was developed when I initiated and gave birth. Nowadays, I do not feel so fixed in my discourses about my personal faith and, for me, humanism allows for personal reflections and autonomy, encouraging free thinking. Personally, the appeal is a celebration of like-minded people, with planetary consciousness without being dictated too or following an approved path that has little meaning to the modern-day world of women. Humanism is not exclusive to women but, for me, that is the central point, it is about myself as an individual, with choices made, navigated by myself. It offers more than the emptiness of not believing anything or having little thought of spiritual thinking and gives weight to what is valued in the here and now. For myself, this is what is important to how I want to live my everyday life as a parent.

Whilst I have focused on pregnancy, birth, and subsequent rituals this is a timely reminder of the complexities arising with the choice of being pregnant. Living in Britain, there are both religious and secular beliefs impacting personal choices about the termination of their foetus and the consequence of those decisions made. For a woman, the conceptual thinking about the emerging or emerged personhood of their foetus will be associated with beliefs of when a life is thought to begin. Those beliefs will have also impacted on reproductive choices relating to contraception, screening tests offered, choices for healthy behaviours and reflections about the desire or termination of being pregnant (Gordon, 2019). The consideration to terminate could be either a result of maternal choice or an offered choice with a health risk and concern towards the wellbeing of the woman or her foetus. A woman who decides to have a termination may choose to actively disconnect from their foetus, although her beliefs about the personhood of her unborn will have been influenced by the societal background as well as her own religious beliefs (Callister and Khalaf, 2010). This will consequently impact subsequent decisions about the continuation and choices about pregnancy.

In Humanism, this complex and deeply personal decision is considered a maternal choice by the mothers, with or without medical advice and recommendations. For those women who are subsequently offered termination for a known abnormality, they may have already reached a place of acceptance and communication with their foetus through their decision-making (Crowther and Hall, 2018).[1] This highlights the challenging narratives regarding humans as equal, within and beyond a religious perspective. It includes the time when personhood is accepted during pregnancy and birth. Women who do choose to continue with their pregnancy despite the diagnosis of a serious life-limiting conditions with their foetus and themselves may be religiously or spiritually influenced and from a Humanistic perspective, this decision remains personal and a right of the mother (Hall and Taylor, 2004).

This further highlights the intricacies in recognising the personhood of the foetus, not just by the mother but also by society. In some societies, there are legal rights and choice towards termination. In Britain, this could be viewed as a more progressive stance than other neighbouring societies where choices and restrictions are denied based on religious authority. This underlines the influence of religion and beliefs at a societal and personal level regarding personhood towards the foetus (Carver and Ward, 2007). A humanist would agree that the discourse should be centralised around women. They should feel and be empowered to make appropriate choices for themselves, irrespective of their decision (Crowther and Hall, 2018).

Transitioning to Motherhood

Hello babies, welcome to earth it's hot in the summer and cold in the winter. It's round and wet and crowded. On the outside, babies, you've got a hundred years here. There's only one rule that I know of babies – God damn it, you've got to be kind. (Vonnegut in Copson and Roberts 2020, p. 11)

Shorter, in his analysis of the mother and babies throughout history, draws on the significance of religion and attitudes towards young babies in the eighteenth century. Francois Lebrun writes of agent centre eighteenth-century peasants:

> [t]he death of a small child, provided it has been baptised is considered on the religious plane as a deliverance, for the baby has had the grace of .... being granted ... directly to paradise without knowing the bitterness of this life and risking his spiritual health. On the human plane baby death is almost a banal accident which a subsequent birth will recuperate. (1976, p. 173).

---

[1] During my own pregnancy I communicated with my unborn twins by singing to them and through touch and speech.

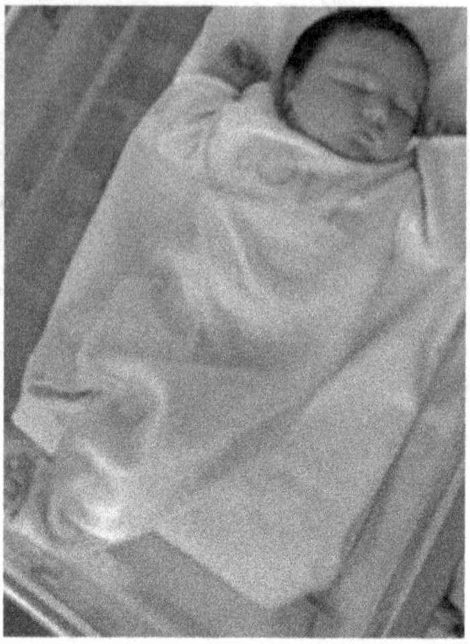

Image 5.1. Hello Baby[2]

In the modern world, an unforeseen and untimely death of a baby impacts and touches the emotional core of a couple.[3] The timely and successful birth of a new being is therefore considered a sacred rite of passage for the mother and baby. It is the acknowledgement of the enormity of a new life entering the world irrespective of religion or belief (Martins, 2018). The religiosity and spiritual experience placed on birth and subsequent upbringing of a young child in modern-day Britain is understood by a milieu of multifaith and non-religious beliefs from mothers and their families. Humanism considers human beings as the starting point for serious moral and philosophical inquiry and provides an alternative life compass in discovering a sense of purpose, ethical values, and morality in life (Wilson, 1997). Baptism is a minority choice for parents in Britain today and this may be attributed to increasingly secular attitudes towards death. However, public rituals bring forth shared experience and some now choose non-institutional religious ceremonies in times of joy and grief (Ward, 1999).

Within the literature, less empirical research specifically addresses birth, motherhood, and religion, with the focus often linked to the differences

[2] All photographs used are my own.

[3] I recognise that the rituals of passage and the acknowledgement of loss are not so well established for miscarriages, still births and abortions in contemporary Britain. The professional support and resources on offer depend on the geographical location of the parents.

between marriage and family relationships (Thiessen, 2016). Among the research findings, mothers have regularly referred to childbirth to some a form of (in some cases a lack of) spiritual experience, with and without religious associations. Reflections on the depth and meaning of how the physical world is experienced through birth was also described, culminating in a spiritual and a deep connection to the earth. Once a new-born arrives, mothers typically seek social support and benefit from a wide range of community networks, including faith community involvement (Koening, McCulloch and Larson, 2001). In pursuing connections and networks aligned to their moral and ethical ways of living, women find solace beyond the traditional organised religious networks readily accessed from previous generations (Athan, 2005).

In the twentieth century, western societies became more secular, with lower rates of church attendance, baptisms, attendance at Sunday Schools and so forth (Brown, 2001). Believing without belonging resulted in a decline being attributed to reduced generational religious beliefs. This resulted in fewer parents successfully transmitting religious beliefs to their children. A small number of studies are starting to address the lack of previous research into non-religious inter-generational transmission in Britain. Strhan and Shillitoe looked at non-religious transmission in primary school-aged children (between 5 and 11 years of age). They found that:

> [n]ot only is a lack of religious transmission occurring but that this takes place alongside and in relation to banal, implicit forms of non-religious socialization in the home together with more explicit forms of socialization occurring in schools (in RE and collective worship in particular), through which children come to articulate their non-religious beliefs. (2019, p. 1105).

For the wider population, evidence suggested transmission was just as weak for those stating they continued to believe but did not attend religious groups. Davie (1994) evaluated supernatural belief remained high but religious practice was substantially declining. Individuals were also associating themselves with a nonreligious identity, with vague alternatives towards spirituality. Day (2011) extended the findings by correlating the reduced regular attendance with a reduction in collective church ritual celebration as a contributing factor to the decline in religious belief. Fuller (2001) supports this by examining the intergenerational influences of religions on non-religious parenting. In the mid-nineteenth century, more than half the adult population of England and Wales would have attended church on any given Sunday, but by the end of the twentieth century, less than one-twelfth were attending a Sunday service (Voas and Crockett, 2005).

Voas and Crocket (2005), when exploring data from the British Household Panel Survey and the British Social Attitudes surveys also revealed a growing population of believers without belonging and concluded that believing without belonging is in decline. However, for many women, including new mothers having a baby may evoke renewed beliefs and faith systems from a religious and a spiritual perspective, possibly identifying, for example, as a Christian Humanist, bridging their own upbringing with their current being (Wojtkowiak, 2018). These are individuals with humanist principles of universal human dignity, individual freedom, and the importance of happiness as essential and even exclusive aspects of the teachings of Jesus (Woodhead, Kowanami, and Partridge, 2009). For others, the complete break from religion has resulted in seeking evolutionary, spiritual, or secular Humanism as an alternative philosophy to living and pursuing something more than simply its absence as atheists often resolve to. Molloy who grew up as a Presbyterian and became a humanist stated:

> I am not vehemently anti-religion. We must respect others and their sincerely held beliefs. I recognise that there are those for whom religion brings comfort, people who face great troubles and couldn't get through it without religious belief. But it's not for me. (Watson, 2008, p. 1).

Women who became mothers took on meanings beyond that of having a baby and according to Martins (2018) as well as Athan and Miller (2005), women spoke of a change in values, behaviour, and outlook on life, all of which were directed toward greater connectedness. The new mothers described a deliberate effort towards faith participation and endorsed the importance of living personal values and beliefs wanting to transmit these to their babies. The women also shared a similar experience of aloneness and need for connection with others, expressed as trying to connect with the sacred. For some mothers, they sought meaning in connection and comfort in the notion that they and their family were not alone in the world. While some referred to a spiritual connection and about going to church and renewing a faith other described feeling a greater sense of connection to humanity through the common and communal experience of motherhood:

> I think I've become more connected, I guess, being pregnant and now being a mum. Just to, humanity, you know. It's like this experience of being pregnant and then having a child, is something completely universal, across all women that have had kids. (Martins, 2018).

As a family group, social identities can change depending on the connections made and the influences around them. They many alter their beliefs from humanistic to agnostic to atheist to SBNR. These findings lend support to the theory that a secular worldview is purposefully considered and transmitted within families. As the number of nonreligious individuals increases in Britain secularity is not merely a default orientation similar to atheism but an actively pursued and sustained worldview (Vernon, 2010). More parents are intentionally raising their children as nonreligious, and that the secular worldview they seek to impart to their children is grounded in their own values, principles, and ideals. These include the independence of thought, treating others as one would like to be treated, an appreciation and care of the earth, valuing science, rationalising problems, and encouraging children to choose their own worldviews. It is important to note that many of the parents teaching their children these values would not be actively identifying as Humanists, even if their worldview could be accurately described as humanist. I propose that they are embracing the tenets of Humanism in the way they want to interpret in their own way, which is the appeal towards Humanism (Luthar et al., 2001).

Research by the Humanist magazine, *Humanist Scot* (2015) asked nine family participants how they would talk to their children about Humanism. Responses ranged from discussing their position to their children from an early age. Some said they did not believe in a god, but that their grandparents and relatives did and that they could make up their own mind when they were older. A core aspect was to be kind to other people. One spoke about coming to Humanism late in life. She felt this was because as a child, a teenager and then as a wife and mother, she had conformed to the family and their associated religion. It was not until having her own children that she began to question her own beliefs. One of the important things she considered was providing her children with the tools to think for themselves, finding their own conclusions and paths. Encouraging them to think that science was crucial, and science was always part of the conversations. They said they preferred to use scientific evidence to try to understand the world. They made them aware that religion could be a controversial subject, and that respect was important when discussing other people's beliefs (Curly, 2007).

Connecting with Spirituality and Humanism

The problem with defining spirituality is that it can be a *slippery* term (Norman, 2012). Social scientists have debated whether spirituality is an alternative to religion or the middle ground between religion and secularity. Zinnbauer, Pargament and Scott (1999) contend that spirituality is a slippery concept, and therefore meanings make it problematic and difficult in providing a clear definition. Many atheists consider the term spirituality to be an inappropriate descriptor for their life experiences because of its association with the supernatural and medieval superstition (Harris, 2014). However, King and Koenig (2009) assert the need to incorporate spirituality in research and health services provision. They consider it as an increasingly valuable aspect of education and care. For many Humanists, the rejection of spirituality also contradicts their individual choice to what they consider as relevant to their beliefs. There have often been various designations conjoined with the term Humanism:

- Scientific Humanism
- Political Humanism
- Naturalistic Humanism
- Romantic Humanism
- Liberal Humanism
- Christian Humanism
- Spiritual Humanism

The three most common groups individuals align to are:

- Secular Humanism
- Religious Humanism
- Evolutionary Humanism (Fowler, 1999).

There is an argument that the word Humanism is important here because these designations tend to stress the importance of the initial term Scientific or Christian. The appended general humanistic outlook is read as a secondary aspect. Personally, I do not consider the two words are presented by preference or significance and, as Fowler (1999) evaluates, free thought and debate are key to a twenty-first-century dialogue. The value of Humanism has come to be referred to as a distinct movement, and the emphasis should therefore not be about the agreements regarding its definition but how it is lived as an ongoing inquiry (Fowler, 1999).

Spiritual Humanism needs to be distinguished from spirituality as portrayed by organised religion. Spirituality in Humanism cannot include any belief in the supernatural or divine intervention (Seltzer, 2013). For many Humanists, it is argued to be preferable to avoid the term spirituality or spiritual because of the connotations associated with it. Although spirituality is an ambiguous term, the concept is argued to be an essential element of humanity within Humanism as for organised religion. According to Dein (2016) members of the British Humanist Association, 35% strongly agreed and

21% moderately agreed that it was possible to be spiritual without being religious. Some respondents asserted that the term spiritual was very vague and therefore was a redundant term. They preferred terms such as emotional connectedness, awe, or beauty, which are commonly included in definitions of spirituality. For me, it is about an enhanced human experience, in this case, triggered by the natural world. It is an experience, personal and with meaning. Many would argue they are concerned their Humanism will somehow be contaminated by religiosity if spirituality is referred to. Humanists would agree that the scientific method is by far the best way to understand objective truths about the world, including an understanding of brain development, through neuroscience, in the twenty-first century. Subjective experience though is not, by definition, open to direct observation by anyone other than the person experiencing it. It is therefore reality for that person and, as far as we know, unique and personal to them and therefore defined by their experience (Mason, 2006).

Elkins (1988) considered the word spirituality derives from the Latin root *spiritus*, which means breath, referring to the breath of life. Spirituality involves opening the heart and cultivating the capacity to experience awe, reverence, and gratitude. Spirituality enables the individual to view the sacred in the ordinary and immerse in feelings of intense sensations (Martins, 2018). Therefore heightened emotions may be also referred to as a spiritual, experience. This could be from hearing a certain piece of music, creating art, giving birth. Fromm (1966) and Maslow (1964) believed spiritual perfection resided in realising human potential feeling and the poignancy of life, thereby, an individual should live their life to the fullest. They also do not anticipate an afterlife. Spiritual perfection, for them, is achieved in the here and now. According to Fromm (1966) spiritual perfection was achieved through humanistic religion and while Humanistic religion is a conflicting term, it is based on humankind and its strengths, such as rationality and artistic creativity. Fromm writes of the *being* mode of existence versus the *having* mode. The being mode is characterised by wisdom, love and care for others, and a philosophical respect for nature. The having mode is marked by the possessiveness of material things, status, and knowledge. Spiritual perfection, for Fromm, is about being human in the deepest and fullest sense, filled with love and contentment (Fromm, 1966). Similarly, Maslow's hierarchal model of needs considered self-actualisation as the fulfilment of our human potential. Self-actualisation or peak experience is a form of spiritual perfection, within Maslow's model in relation to Humanism. Many individuals, whilst not attaining self-actualisation may still have peak experience (Crowther and Hall, 2018; Maslow, 1964). An example being the transformative experience described by a mother after 14 days of pain and strength during childbirth:

> [i]t was exciting I hardly ate or slept.... it lasted for two weeks. I was so happy for having this experience.... it means everything. (Crowther and Hall, 2018, p. 76).

Crowther and Hall (2018) described the mother's labour as her peak experience. Maslow's (1979) peak experiences are characterised by these intense moments in life, involving unexpected and temporal feelings of powerful happiness and wellbeing. It may include possible involvement and awareness of transcendental unity or knowledge of a higher truth during the experience, in this case, labour and childbirth.

While for some women a sense of God's presence may be their reality, for other women during childbirth, there may be an association to a sense of transcendence in emotions. For example, a Finnish woman suggested that while she was not religious her birth experience was far more than physical. She centred herself, listened to her body and was calm, giving herself the strength to negotiate her own childbirth (King, 1989).

Childbirth, for the first time, was therefore considered in many ways as a rebirth, transitioning into the new role of motherhood. Connections was also described during the childbirth experience. Another feeling was the power of creation when they gave birth. (Johnson et al., 2007, p.175). An Australian mother said:

> I didn't think about childbirth being a spiritual experience at the time but looking back I do. I think it's just the way you can connect with your baby in a way you've probably never connected with anything. It gives you a whole different perspective on your spiritual side. (Callister and Khalaf, 2010).

Sellers and Haag suggested spirituality beyond religion is "the centre or core of humanness" (1998, p. 339). A review of the literature revealed only a small number of studies were published on the subjective daily experiences of mothers and how mothering a child facilitates spiritual awareness. Scholarship has attempted to explore this topic generally by following two types: studies of pregnancy-related experiences deemed transcendental or sacred or academic reviews of mothering as a spiritual journey. Researchers, including Crowther and Hall (2018), have provided valuable insights, both from professionals' and mothers' spiritual positions in healthcare. Studies conducted by Spivak et al. (1993) concluded that women in labour regularly and predictably experienced transpersonal shifts in awareness otherwise unusual in their daily lives (Athan and Miller, 2013). Their stories provided revelatory understandings about emotional experiences during childbirth, irrespective of whether they were religious.

Stories in Humanism

Stories within Humanism are valuable as part of understanding human existence. They remind us that we are not alone and that our interactions with others can place us at the heart of the story or as a backstory of another person's story. It makes sense of our lives and allows us to convey and give shape to human experiences in our lived worlds. From telling a story, cyclical connection with others can be formed and conversations created with like-minded individuals (Humanists UK, 2020). Reading the stories of mothers' experiences is valuable in Humanism because they serve the purpose of enabling us to make sense of our lives. Stories give shape to lived experiences. They provide patterns, templates about what we want to tell others and the meanings within them. In reading stories, there is an ongoing connection between the self and others. It provides a platform to understand other individuals lived experiences through real-life biographies and histories. Stories convey what it is like to have a certain kind of experience (Norman, 2012). As an approach to writing lives, I give voice to the *spirit autobiography*, and reveal the why, how, and when in configuring my story around childbirth (Parnell, 2019).

The story I begin with is my own. In reflecting on the beginning of life, I will be drawing on my subjective experiences during birth and ritual in making sense of how I feel I connected to Spiritual Humanism. An auto-ethnographical approach was adopted in consideration of my personal experiences. Method storytelling enables the researcher to make sense of their experiences, although there may be an associated emotional toll to contemplate. Considering this, I have drawn on culturally significant themes to frame my experiences in consideration of Spiritual Humanism. The process of narrative inquiry expands upon storytelling, it involves critical reflection, with personal information whilst making connections between the experience of the individual and the cultural context. When using a reflexive approach to narrative inquiry an acknowledgement of my own identity, culture, values, biases, and assumptions are considered and acted on (Ellis, 2004). A Neoliberalist ideologically informed perspective suggests that the process of reflective practice may *hollow out* learning, and therefore be viewed as being restrictive and simply a confessional narrative (Chang, 2008). However, Moloney (2006) asserts that birth narratives do more than this and present insights into the connection between childbearing and spirituality (Rosato et al., 2006). Birth stories actually offer a powerful and rich source of data. Greater emphasis needs to be accorded to "a valuing of women's stories as data" (Carolan, 2006, p. 66). According to Ellis (2004), autoethnographic texts are often written in the first person and are deeply personal and sensitive expressions of the authors' sense of being.

I have used an auto-ethnographic approach in sharing my story and contributing to the literature of Humanism as a mother. It is an approach aiding an understanding about myself in relation to the self and others (Maloney, 2006). Understanding spiritual Humanism and motherhood is nestled between the existing literature and my own interpretation of experiences. My cultural contextual journey has been reflected on during my experiences as a mother. I say children with a sense of awe at having four healthy, thriving *children*. However, my current position as a mother does not reveal the anguish of treatments, despair, and hope from pregnancy through to birth and motherhood. In seeking treatment and having to accept professional and scientific intrusions, this provided a framework in reflecting on my beliefs, faith, and spirituality. I have chosen to reflect on my last childbirth experience, having twins and the relationship I subsequently made with connecting to Spiritual Humanism.

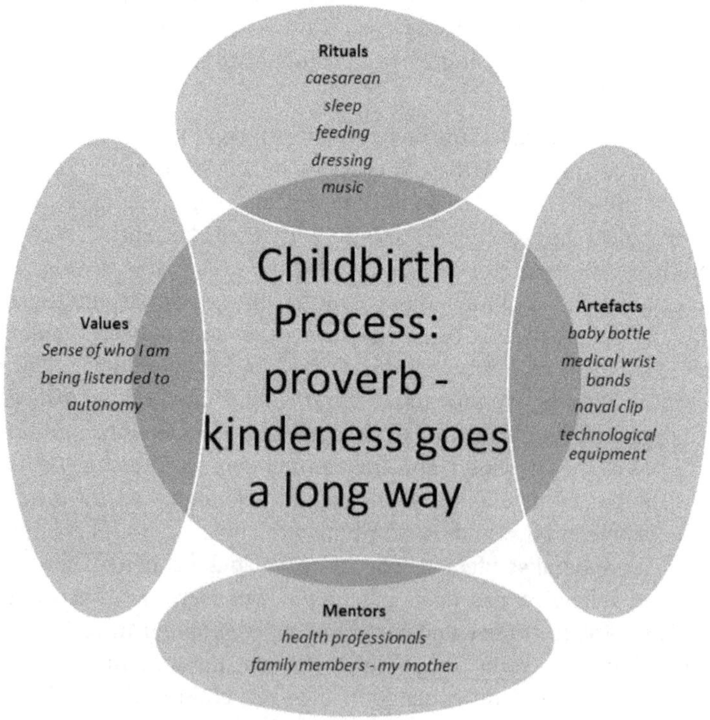

Figure 5.1. Reflections on themes during my personal experiences of childbirth and post-delivery adapted from Chang (2008, p. 76).

The process of my childbirth and subsequent days in the hospital. An ethnographical approach, framed by Chang's (2008) five themes to approaching ethnographical data. The themes are proverbs, rituals, artefacts, values, and mentors. It was a useful approach to drawing on personal key themes, culturally contextualised in my experience of childbirth. In producing this model (Figure), it enables me to reflect on my position.

In experiencing birth trauma, it has aligned my sense of who I am in the present, what I contribute to this life, my values, and the philosophy I convey with my children. Like Wilson (1997), having children is not just the process of childbirth but the responsibility, morality and values that are attached to having children:

> [p]erhaps the most wonderfully exciting thing in the natural world is the ability of living things to reproduce.... human beings are unique in their capacity to make sophisticated decisions about having babies. Most men and women in the country can choose whether or not to have a family, how many children they want and when to have them and how to space them. But with this capacity goes grave responsibility. (Wilson, 1997, p. 1)

My Birth Story

It is the morning of my caesarean and I have been in hospital with high blood pressure for the past few hours. I have had two previous caesareans and concluded with twins this would probably result in another. As a Humanist, Wilson (1997) states active birth is still uncommon in this country, although it has some powerful advocates. Hospital deliveries with the option of an epidural block caesarean section are sometimes essential for the safety of the baby. If circumstances are favourable most humanists would opt for methods that show great respect for the human body and its natural process. It gives more responsibility and control to the parents involved, but there are always exceptions (Wilson, 1997).

I had been advised by a young (in my mind with her painted nails, slick hair and small figure and little visible lines of an experienced life on her face, an assumption I know and aware it may be more about my own feelings perhaps, being 42 years and heavily pregnant) midwife that my imminent caesarean certainly didn't have to be the outcome and a natural birth could be possible with twins. I look at her with a mix of frustration and annoyance as she recalls a couple of studies of success, no doubt from the United States, I think. I recall wondering whether she had given birth herself and how much emphasis was placed on natural birth from her recently completed training. I try to feel calm and think positively as it is her job, and she is trying to present me with options. She chats about a natural birth and the word natural in itself may have already provoked a feeling that somehow my two previous sections had been an option and somehow less natural. I also felt in her view an unnatural mother and caesareans were to be something to be avoided. From my experience in trying to convey the emotions of helplessness and my achievements of having two healthy children already from previous life-threatening childbirth, experiences seemed too much to say and far too dramatic. So, in true British style, I say nothing. I think about how I feel about her comments and consider that perhaps I play a minor role as "patient" in her story, an unfamiliar face with little to offer or need in terms of the patient, professional relationship. I talk and lean to my friends and husband through this period and feel gratitude and at peace with my two previous childbirth outcomes.

Childbirth number three: At the hospital, I prepare for my caesarean. I wash my hair and brush it in preparation, unsure when I may get another chance. I follow the procedures of not eating, being checked, and arranging my home items. I talk to my family on the phone and go through moments of excitement and then calm. I have been in a few days and the decision was for the caesarean to happen with my blood pressure high. Ultimately, I had no voice in what and how I chose to birth, once again a medical procedure to be undertaken. I do not think of what may go wrong but rather visualise the positive of having my babies soon. I recall my previous feeling of love for my daughter and how the process was calm and magical. I feel it will be similar.... I am focusing on my final block as the ritual of the injection commences...I am unduly anxious about the injection that it will not be a success. I feel it is a premonition perhaps and vocalise this to the staff, who laugh and reassure me it is nerves.... Unfortunately, it took four painful attempts, "roll your back", they bark as they try again.... and once achieved I was quickly moved to a bed in preparation – my legs tingling and now accepting the rest is beyond my physical control. I have to allow the professionals to take responsibility for me and my babies. I must trust. I remain calm and enthusiastic. The staff speak all around me but not to me. My husband talks to me, and I am asked if I need more medication every so often.... one baby is not in the best position and the room is filled with an atmosphere of tension and abrupt voices. I am not spoken to, and calls are made. I close my eyes and breathe. I focus on the voices familiar to me and breathe slowly. The collective group of medical professionals continue to talk all around me.... The crash team are notified.... the babies arrive one by one. They are shown to me, held by the midwives, fed by the midwives, and removed by the midwives. Busy and procedural came to mind.... kindness was needed....

I feel a sense of awe and euphoria of childbirth successfully finished, but also a feeling of helplessness and removed in the here and now. Residing in the tension between the two overwhelming feelings. I was not asked much about the babies and felt my spiritual health could have been included. I connect to the mothers who felt childbirth was a spiritual experience but also the complexity and anxiety around medicalised childbirth and the attitudes towards me because of this.

I am taken to a recovery room, my husband and one of my babies were already there, but one has been taken to emergency care as a precaution. It was casually told to me, perhaps deliberately so as not to worry me.... I also felt emotionally fragile at the news, responding as such. During the subsequent eight hours, I am left alone to recover with my husband by my side. I look at my one baby and listen to the midwives as they come in and out of the room talking about their shifts and weekends. Eventually, a nurse comes over and asks if I would like to be cleaned. I remain numb, my thoughts and physical body are not aligned.

My body is responding and reacting to the environment while my head is full of thoughts about the new lives I have produced and the uncertainty of their future at this point. Their future in the short term and long term is unknown to all and I have to accept what will be... in a spiritual but not Godly way....

The nurse cleans the yellowy orange stains that encases my lower body. She is gentle in manner, and I believe she is gentle in her approach. I question her medical role to myself. How many times does she undertake this ritual with unknown women post-operation? She doesn't speak a lot but asked if I would like toast and a drink and her presence is calming. She talks about my babies, and I feel a sense of being valued for the first time. She explains why my daughter had gone to NICU and I am able to ask questions. I would like to see them both but, at that moment, I wait until I am told. I feel I am suspended in time as I recover physically from birth. I will keep their hats and wristbands as a symbolic remembrance of the day.... It was a sacred time, and I was very much in the present, moment to moment. I did not pray or call on God. Rather I appreciated and accepted the situation. I would have liked to be listened to and interacted with more though....

Exploring childbirth and humanism I have also included the spiritual tensions I felt during this time. For me, the initial childbirth journey was intended to be about connecting with my inner self, a spiritual awakening and sense of belonging in the community of mothers. How would I live in the here and now and what ethical considerations about morals and family life would I value and share with my children?

Whilst this was an appealing way to explore my forthcoming transition to being a mother, I had not anticipated the impact on childbirth. The lived experience of childbirth moved from an autonomous and *natural* process to something quite different. With medical attention being necessary within an intimate and personal transition I moved between life and death and the relationships between professional and patient. In reflecting on my experience, my identity has not transformed but rather moved into a more fluid existence of how I want to be, how I want to live and what I value and believe as a woman and as a mother. In making sense of my childbirth experience, I considered what this meant to me as a woman considered a Humanist, where my spirituality was positioned and my sense of belonging in a healthcare setting, a maternity ward. This led me to consider the type of care I received and how this had a personal and lasting impacting on my own faith and beliefs in the transformation from women to mother. It also raised questions about how care is received by medical professionals during rites of passages, including childbirth.

Image 5.2. Twins

Martins (2018) concluded that women portrayed childbirth as a transformative rite of passage marking the transition into motherhood, and attached significance to the act, promoting recognition and celebration of the experience as an act of creation. One woman equated childbirth with empowerment and self-affirmation, describing her experience as an intimate moment between her and her baby. She discussed her experience using words mind-opening, self-defining and creative. They noted all the women in their study made mention of a desire to have a *natural* labour and equated the act with participating in creation. The ability to deliver their child with minimal medical intervention held meaning for these women beyond the outcome of the birth of a healthy child and became a key factor in influencing their transition to motherhood as a spiritual experience. In contrast, not having a natural birth impacted the meaningfulness of this experience with an expressed disappointment and in part, I shared a similar experience of disempowerment and having felt cheated of a vital and defining experience. Throughout my pregnancy, I knew that I had to balance life stresses and to have a positive outlook regarding the outcome. Using creative visualisation to support my well-being and communicating with the twins in utero helped with bonding post-partum.

Crowther et al. (2021) suggest spiritual care has become mechanical with the move toward a *tick-box* culture. Assessment of childbearing women may include the question about spirituality that will help provide better care during pregnancy and birth (Jesse, 2007). Midwives should acknowledge and support women's religious beliefs and be aware of their own personal spirituality during health care. They should be able to support a patient's spirituality even if it is different to what they practice themselves. After a woman gives birth, simply asking about the experience allows the woman to express feelings about the spiritual dimensions of her birth experience rather than just focusing on facts (Callister and Khalaf, 2010). Additionally, during childbirth, women often think about their mothers and grandmothers, but some also feel connected to the distant past. It could be the connected feeling with the beginning of life on earth and what it means to be a human (and a woman) who is a part of that chain of life and who will pass life on to another. In this way, birth has profound personal meaning (Athan and Miller, 2013). This resonated in my own experiences of overwhelming helplessness. However, it also heightened my awareness to remain strong through the process and connect with the environment and what I was achieving, bringing new lives into the world. It was a highly medicalised experience, but I still felt a sense of wonder and emotions in heightened alertness and response to the situation.

Rituals and Belonging

Primarily the focus has been on the mother's experience during childbirth. I now turn to the meaning of pregnancy and birth from a transitional and symbolic perspective. Studying rituals around pregnancy and welcoming the baby provides a deeper understanding beyond a medical and procedural approach. In Western, secular societies, ritualizing birth, such as the baby shower, gender reveal or party for the baby is increasingly popular in the west (Wojtkowiak, 2020). This is when family and friends are all invited to visit the baby for the first time. These are all emerging and renewed rituals associated with transitioning to parenthood. Some have connections to generational rituals like religious celebrations and gatherings by extended families. Others are more unique or conscious diversions to mainstream commercialised ritual celebrations. Within Humanism, the ritual is not expected to serve an agreed purpose or be a compulsory part of being Humanist (Wojtkowiak, 2020).

For some, the seeking of an agreed Humanist ritual is contradictory to Humanism itself who reject the expected religious social rituals imposed. For a Humanist, ritual does remain important to many but it is more about parent choice and individuality, celebrating the here and now, and hence not a collective obligation for validation to being a Humanist. Therefore, the ceremonies discussed are not Humanist ceremonies or rituals but personal ceremonies and rituals that people without a religious belief have chosen to organise and attend because it gives meaning to them and their family. For those that choose a ceremony, it is about marking a special time in life and acknowledging this with others close to them.

On a macro level, it is a remembrance, a shared experience with the aim of creating shared memories. At a micro level, the ritual and celebrations are viewed as part of the baby and family story to be told, creating a time out of the everyday routine of life. The extent to how this addresses a deeper layer of meaning or even spirituality is personal and only meaningful to the parents and those involved (Adams, 1996). Davis-Floyd (1992) contributes to the understanding that pregnancy and birth are highly ritualized in Western, secular contexts and these range from giving a name to the baby to keeping memorial objects such as a sonogram. Interestingly, there is, however, not one collectively shared ritual or ceremony that acknowledges the transition into a new life in western secular societies. Predominately Baptisms or Christenings are acknowledged as the first collective ritual in celebrating the arrival of a baby. For Humanists therefore the emergence of new and alternative ceremonies prior to the start of life is emerging in Britain. These include the *Blessingway Ceremony* or *Mother's Blessing* (Burns, 2015) as well as Humanist or secular Naming Ceremonies for babies (Gordon-Lennox 2017; Wojtkowiak and Crowther, 2018).

Birthing has been mainly influenced by medicine and technology (Davis-Floyd 1992). Grimes (2010) evaluated in contemporary western secularized societies, that birth is more a passage, rather than a rite of passage, due to the lack of collective rituals around pregnancy and birth. However, Davis-Floyd (1992) argued that within western medical settings childbirth is highly ritualized in the practices the midwives do with each birth as part of their health care routine. This includes rituals in the way the mother is prepared for childbirth and post-natal care. These include rituals such as washing, feeding, dressing, monitoring and so forth. This includes not just the care for the pregnant and birthing woman, but also in the way meanings are given to birth. These daily rituals do differ from the participation of a social ceremony and can represent a different ritual layer. A ceremony is intentionally marked as a social gathering and puts attention towards a specific life event.

In consideration of how rituals are defined Gordon- Lennox (2017) considered new tools and categories are needed to measure ritual identity beyond religion. Gordon- Lennox (2017, p. 19) identified four profiles that can be considered as a ritual practice alongside institutional membership:

- Institutional – Individuals who regularly practice their religion at least once or twice a month.
- Distanced – individual who identify with their religion but practice occasionally – once a year.
- Alternative – Individuals who identify with holistic or esoteric practices.
- Secular – Individuals who identify with humanist values and may be against religion.

I propose that in drawing on the fourth profile of individuals who identify with humanist values, the social gathering is often personally chosen by the expectant mother or the parents. This differs from traditional ritual, which is embedded and embodied in the community. Religious rituals, such as baptisms, have not changed over the years, and these evoke memories for those at the gathering. For church communities, the baptism of an infant is the start of a long relationship with that community, "where the child can grow" (Ward 1999, p. 300) and there is a sense of belonging.

Ritual can also be of moral orientation, but this does not mean that it always prescribes to them explicitly. Moreover, in societies where traditional rituals are not common anymore, these moral and social guidelines become more vague or pluralistic and new ways of meaning-making are enculturated (Grimes, 2014). An example of this is the increasing interest in parenting literature and decisions made about the form the ritual takes are drawn from multiple advice offered. These types of rituals are introduced by those who are at the centre. The community that is enacting the ritual needs to learn and embody the ritual, often for the first time. Humanist ceremonies are a movement against traditional, religious ritual, placing a focus on the individual within a social event (Bell, 1997). Alternatively, rituals can also be inspired by traditional, religious (Christian or indigenous) rituals. Ceremonies carried out by Humanists can also draw inspiration from Christian ceremonics. New rituals focus on the individuality and uniqueness of a person, but at the same time, they create a sense of community through this ceremonial social gathering and interaction.

I am going to discuss one ritual increasingly popular during pregnancy and another more established ceremony in Humanism after the baby is born. The wishes and promises of both rituals are symbolically enacted during the ceremonies and confirm that the pregnant mother and the newborn are acknowledged by their social group. Initially, the Mothers Blessing is when a pregnant woman and the foetus are both in a state of transition, with the mother's blessing revealing notions of the community an equal, temporal, cohesive sense of togetherness between her and her baby (Loonsk, 2021).

Mother Blessing

Burns (2015) revealed the female community is an important element in this ritual. A Blessingway ceremony, or more frequently known in the West as Mother Blessing, is a circle of women (and men too) sharing, celebrating, and empowering the pregnant mother as she prepares for birth and motherhood. Fellow women, including relatives and friends are present for empowerment. They are all there to encourage and bless the journey to motherhood. It is the support from the mother's *tribe* as they embark on the parenting journey. It is a ceremony to symbolise the love and support being offered and can be considered a deep and transformational experience. It is also about sharing and celebrating, with the intention of blessing the mother and baby and feeling held and supported by those that love and respect her. I chose a Mother Blessing, creating an informal event and led by friends. It was an opportunity to acknowledge the birth beyond an organised religion, with the process and event organised and managed in a fluid way rather than the procedural baptism. Food and celebration were key, but it was also a way of recognising and giving thanks for a successful high-risk birth. A sense of belonging and connecting with others is then achieved. It is not specifically a Humanist ritual but a ceremony ritual that is designed to provide a deeply meaningful experience for the mother, and this includes Humanists. The focus is honouring the mother's own belief system.

In recent years baby showers have become increasingly popular within the west and a ritual many women have sought in celebrating the preparation of their pending childbirth. However, the celebration has predominately been focused on the forthcoming baby rather than the mother. Subsequently, gifting and the focus on the baby has been deemed by many as an increasingly commercialised ritual with little symbolic meaning towards the mother. Consumerism has led to an increase in baby marketed gifts and promotional advertisements as a way of buying into and normalising the ceremony as part of the pregnancy experience. This has been argued to perpetuate a consummative culture, familiar in the west, rather than sharing and empowering the pregnant mother. In a sense, it was argued to trivialise the mother state of being in preparation for birth with the attention focused on what the baby should be gifted with when they are born.

The Mothers Blessing ceremony originated from the Navajo tradition, although each ceremony is unique with some ceremonies including rituals from other cultures. According to Wyman (1970) in Navajo mythology, the Navajo word, nizho'ni' is translated as beautiful and is a blessing across the life course (Wyman, 1970). The ancient ritual is from North American Indians, who viewed it as the second blood rite for a woman with her first being her first menstruation (Sturme, 2015). Blessingways are a celebration of creation, harmony, and peace. Their original form and purpose were to bless using song and were sometimes referred to as the *singing over*. These rituals celebrated specific, spiritual rites of passage throughout the entire life cycle, not just the passage into motherhood. (Jones, 2004). Although the Mother Blessing retains key aspects to a traditional Blessingways ceremony, it has been westernised and adapted. When engaging with other cultural practices, it is easy to appropriate their practices without honouring them. Using the term Mother Blessing and entering a blessing ceremony, with clarity and conscious intent honours the origins of the Blessingway without appropriation of the ritual in its original form and meaning. The core concept of the Mother Blessing, therefore, is being surrounded by a support network with the expectant mother receiving energy (Biddle, 1996). There are no set agendas in a Mothers Blessing ceremony, but most do include the procedure of beginning, shifting, focusing, and completing.

Most ceremonies are carried out in a circle and include blessings and poems, positive birth stories, empowering words, and songs (Dean, 2020). As a symbolic representation, a birthing necklace may be included with each guest bringing a bead that means something to them and gift it to the expectant mother. The expectation would be to wear this during labour. The beads would then be strung together with a beading thread and each guest would explain the intention or wish behind her choice of bead as she placed it through the string. The finished necklace would then be presented to the mother. During labour, she would wear this necklace, and this would serve as a reminder of all the love, support, and blessings that she had received for her pregnancy and journey into motherhood; a symbolic representation of her belonging to a community of women and mothers (Burns, 2015; Grimes, 2014; Sturme, 2015).

Naming Ceremony

In Western contexts, the emergence and increasingly popular secular or Humanist Naming or Welcoming ceremonies for babies is increasingly evident. Humanist parents, particularly those who were themselves married in humanist weddings may have decided to organise a Naming Ceremony to welcome the new member of their family. This ritual is inspired by the Christian faith, the traditional baptism or Christening. It is however a re-invented way of welcoming the baby into their community. In Britain, this ceremony is offered as an alternative to a traditional, religious baptism. The motivation for a baby Naming Ceremony is described as bringing family and friends together to celebrate the baby's rite of passage into the world, without an institutional religious influence (Gordon- Lennox, 2017).

The process of the ceremony can be accompanied by a humanist or secular celebrant who then leads the ceremony. The organisation of the Naming Ceremony is personalised and unique, created by each family. Parents and other significant others can, for instance, state their hopes and wishes for the baby. Music and readings can also be part of the ceremony. A physical symbol might be given to the baby, for guidance or a letter they can open and read in the future (Grimes, 2014). *Guide Parents* might be presented to the community, and they can also express their wishes to the baby. Unlike Christian God Parents, they do not make promises on behalf of the baby or undertake to see that he or she grows up to be a *Good Humanist.* The commitment is to support both parents and the baby regularly alongside times of crisis. When a Humanist is asked by friends to be a God Parent this can present challenges with their roles blurred, living in a Christian community as a Humanist:

> [a]s Humanist parents we were ourselves asked by two of our friends to be God Parents. They were religious but wanted a humanist input. Naturally we were very pleased to be asked and made our positions absolutely clear. By agreement we did not attend the Christenings, feeling this was our only option or we would in a way have been supporting what was going on religiously. Looking back, I'm afraid we have not been very attentive Non-God Parents and I feel we should have been. It was a lost opportunity. (Wilson, 1997, p. 8).

Additionally, Humanist parents are often invited to baptisms and religious ceremonies such as funerals. This can cause conflicting thoughts about their own beliefs and feelings of belonging especially when observing the unity the church can bring with the sense of belonging within the congregations. However, this also simultaneously creates opportunities for Humanists to reflect on their own personal beliefs, confirming how they want to live their life without a higher omnipresent God. The conflict of feelings are narratives encouraged to be expressed and discussed within Humanism and it may offer one reason as to why Humanists join local Humanist groups. Such groups open opportunities to learn about alternative ceremonies and being able to organise a symbolic ceremony and foster a sense of belonging (Dworkin, 2013).

The families who participated in the previously mentioned research by the Humanist magazine said they were happy to attend religious ceremonies but found much of it irrelevant to them. They accepted individuals had the right to choose and if attending a religious ceremony, the family would listen and follow what was being said. However, they did not partake, for example pray, but reflected instead. Another spoke about their nephew being named at an informal family Naming Ceremony, though not a formal humanist affair, and it was warm and welcoming (Humanist Scot, 2015).

It was through attending a baptism that I further explored Humanism. This, coupled with my non-traditional Las Vegas wedding, led me to joining the British Humanist Society as an online member. I knew that traditional religious rituals and practices did not align with my personal understanding and experience of lived religion. Initially, I was drawn to the British Humanistic Society as more women are aligned to the society both historically and in the present. Writing this section of the chapter made me consider Holt and Greenford's earlier question on my understanding of what it means to be a woman who connects with and secures a healthy belonging within a spiritual group. On reflection, my own spiritual path through Humanism has enabled me to explore the essence of belief and its relationship to belonging. Through membership in an organisation that is predominantly female, I already had a common bond. By utilising the heuristic research process, I could see that I explored and reflected my own spirituality, my personal religiosity. My Humanistic attitude to life allowed me to find an identity and recognition within the group thus establishing a healthy belonging.

In the Naming Ceremony, each aspect is individually crafted for each family, the location, length, content, and other ritual elements are chosen for the occasion. To avoid the contradictions between baptisms the naming ceremonies are often held in specifically nonreligious settings, with the purpose explained to the attendants. Gordon-Lennox considered the naming ceremonies serving two functions, "[t]he newcomer (baby) is publicly received into the group. The group implicitly or explicitly acknowledges its responsibilities for the new person." (2017, p. 94). Gordon-Lennox (2017) further elaborates meaningful ceremonies may include promises, symbolic gestures, and music, coherent with the values of the parents in what they want to transmit to their baby. Moreover, she advises to include a pledge from the Guide Parents with the baby remaining at the centre of the Naming Ceremony. Parents choose what kind of elements they think are meaningful, such as music, text, or a physical symbol. The Naming Ceremony reveals ritualized strategies of giving meaning to birth and this new life, as well as notions of spirituality. The wishes for the baby express a search for meaning and confrontation with the mysterious, as well as moral obligations.

The ceremony shows the importance of responsibility in the life of the baby, also revealing one's social bond with the baby. The ceremony is a space for seriousness and reflection, which makes this social gathering different from a party gathering (Bell, 1997). It is a way of presenting the baby to the community. From a spiritual perspective, it is about potentially recognising the unknown or mysterious aspect of spirituality at birth. It is about the baby's future being yet unknown. By giving them a name and acknowledging their relationships and status in the community, this unknown future becomes tangible and established in relation to others (Theissan, 2016).

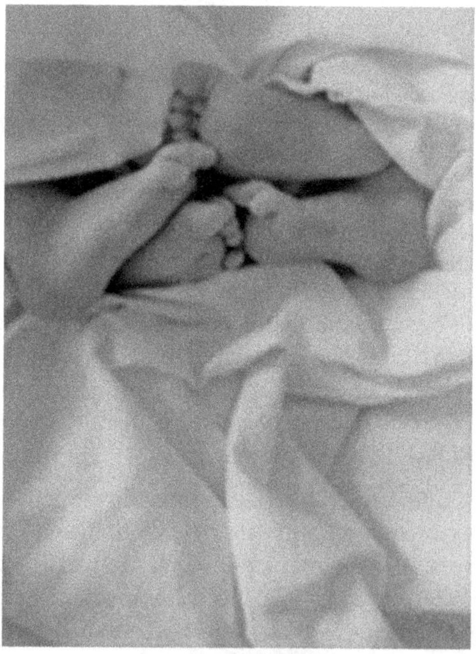

Image 5.3. Together

Stories can nurture the capacity for imaginative identifications and in terms of childbirth, this is the beginning of a story, there are no guarantees, and the story is yet to be revealed, only drawing on the imagination of the outcome.

These stories are found in rituals and ceremonies, with the core values of empathy, compassion, and a sense of justice at the heart.

During the first year of being a parent to twins, I wanted to celebrate their presence in this life and in talking to family members and parents the custom was for a baptism. Having a Christian mother, educated in a convent was an influencing factor in my decision. Whilst I did not believe they needed to be saved or enter the gates of heaven as a baptised individual I felt somehow obliged to follow through with the ceremony. On reflection, I felt I had to conform to my extended family and having been confirmed as a teenager, it was expected and celebrated. In some ways, the journey and life events have reinforced my current position as a Spiritual Humanist. In my journey, my experiences have helped me shape what I believe, so I do not feel regretful. The baptism was carried out by a female priest and ceremony and whilst having a religious order of songs and in a church only formed a small part of the day. The day was centred around the children with cake, gifts, and token stories. Two of my close friends had not managed to attend due to unforeseen weather, although as they are atheists I wonder if the church attendance had in part influenced their unforeseen lack of attendance.

With my girlfriends and close relatives, we had a post Naming Ceremony which was very intimate and less formal. We talked together and made promises to the babies. We welcomed them into the world and celebrated. There was kindness and unity in the ceremony. We also made wooden artefacts for the children to keep, a heart plaque and wooden picture frames. Interestingly those chosen as Guide Parents have remained committed to their role. This has been much more than the allocated God Parents that did attend the church baptism. Within the Naming Ceremony the key areas I reflected on was empathy, compassion, reason, and respect. This was shared with the babies and the way I want to live by:

- Reason: In organising the ceremony we used the capacity to work things out together. We used reason when forming judgements logically and considered each other.
- Empathy: The ability to imagine myself in my friends' position being asked to be a God Parent when they were not religious. A Guide Parent made more sense to me and them. I needed to ask how I would feel if we were in their situation.
- Compassion: This was one of the areas we share during the ritual in our promises and how we hope to help the growing children desire to help others who are suffering.

Respect for the dignity of each person: Another key area we wanted to share with the Naming Ceremony was to sing and draw on poems that promoted the recognition that all human beings are valuable and have a right to happiness (Humanist UK, 2020).

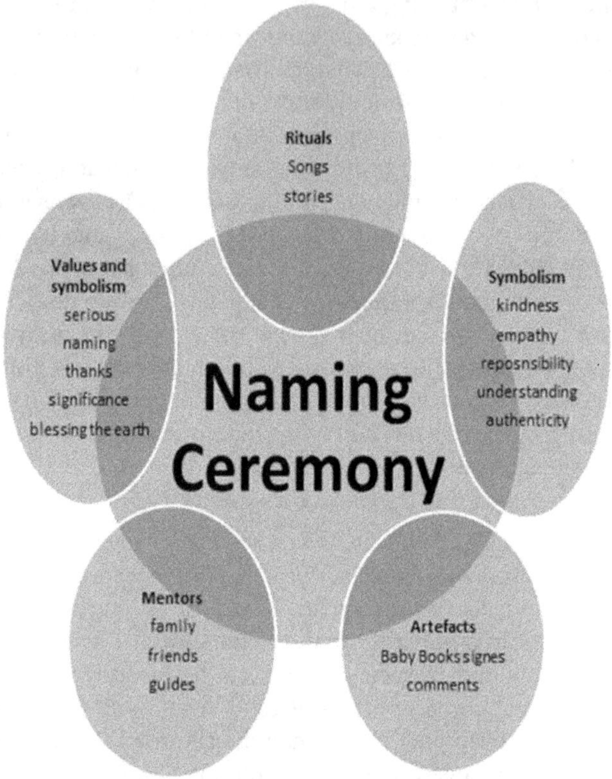

Figure 5.2. The Naming Ceremony and key themes adapted from Chang (2008)

Family Life and upbringing

In Britain today, the growing complexity of human society means we are increasingly dependent on people who we do not know personally for many of our basic needs. With relatives often living in different parts of the country, our support network is not as readily available. This can place a great strain on families, specifically new parents. Many Humanists believe this is a reason we need to care for those beyond our immediate family and support others to have loving and stable relationships. Humanists believe we need to recognise that all human beings are part of one extended family, and very much dependent on each other within and beyond the known family we connect to (Curly, 2007). Actively engaging in a community group, such as Humanist UK or local groups can contribute to positive health benefits, leading to similar social ties and a strong social support network is (Galen 2018; Theissan, 2016). This can foster a healthy spiritual belonging.

In 2015, nine families were asked about how they live with Humanism and published in a Humanist magazine (Humanist Scot, 2015). It provided a rich insight into the narratives of families about their views regarding Humanism, from a family perspective. One family referred to themselves as an ethical atheist, which they described as living one life to the full, without superstition, gods, or doctrine: with intellectual rigour, joy, compassion, and mutual respect. Living a life as a Humanist was also about being motivated to do so purely for the good of humankind, independent of a dogmatic moral code imposed by a spiritual faith system. A further definition of Humanism was conveyed as being a happy non-believer, who wants to do good things. A person who is non-religious, not anti-religious. A person that believes that people are equal and should not judge one another, according to their values. This was described as someone who does not believe in a deity but respects the right of others to do so. Doing good in their lives, for those they love, and the wider community and planet was also considered.

Figure 5.3. Parenting within Spiritual Humanism adapted from Chang (2008) five themes

As Humanists do not believe in an afterlife or rebirth, they do not consider their actions will be punished or rewarded by a god or gods. Rewards and punishments are not, therefore, motivating reasons to behave in a particular way. Punishment and rewards are understood in relation to family, friends, or the law. Laws help as a guide but may be the result of being told what to do rather than acting virtuously. Some humanists believe that doing the right thing simply due to the fear of punishment could be viewed as selfish should be more of a morally virtuous motive. Humanists believe empathy can motivate people to be good at reflecting on other perspectives. The consequences of actions are also an important element; Humanists value happiness, freedom, and justice, making the world a positive place to exist in. It is the individual's responsibility to make the world a better place (Humanist UK, 2020).

In approaching Humanism and parenting in this way I have considered Chang's (2018) afore mentioned five themes within the frame of upbringing:

1. Proverbs:

Treat other people in the way you would like to be treated yourself. We can try to give more than we take.

2. Values:

This can be a personal philosophy. How I want to live my life, what is right and wrong what is the best way to live your life the best way you want to treat other people. I reflect on my moral compass and how I parent within this. I reflect on how best to support esteem by being in the moment and valuing those peak experiences and creating opportunities for my children to experience this too.

3. Rituals: Rites of passage and rituals celebrations

The everyday rituals and their meanings. The celebrations and social gatherings in gaining a sense of belonging. What I celebrate with my children is personal but has meaning for us as a family. This ranges from forest walks and being thankful for our environment to how we eat collectively and celebrate the end of the week with an evening of pizza. It also includes celebrating through social gatherings such as family time when someone has been ill, and those alongside more religious celebrations such as Christmas but with an aligned focus on giving and a reminder of those less fortunate.

4. Mentor

Where you take your guidance from, from friends and thinking about their actions.

Whilst not intended as a dogmatic approach I find value in networking and membership to an organisation Humanist UK and local groups, sharing a common outlook on life. I reflect how I can share the positives and work in harmony with others. This links me to think about my human rights and where I find unity in campaigning, social justice, and environmental concerns. This makes me reflect on my family and the ethics I am promoting.

5. Artefacts

What is significant and personal to the individual, cultural artifacts. For me as a parent, I make and keep my baby biographies in the form of a baby book which is, written in, hats, blankets, and photographs. I keep family objects that have meaning to me and a reminder of a ritual celebration. Sacred to me and personal.

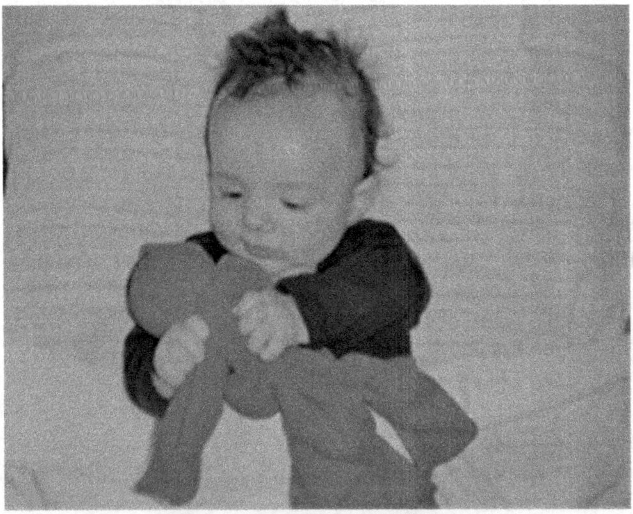

Image 5.4. The cuddle cloth I keep

Conclusion and Reflection

This chapter has discussed Spiritual Humanism from a women's perspective as she embarks on motherhood. By using Holt and Greenford's Complex Reflective Technique (CRT), I have reflected on my own position regarding this belief system. It has highlighted some of the ways I suggest it can be applied in practice. Future research is required into the narratives of mothers experiencing childbirth, and, more significantly, in the lesser researched areas regarding their perspectives towards rituals and family values. The chapter has brought together three broad themes regarding Spiritual Humanism;

childbirth, rituals, and parenting in gaining an insight into broadening and inviting the reader to further explore secular beliefs in its differing guises.

Reference List

Adams, W. (1996) "Discovering the Sacred in Everyday Life: An Empirical Phenomenological Study." *The Humanistic Psychologist,* 24, pp. 28-54.

Athan, A and L, Miller (2005) "Spiritual awakening through the motherhood journey." *Journal of the Motherhood Initiative for Research and Community Involvement,* 7(1), pp.17-31.

Athan, A. and Miller, L. (2013) "Motherhood as Opportunity to Learn Spiritual Values." *Experiences and Insights of New Mothers.* 27, p. 220. Available at: https://www.researchgate.net/publication/288827867_Motherhood_as_Opportunity_to_Learn_Spiritual_Values_Experiences_and_Insights_of_New_Mothers. Accessed: 11/6/2022.

Aune, K. (2008) "Singleness and secularization: British evangelical women and church (dis)affiliation." In Aune, K. Sharma, S. and Vincett, G. (eds.) *Women and Religion in the West: Challenging Secularization,* Aldershot: Ashgate, pp. 57-70.

Aune, K. (2011) "Much Less Religious, a Little More Spiritual: The Religious and Spiritual Views of Third-Wave Feminists in the UK." *Feminist Review.* 97(1), pp. 32-55.

Barlow, J. (2018) cited in Leach, P. (2018) *Transforming baby well-being: research policy and practice for the first 1001 critical days.* London: Routledge.

Bell, C. (1997) *Ritual: Perspectives and Dimensions.* Oxford: Oxford University Press.

Biddle, J. M. (1996) "The Blessingway: A Woman's Birth Ritual." *Master's Thesis,* Oregon State University, Corvallis, OR. USA.

Blackham, H. (1987) *Blackham's Best.* London: Smoker.

Brierley, P. (2006) *UKCH Religious Trends No. 6 2006/7,* London: Christian Research.

Brown, C. (2001) *The Death of Christian Britain: Understanding Secularisation, 1800–2000,* London: Routledge.

Bruce, S. (2002) *God is Dead: Secularization in the West.* Oxford: Blackwell.

Burns, Emily. (2015) "The Blessingway Ceremony: Ritual, Nostalgic Imagination and Feminist Spirituality." *Journal of Religion and Health,* 54, pp. 783–97.

Callister, L. C. and Khalaf, I. (2010) "Spirituality in Childbearing Women." *The Journal of Perinatal Education.* 19(2), pp. 16-24. Available at: https://www.ncbi.nlm.nih.gov/pmc/articles/PMC2866430/. Accessed: 30/6/2022.

Carolan, M. (2006). "Women's stories of birth: A suitable form of research evidence? Women and Birth." *Journal of the Australian College of Midwives,* 19, pp. 65–71.

Carver, N. and Ward, B. (2007) "Spirituality in pregnancy: a diversity of experiences and needs." *British Journal of Midwifery,* 15(5), pp. 294-296.

Cave, P. (2009) *Humanism: A Beginners Guide.* London: One World.

Chang, H. (2008) *Autoethnography as Method.* California: Left Coast Press.

Copson, A. and Roberts, A. (2020) *The Book of Humanism.* London: Piatkus Press.

Crowther S. and Hall, J. (2015) "Spirituality and spiritual care in and around childbirth." *Women and Birth,* 28 (2) June 2015, pp. 173-178. Available at: http://dx.doi.org/10.1016/j.wombi.2015.01.001. Accessed: 14/6/2022.

Crowther, S. and Hall, J. (2018) *Spirituality and Childbirth.* London: Routledge.

Crowther, S. J., Hall, D., Balabanoff, B., Baranowska, L., Kay, D., Menage, J. and Fry, J. (2021) "Spirituality and childbirth: An international virtual co–operative inquiry." *Women and Birth,* 34(2), pp. 135-145.

Curly, S. (2007) *Humanism for parents parenting without religion.* US. Lulu Press.

Davie, G. (1994) *Religion in Britain since 1945: Believing Without Belonging,* Oxford: Blackwell.

Davis-Floyd, R. (1992) *Birth as an American Rites of Passage.* Berkley. University of California Press.

Day, A. (2011). *Believing in Belonging: Belief and Social Identity in the Modern World.* Oxford: Oxford University Press.

Dean, D (2020) *Mother Blessing ceremony.* Available at: https://www.daniella dean.co.uk/mothers-blessing-ceremony. Accessed: 13/6/2022.

Dein, S. (2016) "Attitudes Towards Spirituality and Other Worldly Experiences: An Online Survey of British Humanists." *Secularism and Nonreligion,* 5(1), p. 9.

Dworkin, R. (2013). *Religion without God.* Cambridge: Harvard University Press.

Elkins, D. (1999) In Seltzer, L. (2013) "Evolution of the Self Part 1: Defining Spirituality in Non-Religious Ways". In "Contemporary Humanism and Spirituality, Part 1" *Psychology Today, 2013.* Available at: https://www.psychology today.com/gb/blog/evolution-the-self/201306/contemporary-humanism-and-spirituality-part-1. Accessed: 17/6/2022.

Ellis, C. (2004) *The Ethnographic I: A Methodological Novel About Teaching and Doing Autoethnography.* Walnut Creek: AltaMira.

Fowler J. (1999) *Humanism Beliefs and Practises* Brighton. Sussex: Academic Press.

Fromm, E. (1966) *A Radical Interpretation of the Old Testament and Its Tradition.* Greenwich: Fawcett Publications.

Fuller, R. C. (2001) *Spiritual, but not Religious: Understanding Unchurched America.* Oxford: Oxford University Press.

Galen (2018) In Smith, J. M. and Cragun, R. T. (2019) "Mapping Religion's Other: A Review of the Study of Nonreligion and Secularity." *Journal for the Scientific Study of Religion,* 58, pp.319-335. Available at: https://doi.org/10.1 111/jssr.12597. Accessed: 14/6/2022.

Goodall, M. (2020) *Heroines of Freethought: Women of the Early Humanist Movement.* Available at: https://Humanism.org.uk/2020/11/20/heroines-of-freethought-women-of-the-early-humanist-movement/ Accessed: 15/6/2022.

Gordon-Lennox, J. (2017) *Crafting Secular Ritual: A Practical Guide.* London: Jessica Kingsley Publishers.

Gordon, O. (2019) *The First Breath.* London: Bluebird books.

Grimes, R. (2010) *Beginnings in Ritual Studies.* Waterloo: Ritual Studies International.

Grimes, R. (2014) *The Craft of Ritual Studies.* Oxford: Oxford University Press.

Hall, J. and Taylor, M. (2004) "Birth and spirituality." In Downe, S. (ed.) *Normal childbirth. Evidence and Debate.* Edinburgh: Churchill, pp. 41-56.

Harris, S. (2014) *Waking Up: A guide to spirituality without religion.* London: Simon and Schuster.

Humanist Society Scotland (2015) *Living as a Humanist: The Family Way Part 1* Available at: https://www.Humanism.scot/what-we-do/humanitie/living-as-a-humanist-the-family-way-part-1/ Originally published in the 2013 Summer edition of Humanities magazine. Accessed: 11/6/2022.

Humanists UK (2020) Available at: https://Humanism.org.uk/Humanism/. Accessed: 19/6/2022.

Jesse, D. E. (2007) "The effect of faith or spirituality in pregnancy: A content analysis." *Journal of Holistic Nursing,* 5(75), pp. 1-8.

Joan of Arc, c. (1412 – 30 May 1431) Available at: https://www.goodreads.com/quotes/84842-one-life-is-all-we-have-and-we-live-it. Accessed: 11/6/2022.

Joas, H. and Wiegandt, K. (2009) *Secularization and the World Religions.* Liverpool: Liverpool University Press.

Johnson, T. R., Callister, L. C., Freeborn, D. S., Beckstrand, R. L. and Huender, K. (2007) "Dutch women's perceptions of childbirth in the Netherlands." *MCN American Journal of Maternal Child Nursing,* 2007 May-Jun;32(3), pp. 170-7. Available at: https://journals.lww.com/mcnjournal/Abstract/2007/05000/Dutch_Women_s_Perceptions_of_Childbirth_in_the.10.aspx. Accessed: 30/6/2022.

Jones, J. (2004) *Mother Blessings, Cultural Appropriation and What to Do Instead.* Available at: https://newbornmothers.com/blog/mother-blessings-cultural-appropriation-and-what-to-do-instead . Accessed: 12/6/2022.

King, M. and Koeing, H. (2009). "Conceptualising spirituality for medical research and health service provision." *BMC Health Service,* Res 9: Available at: https://doi.org/10.1186/1472-6963-9-116. Accesssed: 16/6/2022.

King, V. (1989) *Women and spirituality.* London: McMillan.

Koenig, H. G., McCullough, M. E. and Larson, D. B. (2001) *Handbook of religion and health.* Oxford: Oxford University Press.

Law, S. (2011) *Humanism a very short introduction.* Oxford: Oxford University Press.

Loonsk, S. (2021) "Integrating the Navajo Blessingway Rite and Drypainting Thomas Yellowman." Art Therapy Department of Visual Arts. Available: https://minds.wisconsin.edu/bitstream/handle/1793/75753/Integrating%20the%20Navajo%20Blessingway%20Rite%20and%20Drypainting%20by%20Thomas%20Yellowman.pdf?sequence=4. Accessed: 15/6/2022.

Longden, G. (2015) "A Profile of the Members of the British Humanist Association." *Science, Religion and Culture,* 2, pp. 86-95.

Luthar, S. S., Doyle, K., Suchman, N. E. and Mayes, L. (2001). "Developmental themes in women's emotional experiences of motherhood." *Development and Psychopathology,* 13(1), pp. 165-182.

Martins, S. (2018) *The role of spirituality in the lives of women coping with early motherhood and postpartum depression.* Ottawa, Canada. *Available at:* https://ruor.uottawa.ca/bitstream/10393/38457/1/Martins_Sandra_2018_Thesis.pdf Accessed: 12/6/2022.

Maslow, A. (1964) *Religions, Values, and Peak Experiences.* Columbus: Ohio State University Press.

Mason, M. (2006). *"Spirituality" - What on earth is it?* Available at: https://humanists.uk/wp-content/uploads/SpiritualitywhatonEarthisit.pdf. Accessed 16/6/2022.

McGuire, M. (2008) *Lived Religion: Faith and Practice in Everyday Life.* New York: Oxford University Press.

Moloney, S. (2006) "The spirituality of childbirth." *Birth Issues,* 15, pp. 41-46.

Norman, A. (2019) *From Conception to Two. Development, Policy, and Practice.* London: Routledge.

Norman, R. (2012) *Only Humanism.* London: Routledge.

O'Sullivan, C. (2015) "Why Humanism and feminism go hand in hand." Available at: https://humanistlife.org.uk/2015/03/07/why-humanism-and-feminism-go-hand-in-hand/. Accessed: 14/6/2022.

Parnell, J. (2019) *New and Experimental Approaches to Writing Lives.* London: Palgrave McMillan.

Rosato, M., Mwansambo, C. W., Kazembe, P. N., Phiri, T., Sokso, Q. S. and Lewycka, S. (2006) "Women's groups perceptions of maternal health issues in rural Malawi." *Lancet,* 368, pp. 1180–1188.

Rosen, M. and Young, A. (2015) *What is Humanism, How Do You Live Without a God and Other Big Questions.* London: Wayland.

Sellers, S. and Haag, B. (1998) "Spiritual nursing interventions." *Journal of Holistic Nursing.* 16(3), pp. 338–356.

Seltzer, L. (2013) "Evolution of the Self Part 1: Defining Spirituality in Non-Religious Ways." Available at: Contemporary Humanism and Spirituality, Part 1' *Psychology Today.* Accessed: 17/03/2021.

Sherwood, H. and Roberts, A. (2020) "Atheism is defining yourself by an absence. Humanism is a positive choice." Available at: https://www.theguardian.com/books/2020/aug/31/alice-roberts-atheism-humanism#:~:text=Humanism%20is%20a%20positive%20choice',-Harriet%20Sherwood. Accessed: 18/6/2022.

Shorter, E. (1976) *Making of the Modern Family.* London: Harper Collins.

Spivak, D., Spivak, L. and Wistrand, K. (1994) "Altered psychic states in physiological delivery: Definition of the problem." *Human Physiology.* 20(4), pp. 314-318.

Strhan, A. and Shillitoe, R. (2019) "The Stickiness of Non-Religion? Intergenerational Transmission and the Formation of Non-Religious Identities in Childhood." *Sociology* 53 (6) pp. 1094 – 1110. Sage Available at: https://journals.sagepub.com/doi/pdf/10.1177/0038038519855307 Accessed: 11/6/2022.

Sturme, A. (2015) *A Time to Heal: Mother Blessing.* Available at: https://homebirth.org.nz/magazine/article/a-time-to-heal-blessingway/. Accessed: 16/6/2022.

Thiessen, J. (2016) "Kids, you make the choice: Religious and secular socialization among marginal affiliates and nonreligious individuals." *Secularism and Nonreligion.* 5(6), pp. 1–16. Available at: http://doi.org/10.5334/snr.60. Accessed: 14/6/2022.

Thompson, R. (2021) *Latest British Social Attitudes survey shows huge generational surge in the non-religious.* Available at: https://humanism.org.uk/

2021/04/01/latest-british-social-attitudes-survey-shows-huge-generational-surge-in-the-non-religious/. Accessed: 09/11/2020.

Vernon, M. (2010) *Understand Humanism.* Oxan. Abbingdon.

Voas, D. and Crockett, A. (2005) "Religion in Britain: neither believing nor belonging." *Sociology,* Vol. 39, No. 1, pp. 1–28.

Ward, K. (1999) *Religion and Community.* London: Clarendon Press.

Watson, A. (2008) "All change: Trevor Molloy grew up as a Presbyterian but became a humanist." Available at: https://www.belfasttelegraph.co.uk/imported/Humanism-the-alternative-to-religion-28217202.html. Accessed: 19/6/2022.

Wilson J. (1997) *Parenting without God. Experiences of a Humanist Mother.* Nottingham: Educational Heretic's Press.

Wojtkowiak, J. and Crowther, S. (2018) "An Existential and Spiritual Discussion about Childbirth: Contrasting Spirituality at the Beginning and End of Life." *Spirituality in Clinical Practice.* 5, p. 261.

Wojtkowiak, J. (2020) "Ritualizing Pregnancy and Childbirth in Secular Societies: Exploring Embodied Spirituality at the Start of Life." *Religions* 11(9), p. 458.

Woodhead, L., Kawanami, H. and Partridge, C. (2009) *Religions in the Modern World: Traditions and Transformations, 2nd Edition.* London: Routledge.

Wyman, (1970) *American Anthropologist.* Available at: https://anthrosource.onlinelibrary.wiley.com/doi/pdf/10.1525/aa.1971.73.6.02a00520. Accessed: 11/6/2022.

Zinnbauer, B. J., Pargament, K. I. and Scott, A. (1999) "The Emerging Meanings of Religiousness and Spirituality: Problems and Prospects." *Journal of Personality,* 67, pp. 889–919. Available at: https://doi.org/10.1111/1467-6494.00077. Accessed: 14/6/2022.

Chapter 6

"The Nativity" by Ahdaf Soueif: Egyptian *Zār* as Heterotopic Space

Ayse Çirçir

Erzurum Technical University, Turkey

Abstract: Ayse Çirçir uses fiction to explore, in more depth, elements of religiosity from the experiences of women migrants in contemporary Britain. The last story in *Aisha*, "The Nativity", demonstrates a religious ceremony with scathing elegance. The story describes *zār*, a female-only ritual, and at the centre of the depictions are biblical, Islamic, and mythological overtones and perennial contradictions. Aisha, a childless woman, also a graduate of English Literature, returns to her native land Egypt after spending some time in England. She visits the mosque of Sidi Abul Suoud, the Healer of Hearts, to break the knot and thus have a child. Her nurse Dada Zeina, a lower-class character, encourages and presses her to visit the saint to overcome her childlessness.

Aisha attends zārs and presences, recites English Romantic poetry during *zikr* and dance, whispers verses from the Qur'an while thinking about sacrificing sheep for the saint and questions the suggestion of bribery. There are paradoxes in the story, cathedrals and mosques, Bacchanalia and Islamic recitations, the city of the living and the City of the Dead, jinni and human beings, withdrawal and rape, and life and death. Fittingly titled "The Nativity", the story looks at birth, death, and fertility and, as a Muslim woman, Aisha realises that she can neither set up a zār of her own, nor join the zārs of others. She is trapped in-between, just like the jinni who wants to own her but has to destroy her in doing so. In closer focus, the reader recognizes that the story is narrated by a jinni who obsessively follows Aisha, the narrative actually starts with a prologue. Although the ending is tragic, she draws attention to the fact that zār is constructed as a liberating space. As lived religion, zār has provided solidarity and support for women since colonial invasion and, by looking at religion from this perspective, Soueif shows that an activity that is described as irrational could be subject of literature.

In this light, Dr. Çirçir's study argues that zār in "The Nativity" is addressed not only as an answer to the patriarchal and hegemonic discourse of official Islam, but also as subject of English Literature. Fact and fiction in this chapter are interlinked. Although written in the past, "The Nativity" continues to bear relevance with today's British women. The debate continues on Muslim women wearing the veil. Conflict, in Syria has seen many leave their homes in search of safety. Yet how many feel a sense of belonging in their new countries? How many are viewed as a threat, or are *othered*? We can learn much from the pages of a book, be it fact or fiction.

Keywords: birth, Christmas, colonial, dance, death, Eid, female only, fertility, heterotopias, Islamic revival/ resurgence, Muslimness, Orientalism, possession, Qur'an, Ramadan, ritual, Shaikh, solastalgia, spirits, zār, zikr.

***

The Nativity: Zār

So when her old nurse whispered in her ear that
maybe someone had laid a curse on her so that
she would not conceive, she listened.
"The Nativity"

A zār tent in Cairo, 1980s.[1] There are four men and a woman on stage in a marquee. They hold drums and tambourines. Aisha smells hashish for the first time and, unlike the other women who sit on the floor, she is standing and observing. When the female musician gives a few tap-tap-taps on her tambourine, some of the women become animated. They detach themselves from their groups and move towards the rectangular stage. This rhythm belongs to their zār spirits, they obey and dance. They are whirling, twisting, and stamping. The beat gets louder and more commanding and the zār masters demand their bodies.[2] Their eyes are closed, and they surrender themselves to the spirits who take them all in - and understand. Aisha thinks this is Bacchanalia and says that social anthropology books talk about these demons. She thinks about Cathy's ghost that taps at Heathcliff's window in

[1] Zār, also *zar*, plural *zayrān*. Arabic and non-English words are spelled as they appear in publications.

[2] *Zār* spirits are addressed as master, *sayed* in Arabic (Constantinides 1985; Nelson 1971).

Wuthering Heights. This is how Aisha describes zār in "The Nativity", the last story in Ahdaf Soueif's *Aisha*.

Zār is a type of spirit. It is both an illness, that it causes by possessing humans, and the ritual by which the illness is appeased. Partly told from the perspective of a zār spirit, this short story about possession resists interpretation with its uncanny setting, opaque characters and supernaturalism blended with realism. Zār possession pervades the story as the spirit insistently claims the narrative alongside Aisha's body. Soueif does not afford the reader a clear explanation nor a satisfying ending. The reader is left alone on the threshold of a new rationality as they make sense of the events inside and outside the zār tents, since a zār spirit is an omniscient and reliable first-person narrator. The extraordinary narrator of the story never stumbles while relating the plot and he can describe realistic scenes on crowded buses where passengers exchange polite smiles as they stub each other's toes.[3]

To exemplify a similar account, Jokha Alharthi mentions zār in her Booker International-winning *Celestial Bodies* (2018). Zar stands as a split, and a metonymic gap, in her novel's many subtle references to Muslimness in twentieth-century Oman. For Alharthi, zār spirits are untranslatable entities and the women who engage with them are ungovernable and powerful speaking subjects. This context shows that zār instances and presences are defining moments for Muslim women in certain parts of the world and my chapter seeks to understand zār as practised, remembered and experienced by women in Egypt as a female-only cult and as interpreted, recounted, and understood by Egyptian women. These women speak English, study the English language and literature in England and identify as Muslim in the decolonising state and the metropolitan centre. It is my understanding that Aisha is the embodiment of these women and that zār is connected directly with cultural belonging. A manifestly thorny issue in Soueif's writing.

However, the point to consider is not a supernatural element, but rather how spirits operate in the story and complicate the ways we read fiction. Zār is a rarely explored subject in fictional writing and literary criticism and it is important for my research for two reasons: it carries the imprint of colonialism and slavery in the history of its formation and will be interpreted as female agency. Undoubtedly, the intersection of gender and slavery in the zār cult makes a literary exploration interesting for Post-colonial Studies. For all these ends, I organize my chapter to first picture the late 70s and early 80s

[3] *Zār* spirits have genders and ethnicities.

when what political analysts call Islamic resurgence was the defining spirit in the Muslim world and, secondly, to re-construct zār as a form of performance and observance of Muslimness for women. I will base my interpretations on the research of two anthropologists, Jane Boddy and Susan M. Kenyon, whose scholarly work is insightful for a literary-religious reading.

My aim is to write against Islamic determinism as defined by Victoria Bernal and to show the connecting thread between religious transformations and gender relations in Muslim communities. As Bernal (1994) suggests, Islam is not solely about texts, and it is misleading and ahistorical to think about Muslims as a text-driven society. Zār, in that sense, helps us recognise the fluidity and change in Islam because it shows that faith is understood differently within different religions and Islam is taking on new meanings with divergent religious acts. Significantly, Soueif writes about zār in the 80s when Muslims were moving toward a more scriptural construction of faith as the result of Islamic resurgence. Of interest is the way women are constructed as traditional and therefore associated with established practices in Muslim societies. Zār, on the other hand, is an exclusively female activity, and this has led to the assumption that women are conforming less with new definitions of orthodox Islam and are therefore not good Muslims. This lack of conformity has been put forward as to why they are visited more by spirits than men (Muhammad, 1993). With zār, it is possible to see social and religious changes as building a gender gap and my argument is that zār is not a redefinition of orthodox Islamic practices, or a significant disparity, or new orthodoxy and a peripheral cult, but that it survives the changing configuration of Islam which breaks faith from life through discussions about what is correct Islam and what is not.

From this inception, I point to the profound connections between Islam and zār practices alongside its effects on women's lives and the forging of social relationships. My research looks at zār historically and anthropologically to construct it as another space where Muslim women freely create and control meanings outside the patriarchal religious discourse. I will map the mythology around zār, its cosmogony, glossary, rituals, and brief history which, I propose, make it into a heterotopia. I frame it specifically around Michel Foucault's *Of Other Spaces: Utopias and Heterotopias* with the recognition that all cultures constitute heterotopias. I also put forward that zār is involved with the colonial history of Egypt and slavery and this understanding will shape my textual analyses. Before combining Foucault's arguments with anthropological literature and aspects of religion in "The Nativity" it is useful to examine Soueif's implications about religion in *Aisha*. I should be clear on this point that I use contested words such as *Islamic* and *Islamist* and confront my own situatedness while critically examining spirit possession and female agency during the Islamic revival. My research is ethnographically informed and, although I interpret zār as an active female act against hegemonic male cultural/Islamic norms, I am aware that there is a fine line between etic and emic interpretations, and I do not want to impose western common sense while discussing the notions of autonomy and agency.

The Religious Undertones in *Aisha*

Ahdaf Soueif is an Egyptian-British novelist, short story writer, cultural commentator, and activist. She was shortlisted for the 1999 Booker prize for fiction with her *The Map of Love*, a Historical novel that explores the Egyptian-British conflict during the late nineteenth century and its repercussions in the twentieth century. Alongside her radical, and more political, *The Map of Love*, Soueif writes on nationalism, Orientalism, and the intersection of gender and religion. Published in 1983, *Aisha* includes eight stories that share characters, narrators, and themes. Focusing on religion and culture in Egypt mainly during the Islamic resurgence, the stories are about the coming-of-age of Aisha, an everyman-type Arab/Muslim who spent her formative years in England. Sometimes, she is removed from Egypt, the central setting of the collection, and placed in England that turns into a periphery. She becomes, at other times, a minor character in a story in Cairo and the narrator refers to her in passing remarks only. However, as the title suggests, Aisha is always present, and she is a crucial element to all the stories. I must point out that we see a continuation of this in Soueif's other publications as she writes, and rewrites, the story of Aisha in entangled narratives. I will remain largely within the context of "The Nativity" considering the boundaries of this book, but it is helpful to look at the other stories, especially the opening story, "Returning".

Soueif is primarily known for her varied portrayals of Muslimness, and her fiction and non-fiction enlarges on the lived religious experiences of Muslim women in Egypt and England. Likewise, *Aisha* is loaded with Islamic material, tropes, and undertones. In "Returning", Aisha comes home to Egypt after completing her studies in England to collect books from her house, a house that she used to share with her absent husband. The title suggests that the inevitability of returning home, to memories, trauma and past cannot be eschewed for the post-colonial subject. It is the late 1970s and Aisha observes the streets of Egypt. She flashes back to past memories and contemplates on the suffocating atmosphere in the country. She informs the reader that she always imagined the scene of her homecoming in every detail, but it turns out to be a disappointment and her frustration is in marked contrast to her expectation. The intensifying religious revival in Egypt at that time is explained through *solastalgia* as she reflects on the beautiful gardens of Cairo that are replaced by construction sites for grand mosques and religious institutes.

Soueif depicts her emotional weight with interior monologues. Aisha asks rhetorical questions about the degree of importance and wealth that allows Mr. Ismail to build a mosque in his name in the middle of a place designed as a recreation ground. The Mosque of Ismail and the Islamic Institute projects take up five-sixths of the garden and Aisha says it is more "like a demolition than a construction site" (Soueif, 1995, p. 4). This is perhaps a reference to a significant incident in mid-1860s Egypt when Khedive Ismail "remodelled Cairo along the lines of Hausmann's Paris" (Brennan, 2021, p. 6). Ismail had studied in Europe and built Cairo "in the image of Paris under the Second Empire" (Mattar 2004, p. 281). Nash describes his European-driven innovations as "pretensions" (2016, p. 83) and Melman states that Ismail's study is "something between a taxidermist's shop and a hall of curiosities, packed as it was with the Khedive's stuffed game and mechanical toys and automata." (1992, p. 151). Leila Ahmed indicates that importing the European ways in the nineteenth century brought about changes in Egypt that extended beyond transforming Cairo streets:

> Cairo was becoming altogether too Europeanized. The Orientalist Edward W. Lane wrote that officials in Egypt were now abandoning native dress (just as they had done in Istanbul) and were taking to wearing European clothing. Lane (who himself always abandoned what he considered uncomfortable Western dress the moment he arrived in Egypt in favour of the loose and comfortable robes of that country) found this change in local dress ridiculous.... People, especially the well-to-do, were even changing the furniture of their houses. Divans were being bundled out of doors, replaced by chairs and tables. Some people in Egypt, Lane further noted, were "very angry" at these changes, rightly (in his opinion) regarding them to be signs of deeper and more important changes that were now. (2011, pp. 27-28)

Ismail's passion for rivalling Europe resulted in debts, led to the arrival of the British forces in Egypt, and finally, occupation in 1882, an occupation that lasted until 1954. During these times, cities were changing, as were fashions. There were heated discussions on women's liberation and the Islamic practice of veiling initiated by "the colonial critique" of it (Armanios, 2002, p. 113). It can be argued that Soueif juxtaposes the changes in the mid-nineteenth century and the late 1970s to emphasise that a comprehensive social, political, and decolonizing transformation necessitates more effort than the correction of Europeanized fashion, dress and architecture or reinstalling previous and allegedly pure culture.

In "Returning", though a century apart from Khedive's Cairo, Aisha is uncomfortable with the white Islamic head-dress that is spreading rapidly in the streets of Egypt. The Islamic revival, as Saba Mahmood states, refers "not only to the activities of state-oriented political groups but more broadly to a religious ethos or sensibility that has developed within Muslim societies more generally, particularly in Egypt, since the 1970s" (2006, p. 32). For Mahmood, the adoption of the veil is an example of this sensibility. Leila Ahmed (2011) also interprets hijab as the emblem of Islamist movement in the decades of the 1970s and 1990s. Hala Shukrallah holds the view that the Islamic movement in Egypt affected women and Christians more and the imagination of an Islamic community had serious implications on both:

> [w]oman's dress and behaviour in public also became the subject of great debate. They symbolized the release of rampant forces causing fitna (disruption) in society. Women therefore became the symbols around which control over society could be exercised. They were the models of virtue, if controlled, or the instigators of disruption if uncontrolled. (1994, p. 27)

This is important because, as Al-Arian observes, student activism played a central role in the Islamic resurgence during Sadat's era, a largely male domain, although its success is measured "partially by the visibility of female religious observance" (2014, p. 66). For Aisha, women inhabit new Islamic norms by wearing the headscarf and her anxiety can also be read as insecurity in the face of encroaching religiosity which, we are led to feel, does not disappear when she enters the house. There is a vivid sense that although women are more visible on the streets, questions resonate about female agentival capacity regarding veiling. Aisha's uneasiness in the changing Giza streets is an unequivocal sign that home is no longer a safe place. This remains an area for debate in Britain today. The visual image of a woman wearing the veil is perceived, by many in British society, as a sign of oppression. As Mirza and Meetoo note:

> [r]eligious dress from the hijab to jilbab and, more recently, the burkini, have been the subject of virulent political, policy and media debate in western societies, as symbols of Muslim women's lack of agency, and more recently as a threat to national security. (2018, p. 228)

In Britain, the veil immediately identifies the woman as Muslim, as non-Christian, as an immigrant. It alters the sense of belonging within a British setting.

With each page, the reader becomes conscious that her flat is unreal and claustrophobic. It has "ghost smell" (Soueif, 1995, p. 7) and Aisha cannot recognise her reflection on the mirror. There are two things that push her insecurity one step further: her thoughts on the sterile wife of the caretaker – sterile women are frequent participants at zār– and her husband whom she imagines as Shahryar, the threatening sultan in *A Thousand and One Nights* who kills his faithless wife and, as an act of revenge, sleeps with a virgin maiden each night, only to kill her, too.[4] Nonetheless, Aisha's imagined Shahryar believes, as a reversal of the *Nights*, in the chastity of his wife, but Aisha is no Shahrazad. She will not save herself and the Muslim women by telling stories. She is an English professor and an adulteress. She thinks more about George Eliot's *Middlemarch* and Dorothea Brooke, the adulteress in it.

With these two specific characters, Aisha unmasks her feelings on adultery and childlessness.[5] She is trapped inside an insecure and childless marital relationship, and as we know from "In the Eye of the Sun" in which she, named as Asya, has an affair with an English man. Soueif brings her Arab/Muslim adulteress into a sharper focus as painful memories sprang to her mind. Aisha cannot ignore conflicts and feels that she has no memories because she had no time to have a past. To the contrary, she feels that her husband's memories are vivid and, as she says, his past devours her present. She keeps thinking about double beds which, she bemoans, mock her and she knows that Shahrazad does not produce an heir for Shahryar. "The Nativity" shows that Aisha will produce an heir, but this baby destroys her.

Aisha wanders in the house as if she never was there and finds her bridal veil and Juliet's cap covered with black moths. She immediately sets them to fire. In Sufi religious poetry, moth is:

> understood as a symbol for the soul of a mystic, drawn and reduced to ashes by Divine Beauty" as well as "an image of the poet's heart set on fire by adolescent beauty, helpless in his faith as a moth by a flame. (Abahsain, 1993, p. 22)

Accordingly, the paired moth-flame symbol in the story reveals the tension between the couple and is meant to be understood as Aisha's decaying relationship with her distant husband. Above that, moths can be taken as a symbol for the deteriorating conditions in Egypt during the period of Islamic

---

[4] Shahryar is a cruel sultan who kills a succession of wives on the morning after the consummation. Shahrazad, the inner-frame narrator of the *Arabian Nights*, has to tell a new story each night to defer a similar execution (Amigoni 2000, p. 139; Ingham 2006, p.141; Andrea 2007, p. 101; see also Nash 2007, p. 114).

[5] Asya identifies with upper-class adulteress protagonists in fiction such as Dorothea Brooke and Anna Karenina. As Edward Said showed though, "Asya is her own Casaubon" (2012, p. 409).

revival. Soueif juxtaposes the radical claims of the post-colonial state with lived experiences: the state inflicts emotional and physical wounds on its citizens.

Aisha's homecoming impinges on her a sheer physicality that she cannot handle, and it is tempting to suggest that her return resembles Mrs Drover's in Elizabeth Bowen's "The Demon-Lover" when the war-traumatized protagonist comes back to her house in Kensington to collect some stuff during the Blitz and feels out of place. Heavily bombed London streets are indistinguishable from cemeteries and Mrs Drover feels insecure when she nervously waits for her ex-lover but cannot confront her wish and fear. She receives suspicious letters addressing her with her Christian name and hears someone leaving the empty house. Suddenly, a taxicab appears in front of the house and takes her to an unknown place as she screams to no avail. Mrs Drover is not a reliable character as one of the multiple narrators of the story, but her state is characteristic of war that can be held responsible for her nervous breakdown and trauma.

I suggest a relationship between Bowen's gothic modernist picture of the Blitz and Soueif's "Returning" because both stories address betrayal on a personal and national level. Mrs Drover feels that she betrayed her soldier ex-lover by marrying another man and is obsessed with his return for revenge as depicted in a seventeenth-century gothic ballad (Masahiro, 2011).[6] Bowen reinforces the sense that war resulted in feelings of guilt and betrayal in the collective subconscious of English women and, more intensely, she shows that the Blitz Spirit is a myth. A similar insight is expressed in "Returning" as Soueif insinuates that Egypt's failure during the 1967 Arab-Israeli War was humiliating despite the government's efforts to hide it.[7] The success of the Egyptian army was a myth and the continuous wars with Israel changed maps and brought more political frictions, poverty, forced migration, failed reforms and underdevelopment. To illustrate the post-war human plight, Aisha's new caretaker informs her that the former janitor Had Abdu was taken to army long ago and his wife returned to her village to live with her family. It is not clear whether Had Abdu will return or not and Aisha's dream of reuniting with this childless couple is shattered. This testifies that Egypt is a post-colonial state under construction and the consequences of this are not alleviating for the post-colonial subject.

---

[6] See also Sadler 2021; Reed 2009.

[7] Nelson states that the changing characters and imagery of the *zār* spirits mirror changing circumstances. A woman informs her that she was possessed by an Israeli spirit during the 1967 Arab-Israeli War (1971, p. 208).

The body and the mind of the post-colonial subject bear visible traces of trauma and Soueif affirms so conclusively that it is difficult for the post-colonial subject to create meanings in unsafe places, or to find a secure space in the post-war state, or to belong. There is no safe haven but only a cycle of returns to war, trauma, loss, and risks. Aisha feels, like Mrs Drover, betrayed, disloyal, and insecure at home never leaving aside the fact that she is culturally unbelonging as a Muslim woman. She is caught in the dilemma between her sexual and cultural identities; between two opposing loyalties. She is forced to choose between "[b]etrayal and betrayal" (Ahmed cited in Shukrallah, 1994, p. 26). Soueif's emphasis on the disappearing public-private dichotomy is therefore not inconsequential if read from a post-colonial standpoint.

In "Returning", there are both realistic and supernatural reminders of decadency resulting from Islamic resurgence and relentless wars, and I should forthrightly point out that the semblance with "The Demon-Lover" can be carried to "The Nativity" with similar implications of geopathology and female agentival capacity. Here lies a significant paradox about the sense of belonging those redefinitions of Islam set out to promise. The zār spirit operates like Mrs Drover's demon-lover and eventually leads to Aisha's death thereby opening enquiries on its healing power and interpretation as a conscious female act.

It is evident that "Returning" and "The Nativity" simultaneously express views on female agency during popular Islamic activism in Sadat's presidency. I strongly affirm that the period between the 1967 Arab-Israeli War and the assassination of Sadat in 1981 deserves special interest to understand Islamic activism alongside deviations from Islam and how Muslim women define themselves at the intersection of competing discourses. Once again, I draw parallels with British Muslim women. The media contains articles on Isis brides, questioning their belonging and allegiance. This fosters a sense of distrust:

> it is important to consider how wider constructions of Muslim women in public discourse have taken shape amidst the backdrop of shifts in multiculturalism and the production of "dangerous" Muslim "Others". (Mirza and Meetoo, 2018, p. 228)

"Returning" is set in 1978, shortly before the Iranian Revolution and, as aforesaid, Soueif is critical and vocal in her portrayal of Islamic resurgence. The other stories are not directly engaged with the political climate of late 1970s and, the following story, "1964", takes us to a time before the war of 1967. Aisha is a teenager of the 60s now and studying for her Egyptian preparation certificate in England because of her parents' post-doctoral research. She loves reading *The Mill on the Floss, Anna Karenina* and *Madame Bovary* alongside Harlequin romances and has a romantic sense of adventure that she hopes to realize in England. To her disappointment, her parents do not approve a friendship with a boy from India who travelled on the same ship with them to England. Another potential adventure is destroyed when her English physiotherapist turns out to be not her dream prince, but a toothless old man.

Behind each of Aisha's statements, there is an incisive sense of unbelonging, and, despite the hostile border barriers of England, she senses "a palpable air of superiority" towards the other passengers beneath her mother's surface friendliness (Soueif, 1995, p. 24). Aisha hesitatingly introduces immigration vocabulary: her Indian friend is a *would-be immigrant* and there are *would-be Australian settlers.* This marks the historical moment when Britishness was defined and redefined after the Second World War. People from the former colonies arrived in Britain as workforce following the British Nationality Act of 1948 that declared all subjects of the empire citizens. Aisha's observation confirms that there are schematically organized categories for new arrivals and that the hostile environment was in the making. There is little ambiguity that the 1948 Act was intended to welcome white subjects from the Commonwealth although every British subject might exercise their legal right, too –and thousands of them did. When we look at Aisha's examples, historically speaking, Australia was part of the Commonwealth realm in 1964 (and still is) and the British rule in India had ended in 1947. Egypt was no longer a British Protectorate and had declared independence in 1956. For Aisha, it is difficult to understand who a settler, an immigrant or a citizen is. Also, she does not categorize herself and her family because they are academics and immigration rules do not apply them.

For Aisha, England stands for adventure, change, music, films, and night-outs. It is more a novelistic setting than a real place very much like her toothless physiotherapist who could have been as dashing as Mr Rochester or Mr Darcy. A crucial impediment is that England also presents an index of alterity on a daily basis. One day, the neighbouring vicar's kids invite Aisha for an evening out and she dreams of going to the liberated youth clubs of England, or to a film. To her surprise, they take her to a modern and bare church, and she is distraught because it is "not even an old, picturesque church" (Soueif, 1995, p. 26). In any case, Aisha tells herself that she is not as different as she fears to be and that she belongs as a Muslim. There are, however, numerous instances that, I propose, reveals that she does not. In the first place, the Vicar speaks of alien races and alien beliefs and Aisha feels that everybody is large and pale and that she is excessively small and dark. This remains a feeling for immigrant women in Britain where "[w]hiteness is a yardstick for beauty" (Campion, 2019, p. 200). Aisha defines both her appearance and her hair as alien and states that she is betrayed, not sought out and guided into the love of Jesus Christ as the vicar promised. This equates with recent literature on Muslim women and their sense of belonging in Britain today (Nyhagen, and Halsaa, 2016).

Discontented and disillusioned, Aisha then cherishes hopes of befriending Teddy boys and the rockers, but her parents again disapprove. Aisha labels herself misfit because her manners of an inexperienced Westernised bourgeois intellectual are not compatible with her soul of a rocker. On the other hand, she responds to the post-war youth cultures in England as an Arab/Muslim immigrant and feels somehow connected. Aisha is troublingly unaware however that Teddy boys, of the 1950s, were responsible for race riots, the most notable being the 1958 Nothing Hill Riots. After this event, they constructed an image of themselves as the protectors of a white, working-class, and masculine Britishness. Teddy boys had anxieties about the effects of specifically black immigration on employment (Hebdige, 2002). As Ross states:

> [c]ontrary to what many thought at the time, and what most commentators since have continued to assert, the Teds sought not only to break with the past, but also to anchor their claims to authenticity in a nostalgic vision of the summer of 1914. In doing so, the Teds introduced the problems that would dog youth cultures for the rest of the century: Crises of masculinity, class and national identity provoked by Britain's changing place on the world stage; shifts in women's status and rights; massive immigration; post-war prosperity; and the horrors of the Holocaust. By asserting allegiance to Edwardian values in their choice of clothes, Teddy boys also declared a clear, elemental model of masculinity and national identity. (2019, p. 39)

It is problematic that Aisha equates belonging with the anarchic Teddy boys and rockers because her engagement excludes an anxiety about immigration, racism, and nationality. This missing sense is revealing of other disappointments to follow; she bathes herself "like a concubine" (Soueif, 1995, p. 28) for an English boy. A teacher at the girls' school tells her that she can be excused from Assembly because she is *Mohammedan* like the Pakistani girls who wear white trousers underneath their skirts. Despite her attempts to silently blend in and belong to the crowd, and not to declare herself "a Mohammedan, or even a Muslim" (Soueif, 1995, p. 30), her peers ask Aisha about camels, tents, and the number of her father's wives. Each encounter with English people imposes a reduced Oriental background and a static identity on her and she understands that she is on shaky ground. Feeling an unwanted wallflower, she talks to Catherine Earnshaw in *Wuthering Heights* as the white girls live their own lives and the coloured girls live theirs. In a coup de grâce, Aisha is condemned as the Egyptian who excels in English, a fact that her teachers do not like, "[t]he Egyptian gets it every time. It takes someone from Africa, a foreigner, to teach you about your native language. You should be ashamed." (Soueif, 1995, p. 33). She quits school as the hostility grows and spends the rest of the year reading erotica and passes her exam. Aisha is *othered* by both the students and the staff. Her sense of belonging through her love and knowledge of English is not only denied but it is what condemns her.

Aisha's Orientalism-tainted romantic imagination and the Orientalist prejudices of the English people against Arabs/Muslims at school seem to unite in this story. She is unbelonging although she describes herself as too *middle of the road.* On the other hand, she controversially carries an air of superiority with a persistent emphasis on her proper English, good manners, classlessness, and intellectual parents who are eager to put her to a school with liberal and enlightened ideology. This paradox confirms that the other characters in the story are not measured against Aisha, but in themselves. "1964" is therefore more about the assumptions of middle-class English people in post-war England than Aisha's coming to terms with England. Soueif shows that religious/racial discrimination is inescapable, physical and an everyday reality in England following the influx of immigrants after the *1948 Nationality Act.* She does this by turning our attention to the linguistic and cultural register of English people and by underlining how this strengthens Aisha's alterity.

Aisha features in other stories, she is a minor character in "The Suitor" and, in "Knowing", we see her as a toddler as she struggles to reconcile with the two different aspects of her life: one in Egypt and the other in England. The story is largely about her love of reading as a child and Soueif shows that religion has an obvious significance in a toddler's construction of identity. Aisha recalls that her grandfather is known to be irreligious and that he does not pray. His title therefore does not go as *sheikh* or *hajj,* but as *am* for respect. She remembers her grandmother visiting the Holy Makkah, but past Eids and Ramadans are distant memories, instead, she has the paraphernalia that surrounds Christmas.[8] There are no troubling contradictions: her

---

[8] *Hajj*: Arabic title meaning a person who has performed the pilgrimage to Makkah. *Am*: paternal uncle, also an honorific title used to address an older man.
There are two feasts on the Islamic calendar: *eid el-adha* and *eid al-fitr* (See Adamec, 2009, p. 144)

memories of Christmas and Ramadan exist side by side. They overlap, but do not overwrite one another. In England, though, Aisha is introduced into the world of Lane's *Arabian Nights* and *Vathek.* We see here Soueif's literary fixation on Orientalism as she hints at the material she read as a child. It is discernible from the repetitive references to the *Arabian Nights* and *Vathek* that her larger concern is Orientalism that informs, affects, represents, and speaks for Arab/Muslim people. This Orientalism continues to pervade British views on Muslim women. Mirza and Meetoo identify this blinkered within the British school system:

> [t]he headscarf, as a signifier of Islam, was an "identity site" where some teachers not only felt free to openly contest the young Muslim women's religious identity, but also use it to regulate their emerging sexuality. In the schools, the young women's faith constantly had to be tested. (2018, p. 232)

These two pieces are the closest in both theme and characterisation to "The Nativity" and, in these stories, Aisha is introduced to lower-class Egyptian life and religious patriarchy. To fall in line with the class sentiment, she is absent from the narrative and becomes a listener. As in "The Wedding of Zeina" and "Her Man", there is a dyadic interaction between "Returning" and "The Nativity" and it is useful to explore them as a pair. An adult Aisha is the shared protagonist, and the plot revolves around her return from England and her wrestling with Egypt where religious extremism and nationalism evolve as pressures. These examples show that women are Soueif's focal characters in *Aisha,* revealing a density of religious material in connecting the lived religious experiences of Muslim women before and during the Islamic resurgence in Egypt. In the following sections, I turn my analysis to the Egyptian zār and Michel Foucault's heterotopia as other space.

Zār and Heterotopia

Spirit possession is a phenomenon that occurs in many societies. Zā*r,* as a possession belief, is worthy of study because it provides us with alternative epistemologies. It is comparable to the phenomenon of Voodoo, Candomblé and Santeria (Kenyon, 2012; Boddy, 1994; Elhassan, Safit, and Khairi, 2019). Zār has ancient origins and is translated as *visit* (Natvig, 1987; Fakhouri, 1968; El Aswad, 2002; Nelson, 1971; Seligmann, 1914) or *to become visible* (Boddy, 1989). As a complex and dynamic ritual, it can be understood as "ways of knowing" (Boddy, 1994, p. 42) and remembering. In Muslim, Christian, and animist societies that are situated around the Red and Arabian Seas, and the Persian Gulf, zār spirits are believed to take possession of human bodies and bring sickness that has "physical, emotional, and behavioural manifestations" (Constantinides, 1985, p. 685). Zār is not a uniform phenomenon confined to monolithic interpretations and occurs among Muslims, Christians, Falashas, and adherents of tribal religions in Ethiopia, Eritrea, Djibouti, Somalia, Arabia, Sudan, and Egypt (Natvig, 1987, 2003), southern and south-western Iran (Muhammad 1993, p. 50) and Libya, Tunisia and throughout the Sahara (Grotberg, 1990). Zār refers to both the possessing spirit, the illness and misfortunes, and the various reconciliation-pacification rites. Kenyon defines it as "one of the widespread spirit possession religions" (2012, p. 3) with Werbner adding that it is "not strictly Muslim, yet a therapeutic and transformative space for Muslim adherents" (1996, p. 72). For Nelson, it is largely a woman's activity with "less or little relation to formal Islamic practices" (1971, p. 194).

Zār is thought to have originated in Ethiopia, introduced into the Middle East by slave trade in the nineteenth century. Today, the new zār leaders observe the ritual script, which is both a record that their forbears were enslaved and a reminder of what they accomplished. That its history is embedded in slavery affirms that "the possessed becomes the possessor in the mimesis of zār" (Kenyon, 2012, pp. xviii, 219).[9] Zār is an encounter with the Other and, as Edelstein states, people temporarily embody difference through zār and their "behaviour is reshaped to allow forays into this other world" (2002, p. 165). Early scholarly work on zār, however, failed to notice its representation of otherness and, as a result, it continued, for many years, to be considered by anthropological enquiry as an exotic, incomprehensible, unintelligible, and unrecognisable phenomenon (El Hadidi, 2006). Indeed, as Boddy indicates, zār was "subordinated, rendered illegitimate by Western scholarly paradigms, and depicted as exotic, even aberrant like other possession and indigenous aesthetic genres." (1994, p. 424).

The two explicitly feminist English-language ethnographies of zār are Janice Boddy's study in Hofriyat (a pseudonym) and Kenyon's in Sennar, both situated in the Sudan. Their historical ethnography explores a wide range of problems brought largely by women and addressed by zār. Boddy interprets zār as a metasocial, metacultural and allegorical production, and as a subordinate (subaltern) discourse (1994; 1989). Kenyon traces its origin as a ritual with a subaltern past that continues to be remembered with possession rituals. Boddy sees women's amplification of zār into a possession cult as a counter-hegemonic process. She states that it is "a feminine response to

---

[9] See Boddy 1994, p. 425.

'hegemonic praxis' despite inherent 'gender-appropriate meanings', 'gender asymmetrics' and 'sexual segregation' in the Sudan." (1989, p. 4).[10] Kenyon contends that zār is a type of embodied knowledge completing and enlarging the formal historical record:

> it 'gives voice (albeit in mainly unspoken forms) to those who have otherwise been silenced.... women's knowledge and experiences, of past and present, women's creativity and dynamism, find some of their richest expression in zār. (2012, p. xix).

These ethnographies challenge the traditional Western reductionist treatment of possession claims.

When zār spirits enter/visit bodies, they can never be expelled, but only mollified by ritual. As Kennedy indicates "the whole tone of the ceremony is one of propitiation and persuasion rather than coercion" (1967, p. 186). Nelson similarly underlines that "all an individual can do is perform certain rituals to *pacify* not cure" (1971, p. 205). Seligmann states that "if [zār spirits] are propitiated, all will go well, they will be friends and protectors as they are in life, hence libations and sacrifices are offered." (1914, p. 314). As these spirits manifest their anger through ailments, people suffering from possession seek help from organized cults to enable them to understand the wishes of the invading spirits. This is carried out under the guidance and direction of the zār leader; *shaikh* (Arabic for priest), or *shaikha* (Arabic for prietess).[11] Due to the life-long involvement with the spirits, zār practice "establishes and maintains membership in a cult" (El Hadidi, 2006, p. 30). When *zayrān* possess the human host, they visit the zār leader, like a visit to the doctor's office. Here the spirits manifest themselves to the leader in a dream, illuminating the nature of the possession. They are then summoned with incense pots and other zār equipment. There is a specific order in which this is done (Kenyon, 2012). In the descent of the spirits, there is also an order and the summoning of zayrān includes "proper use of incense, correct drumming and song procedure and distributing appropriate accessories to each arrival." (Kenyon, 2012, p. 115). Boddy (2003) informs us that, firstly,

---

[10] Boddy interprets spirit possession in Hofriyat as incipient feminist awareness. She responds to Saba Mahmood's criticism regarding her outlook in *Wombs and Alien Spirits* in an article titled, "Clash of Selves: Gender, Personhood, and the Human Rights Discourse in Colonial Sudan" (Boddy 2007, p. 408).

[11] Constantinides points to the overt homosexuality or transsexuality of male cult leaders in Sudanese *zār bori* (1985, p. 685).

each box has its own history, elaborated contents and intangible assets known only to the zār leader. Secondly, the zār pot-box, a medium to access the zār domain, is usually inherited through the maternal line as power and status within each box are also inherited.

Zār possession is an intrusion for which nobody is responsible, and it is possible to be visited by more than one spirit at the same time. The relationship with the spirits is based on negotiation and trade in which zayrān are given their dues and, in return, they give their trust. The spirits, however, might not respond to the bargain:

> [t]he basis of contract in zãr suggests a recognition of equity with the spirits; a way of controlling them, or at least temporarily bringing them under control, but also of expecting them to keep their side of the bargain. At the heart of zãr ritual is the expectation (based on past experience) that zãr can be negotiated with, induced to reciprocate. (Kenyon, 2012, p.148)

> [p]ossession is a lifelong affliction which, however manageable, intensifies the already tangible constraints on her behaviour. The rituals and daily observances essential to restore and maintain her health are both costly and time-consuming. Yet even assiduous fulfilment of the spirits' requests cannot guarantee her freedom from further attack. Zayrān are inherently amoral; their behaviour is predictable only in its caprice, despite occasional professions of Islam or well-intentioned bargains struck with humans. Further, since an individual may be host to several different spirits, achieving stability in her relationship with one zār does not preclude invasion by another. (Boddy, 1989, p.145)

It is believed that certain kinds of spirits give the adept discomfort and nervous disorders until their demands are met. Kenyon (2012) points out that zayrān are known to affect the human host in countless ways. The possession may be contagious and responds to no other form of treatment. Some disorders are associated with pregnancy, sexuality and fertility problems, or marital unhappiness and divorce. They are described in relation to stress symptoms and as sterility, hallucinations, convulsive seizures, extreme apathy, chronic headache (Fakhouri, 1968); inability to find a husband, being prone to accidents (Nelson, 1971); miscarriage, lassitude, depression, amenorrhea (Boddy, 2003) and anorexia sleeplessness, unspecified aches, rapid heartbeats, palpitation, and vomiting (Kennedy, 1967). Manning (2015) noted that early studies stated that women are more susceptible to zār than men because they are the more nervous sex.

Women, in particular married women, are seen as naturally more vulnerable to spirit attacks as a function of their femininity because possession is associated with the loss of virginity and as "an assault on women's reproductive health" (Boddy, 2003, p. 74). Boddy's study links zār with reproduction, particularly through the act of pharaonic circumcision as both bespeak the importance of fertility for women in Hofriyat.[12] She points to the morally appropriate fertility, enclosure, and cleanliness symbolism through zār. Boddy's research shows that zār leaders have mediating roles in society in which men have control over women's sexuality and fertility through female infibulation, reinfibulation in the case of divorce, marriage, and childbirth. Similarly, Constantinides (1985) indicates that zār women hold inarticulate powers that allows them to maintain control over their kinswomen although they do not have institutionalized power or authority. Ejibadze adds to the discourse when writing that zār for Muslim women "became a means of certain dissonance into the patriarchal structure" (2011, p. 142). Muslim women in today's Britain continue to occupy women only zones which give them a degree of autonomy.

Zayrān are of types, genders, nationalities, and colours. In Boddy's study, for example, they belong to the "culturally foreign" (1994, p. 417) non-Hofriyati ethnic groups such as Ethiopians, Westerners, Hindus, Chinese, Pashas (Egyptian, Turkish, or colonial officials), desert nomads, gypsies, and western and southern Sudanese. Similarly, Kenyon states that zayrān represent various strangers encountered in the formation of zār such as dervishes, Ottoman and Egyptian officials, Europeans and Ethiopians who embody various waves of foreign invaders and migration.[13] Zār spirits are "ethereal analogues and powerful 'others' who have influenced local communities in the past" (Boddy, 2013, p. 445). These include crocodiles, electricity, and Toyota tracks. Nelson (1971), Muhammad (1993) and Grotberg (1990) write about similar spirit groups. Zār, as Kenyon underlines, is a palimpsest of

---

[12] Pharaonic circumcision or purification is a form of genital cutting in which the vaginal opening is obscured (Boddy 2007, 403).

[13] Ottoman authority in Sudan begins to crumble in 1970s: "A nationalist religious movement was gathering momentum, led by the devout Sufi scholar Muhammad Ahmad ibn 'Abdullah, known as the Mahdi ("divinely guided one"). Driven by a variety of motives—a messianic vocation, a calling to reform Islam, a desire to expel Ottoman rule, even a desire to protect the slave trade (the banning of which threatened powerful economic interests in northern Sudan)—he attracted a large following" (Kenyon 2012, p. 31).

memories about "civil war and conscription, rampant inflation and concomitant poverty, migration and family dissolution, global pressures, and increased expectations." (2012, p. 20). Since its early days, there is an apparent link between slavery and zār practices and, in that sense, it is explicit that zār is cathartic.

Zār spirits become visible when they possess the human host and are recognizable through the the adepts' speech and body language. Natvig (2013) writes that they are fond of flattery, and they characteristically demand acts or items. Some are appeased by chat, tobacco, special clothing (Edelstein 2002); or jewellery, wine, a red cloak and sacrifice of turkey or a black goat (Fakhouri 1968).[14] They are given socks, shoes, imported brandy, whisky, and watches (European spirits); bread, fried chick-pea patties, clean food, coffee beans (Ethiopian spirits); and cigarettes and local alcoholic brews (Black spirits). The ultimate gift is blood (Kenyon 2012).[15]

Although there are ceremonial differences, zār ritual usually combines costumed dancing, drumming, singing, smoking, blood anointment, food offerings, candles, incense, dance, and trance followed by the application of henna. (Boddy, 1989; Kenyon, 2012, Kennedy, 1967; Nelson, 1971; El Hadidi, 2006; Natvig, 1987). The goal in the healing ceremony is to enter a trance state hat Boddy describes as "a practised and learned behaviour shaped by knowledge of spirits and consistent with a certain understanding of the spirits." (1989, p. 133). In the Egyptian cult, sacrificial animals are brought into physical contact with the sick person who either rides it, leads it by the hand, carries it in his or her arms, shoulders, or the head. The blood of the sacrificed animal is poured over the sick person, who rubs it into the skin and drinks some of it – though more rarely today.[16] Natvig (1987) informs us that the ceremony ends when the meal prepared from the sacrificed animal is served.

As a complex category of spirits, zār was first reported in Egypt by Europeans in travel accounts as evil demons that afflict human hosts and cause illness. Native commentators, mostly men, were critical of the Egyptian zār variant and set it "within a discourse of nationalist reform against colonialism" (El Hadidi, 2006, p. 32). Zār persists in Egypt as an important cultural form despite a century-long state repression, social change, and

---

[14] *Ch'at* is "a leaf with mild stimulant properties" (Edelstein 2002, 165).

[15] Foods that are clean bring blood and they are white or tinned goods or certain fruits enclosed and protected by natural and artificial casings. Clean foods are beneficial for women's fertility (See Boddy 1989, pp. 61, 109, 115).

[16] Drinking blood is forbidden by Islam.

criticism particularly from the constant reformulations of orthodox Islam. Today, it expands into various parts of the world with expatriates who bring back new practices and spirits. Having established this background to zār, I want to provide a brief introduction to Michel Foucault's lecture on heterotopia to construct zār as heterotopia.

In *Of Other Spaces: Utopias and Heterotopias,* Foucault points to the importance of space by speaking about the contemporary debates between structuralists and phenomenologists. He shows that space is not an empty container, but a product and productive (Tally, 2013). In *Of Other Spaces,* Foucault subverts the reality/utopia pair with utopias and heterotopias and indicates that some special sites are semiotically significant because they are in relation with all other sites, but to suspect, neutralize and invent a set of relations that they happen to designate, mirror, and reflect. Utopias are fundamentally unreal places, sites with no real places. They present society in a perfect form or turned upside down. Heterotopias can be viewed as counter-sites and Foucault describes them as "a kind of effectively enacted utopia" where real sites can be found within the culture. He suggests a systematic description for heterotopias with sixth principles and calls it heterotopology.

Its first principle is that all cultures constitute heterotopias that can be classified into two main categories: crisis heterotopias and heterotopias of deviation. Crisis heterotopias are privileged, sacred and forbidden places reserved for individuals who are in a state of crisis such as adolescents, menstruating or pregnant women, or the elderly. They are steadfastly disappearing though some remnants can be found in the examples of the military service for young men. Foucault suggests honeymoon trips as heterotopia of crisis, linked to the deflowering of women. Crisis heterotopias are being replaced by heterotopias of deviation. These are places, such as prisons, rest homes or psychiatric hospitals, where individuals whose behaviour is considered deviant in relation to societal norms are placed.

The second principle in the heterotopology is that an existing heterotopia might function in a society in a different fashion. For this, he points to the changing function of the cemeteries in the nineteenth century when they began to be located at the outside border of the city, unlike in eighteenth century when they were next to the church at the heart of the city. The third principle is that heterotopia can juxtapose several incompatible spaces in a single real place. The garden, a contradictory site, and a sacred space in the Orient, is the oldest example of these heterotopias. The theatre, in that sense, is also heterotopic space. The fourth principle is about time and Foucault notes that heterotopias are linked to slices in time and open into what he calls heterochronies. Cemeteries, again, are highly heterotopic places. Museums and libraries are also heterotopias in that time never stops building up there. Opposite to these two heterotopias that are linked to the accumulation of time are fairgrounds that are oriented toward the temporal.

The fifth principle is that heterotopias always presuppose a system of opening and closings, thereby making them both isolated and penetrable. Heterotopic sites, in general, are not freely accessible as public places and, in the case of entry, the individual must submit to rites and purification. Entry is an illusion, and these places generally hide curious exclusions. The last trait is that heterotopias have function in relation to all the space that remains. Two extreme poles unfold in this function: the role of the heterotopia is either to create a space of illusion, or to create another real space that is perfect, meticulous, or, ill-constructed and messy. Foucault indicates that certain colonies such as the Puritan societies founded in America and the Jesuit colonies in South America have functioned in this manner. Brothels and colonies are two extreme types of heterotopias for Foucault, and he concludes his discussion with ship as heterotopia par excellence. Foucault's contestation of space with a systematic description of heterotopia helps us understand zār and, in the following section, I will read zār ritual as in Soueif's "The Nativity".

Zār as Heterotopia

The symbolism of zār clearly echoes the link between human fertility and possession and my chapter analyses Soueif's ambiguous relationship with zār, Islam and Muslim women's anxiety with fertility. "The Nativity" starts with an omen "[y]ou carry darkness, my child" (Soueif, 1995, p. 138). Following a party, Aisha is standing in the rain wearing evening dress. She rejects the protection of the umbrella her husband offers. Her refusal carries deeper meanings because we previously read about the couple's uneasy relationship in "Returning". The husband's dull silence is a self-evident reality that they are emotionally distant. After all, he thinks that what she wants is impractical: they should not have left the car on a dark street and climbed the two hundred steps up to the top of a hill to see the full moon. To prove his concerns, a woman emerges from the dark as they leave the cathedral above the hill and asks for money to tell Aisha's fortune.

At this moment, it is difficult to figure out who the narrator is and, to make things more complicated, the narrator's voice appears in italics and divides the narrative space. We also feel that this narrator is dangerously attracted to Aisha and places themselves physically between her and the fortune-teller as if to protect Aisha. The fortune-teller is as incomprehensible as the narrator is physically obscure and her warnings find embodiment in his unsettling existence "[i]n season, with the year. In its beginning its end will be. Too close. You should not have gone so close." (Soueif, 1995, p. 138). The speaking voice, we understand, is a zār spirit.

While describing Aisha, he affirms his existence as a zār spirit and, ironically, as he is so eloquent, we trust him. Aisha's zār master says that he watched the couple over the years, and he is unhappy because she avoids him. There is a real sense in his observations: like zār inflicted women, Aisha has enthusiasms, excesses, and tears. Aisha is angry and she bursts into tears as her husband speaks against the Third Eye, or a long-dead Eastern music. The spirit understands how she feels and tells us that she is afraid of him and for her husband. He is sure that Aisha is aware of him because, he says, he is lurking in dark corners until she comes upon him. Aisha, however, denies him. He is a mean zār spirit like all the zayran who enjoy the business of possession because it is only in despair the victim-host is with them. On the other hand, the spirit does not think that Aisha's unhappiness is his fault "[i]t did not have to be so" (Soueif, 1995, p. 140). In the context of possession, this makes sense because the adept is not responsible for the intrusion and Aisha's spirit makes it very clear that he wants a bargain. As such, the exposition of the story projects how Aisha's darkness, to use the fortune-teller's words, will result.

The turning point is when Dada Zeina, Aisha's nurse, a lower-class woman, associates infertility with the Evil Eye. This reveals that there is a culturally overdetermined sense of women to be inherently fertile in Egyptian society. It is also evident from the story's title that Aisha's fertility is under threat and that it should be protected. The "Nativity" is the birthday of a local saint and Soueif plays with the biblical nativity story to point to the hope of a promised child, a running theme. Dada says that beauty attracts the Evil Eye and this, in return, harms a woman's fertility. She places infertility as a contravention of femininity, and this is indeed not a consensually validated view for Aisha. She asks why she is cursed in this "particular" thing. Dada, on the other hand, does not need to rationalize this normative representation because these are the values of her culture and women are the living vessels of these values.

Dada is particularly critical of biomedicine regarding zār and portrays the doctor's office as a dangerous space of penetration. As stated before, Boddy's research on zār in *Wombs and Alien Spirits* underlines the importance of enclosure and cleanliness and Dada's linguistic register is filled with threats invoking intrusion "[y]ou have done everything the doctors asked, poor child. Everything. Haven't you? They have poked and prodded and burnt and painted. Is that not the truth?" (Soueif, 1995, p. 141). Dada associates reproduction abnormality not with the body, but superstitiously with a knot that must be broken, and with Aisha's zār. Her attitude is emblematic of androcentric anxieties:

> [h]e [Aisha's husband] let them [doctors] look at him, handle him, squeeze him. He can't have liked it, you know. Men do not like that sort of thing. Do you want him to doubt himself? That's no good for a man. You must do something. (Soueif, 1995, p. 141)

This attitude is also written in the narration of the zār spirit "[w]hen he enters her, she is closed to him" (Soueif, 1995, p. 140). Closed here implies a negative sense, not valuing purity and closeness expected of women. The essential enclosure/penetration dialectic indicates that zār is more a text, learned behaviour and performance. It is a behavioural niche never divorced from social realities as spirits personify fears about women's fertility. In this regard, Aisha's zār spirit says something fundamental about Dada's, and Egyptian society's at large, cultural constructs. If fertility is inaccessible and uncontrollable, this jeopardizes masculinity, marriage, and ideals of womanhood. Dada also implies that Aisha made *them* angry –them being spirits. Aisha objects saying, "We left all that behind long ago" and Dada's descriptions thematically echo a shared *zār* understanding:

> [h]ush child do not talk like that. They hear you; God forgive us. They are our familiars, my darling, our masters. And we have to please and satisfy them or they clamp on our heads and never let us rest. You know all this. I've told you a thousand stories since you were tiny. And you used to listen and ask for more. (Soueif, 1995, p. 142).

As Dada indicates, spirits descend when they visit, and they come down into a person's head. Most notably, she talks about zayrān as masters and warns Aisha about how to address them and how to bargain with them. Although she reprimands Aisha of atemporality, it is obvious that Aisha is familiar with this everyday context. She heard about Abul Suoud and his wife, Set Habiba, and loved Dada's stories as a child. In the main, Dada's diagnostic context is filled with possession vocabulary: she does not want Aisha to set up a zār of her own, a full-scale ritual – this pushes the limits for her class – but to visit Sidi Abul Suoud, the healer of the hearts, pray for his wife and tell her how much she *needs* a child. There are presences every Tuesday and, perhaps, her knot will be broken, and Aisha listens to her.

The world of the presences is a heterotopia that Dada belongs to and comes from. She blends in easily with her black *galabia tarha* and knows how to behave there. Zār possession as learned behaviour also comprises a set of roles and attitudes in the zār tent. Unlike Dada, Aisha is not initiated into this world, and she cannot decide whether to sit or to stand; to recite Qur'an or to observe the other women of the heterotopia. Soueif importantly adds that "[n]o men are there except the ones with business: the ones with something to sell" (1995, p. 143). The gathering is on a hill that separates Cairo from the City of the Dead, a cemetery in which people live, and this strengthens the idea that zār tents are heterotopic spaces. Some people in the tent think that Aisha is not native and does not belong. They mistake her for a journalist and angrily yell out that they do not want journalists there for obvious reasons. Aisha is excluded in this women-only space that virtually excludes males and it is not difficult to understand because she wears European fashion.

Her spirit is also there, and he is proud and expectant "I am hoping that today she will give me some sign; say some word that she will not be able later to recant or disown." (Soueif, 1995, p. 144). With Dada, Aisha enters into a presence first, and there is a fee to pay as if to imply the borders of this heterotopic space. The air is full of smoke, Aisha is smelling hashish and some women start a wild dance on the floor. Aisha is interpellated like the women who respond to a familiar rhythm, but she resists. She interprets this open zār ceremony as *Bacchanalia* and the angry spirit wants to erase the effects of alienation on her. The spirit explicitly confronts Aisha as the coloniser "Other" and the fundamentalist who reduces *zār* as irrationality:

> [h]ow strange that you should have read about it; that as a child you should have brooded over pictures in big, fat books. While I waited. All those years I waited. And then you dismissed it all. You decided it was a world that happened long ago, long ago in far-off places. By what right did you decide? With what knowledge? (Soueif, 1995, p. 147)

The *you* in the first sentence is Aisha's voice and Soueif smoothly integrates the voice of the spirit into Aisha's speech that eventually produces a complex inner monologue. The zār spirit and Aisha become a whole, but she is culturally disinherited by the spirit. In what follows, she meets Farag, a butcher, inside the zār tent who will take her to the Saint, and later to another and bigger event, the Nativity to celebrate the birthday of Sidi Ali, the grand-nephew of the Prophet. Hence, the title of the story. The intrusion of Farag in this female-only space is a harbinger of disasters to come. There is also class anxiety in Aisha's entry into the heterotopia as we read along. She talks about herself as an object while the butcher talks about zār masters and how they pick certain beats. Aisha's inner voice is filled with fragmentation "[w]ell, well, Aisha. Attending a zār. Squatting in the dust. Making friends with a butcher –

a 'master' butcher. Oh dear, oh dear, what will your husband say?" (Soueif, 1995, p. 152).

It is at this point that zār turns into a ritual of reversal for Aisha. She questions her sense of belonging while quoting verses from Coleridge's "Kubla Khan" and feels surrounded by life –and this heterotopia is life. Aisha is on the margin though and she reveals her desperate alterity and in-betweenness as she prays for Set Habiba. She speaks to her as one woman to another, but Habiba's tomb becomes a concrete and familiar fear "the frilled tomb reminded her terribly of bridal headboards and quilts and naked female who adorned the bedheads of many Cairo bedrooms" (Soueif, 1995, pp. 160-161). Aisha's language mirrors the harshness of proper sexuality notions in the Egyptian society when she addresses questions to Set Habiba "[m]aybe she faked. Have you ever faked an orgasm?" (Soueif, 1995, p. 161). Perhaps, it is in this form of religiosity that Aisha feels comfortable and, by reciting the first verse from Qur'an, she talks to Set Habiba:

> I want to have children. But I don't know what to do. Maybe.... maybe it's wrong.... Maybe I shouldn't.... but he is a good man.... he is very fond of me. Everybody says so.... But I, I.... I don't want.... I never want him to .... but I should have a child. Set Habiba... there is no one I can talk to. Even my nurse.... they all say, "You should have a child. A child will make you sane." Even my doctor says that. I don't know what to do. (Soueif, 1995, p. 162).

I propose that Aisha's anxiety is a comment on social and cultural realities which construct childless marriages as potential deficiencies. At the end of the story, she is raped by Farag at the cemetery where the Nativity takes place and, although she is pregnant, we do not know the father's identity or whether the baby will live or not. The story ends as Aisha lies dying on the operating table of a private clinic and the zār spirit telling, that he waits for Aisha desperately, and that she always comes back to him. "The Nativity" shows that Islamic incantations and practices are embedded in the salient features of zār turning it into a counter-hegemonic and heterotopic space during the Islamic resurgence. Although zār is a system of knowledge and a form of remembering the encounter with the Other, what is at stake in Soueif's handling of zār is that it exists both because of essential beliefs on womanhood and fertility and because of Islamic revivalism. We are left with an ineluctable conclusion that zār is a text and, Aisha, a graduate of English Literature, fails to read it. At the same time, I argue that Aisha appropriates zār to question notions of procreativity in Egyptian Muslim society. Her redefinition challenges Dada's and the relationship of these two Muslim women with zār enriches the meaning of zār during the Islamic resurgence.

Zār manifests, negotiates, and realizes aspects of Egyptian Muslim identity to some extent. Yet, it is as unintelligible for Aisha as it is for the international reader. She cannot derive meaning from her native culture despite the stories Dada told to her as a child and Dada's efforts to sustain and justify zār. After realizing that Aisha is culturally disinherited from zār heterotopia due to her education, we also see how this intersects with her religious unbelonging. Soueif's stance is ambiguous, and this keeps the difficulty of understanding zār's function for the story. On the one hand, Soueif clearly shows that zār spirit is ontologically there because the story is tied to his consciousness at certain parts. On the other hand, Aisha insists on zār's supernatural status and is obviously articulate about her criticism. This ambiguity compels us to think that Aisha does not understand and embrace zār and is punished because of this. Or zār is not recuperative for Aisha and we should not confuse its rituality with its healing power. So too, Aisha appropriates zār for her purposes and redefines it. The story exhibits qualities associated with all of these. Soueif explicitly shows that it is not enough to discover a logic for zār, and we need to consider more how its meaning is created and expressed with Dada and Aisha.

What is implicit and of great concern for this chapter is that Aisha never questions *zār* from within orthodoxy. She feels that it is superstitious, and a form of spirit possession taken for granted in many cultures across the world. Aisha fails to see that zār is ritualized behaviour and departure from patriarchal discourses on religion. Emotionally and cognitively, she sees a pattern that strikes her as chaotic, illegible, lower-class, and exotic, perhaps Oriental. The cries of women during possession and trance are unreadable for her. They are also untranslatable for her role as the narrator. She is interested in zār only from outside, and as an ethnographer and anthropologist. For her, zār is not religious competence but a cultural short-coming, a substantial lack in her society. In fact, zār makes sense when you look at it from inside and Aisha fails to see the crystallized cultural and symbolic meanings in it as she looks from the outside. This outside-inside dichotomy is revealed on a narrative level. Aisha is both narrator, character, and a failed translator.

Another dichotomy is with the two zārs that Aisha attends. In the first one, she is playing the distant anthropologist with a keen sense of humour. She never abrogates her role and attempts to make a cultural sense of what she sees. In the second zār she attends after befriending Farag– the Nativity is seemingly rather different than women's zār, Soueif is resistant with details – Aisha's way is smoothed down by him and her experience is very limited. In the zār heterotopia, the Nativity is a labyrinth. She alerts the reader to the fertility register of the singer who praises not the personal qualities of Sidi Ali as a holy man, but his manhood. He cries "[b]ehold your virility, Oh behold your strength" (Soueif, 1995, p. 178). In this can be discerned the implicit function of zār rituals and presences that do not and have never reconciled with mainstream Islam. Here, Aisha also does not link possession to marriageability, pregnancy, or childbirth; she is not exceptionally perceptive. The pattern of nemesis is complete and several points in Aisha's encounter with Farag and in the Nativity suggest that she is in danger. Hence the narrator says "[s]he did not feel very confident. Or steady" (Soueif, 1995, p. 178).

Aisha has a turbid past, an unsettled present and a threatening future. She is obviously under considerable pressure from external sources that declare sexuality and fertility as the two sides of the same coin. She is seen less Muslim and less Egyptian by people who attend zār. Also, less women because reproduction, she is frequently told, is the normative activity of women. Besides, only zār amends the problem it causes –infertility– and the answer to her lack is so obvious for Dada. It is also possible that zār allows her to achieve agency, security, and perceived belonging despite the strong suggestion for zār nemesis. Aisha does not search for complementarity within the Egyptian Muslim world suffused by gender. Her resistance to zār can thus be read as resistance to the concern with reproduction. She evinces a style that is more modern and less superstitious.

From this, I can also outline a puzzling connection between the more modern, less superstitious, and more fundamentally Islamic lifestyle as declared by the state. For this religiously approved style, zār is contrary to Islamic tenets. By the time the story was first published, the association with zār and superstition had already been established by both colonial invaders, anthropologists, and fundamentalists. Aisha has been familiar with its notoriety and challenges zār from a socially superior position. For her, zār is pervasive only in everyday life of lower-class people. It is a story that Dada tells till it becomes graphically clear in the zār tent where she sees the assets of her Muslim society with its notions of idealized femininity. For Aisha, this new religiosity does not imperil aspirations for Islam proper. She also does not appreciate the redefined religiosity with zār.

Zār's complex rationale is completely missing for Aisha which makes her vulnerable. The first scene with Farag, the butcher-rapist, is self-explanatory. He says "You didn't dance" and Aisha states "How do you know?" (Soueif, 1995, p. 164). Zār is an articulation of a certain range of experience and, obviously, Farag is trying to learn whether Aisha is married/virgin since spirit affliction is associated with the loss of virginity. A single woman would be ashamed to admit she might have spirit affliction because defloration is a condition for acknowledging possession. Farag expects that Aisha is not married as she does not dance, and he does not question any further. On another scene, he talks to Aisha about the Nativity of Sidi Ali saying men do not get sent. Aisha believes women have more fun in their tents and she is eager to know if men dance, too. Farag only says that the dance is too *tame* for him. He does not know why Aisha attends the zār, if for a cure, then for which problem. Aisha cannot connect the link between men not being sent as women are and the nature of the tame dance. Farag expresses, I suggest, there is another zār specific for men, but Soueif is not forthright with it. His presence in women's tent makes Dada keenly uncomfortable. His untoward behaviour as they visit the tomb of the saint infuriates her. We are to assume that Aisha cannot attend the Nativity alone as a woman, so Farag attributes himself a legitimate and higher status in this complex structure. He is a trickster, and the borders of the Nativity tent declares Aisha an outsider. To consolidate her belonging to the heterotopic zār space, Aisha should accept her limitations and realize Farag as a masculine, external power to outsmart. This, however, might be a losing game. Aisha might succeed, outwitting Farag, but be hurt when understanding the values of femininity, fertility and other qualities associated with Muslim women in Egypt.

Aisha cannot read zār idiom and vocabulary and the implication is that there is a context of hazards for her – a zār nemesis. I also argue that Aisha represents the essentially masculine and colonial point of view with her practical realism. Paradoxically, it's through her zār that we hear women whereas she does not. Aisha is taught by female informants about fertility, the ticket for social adulthood as rightly observed by Boddy (1989). Dada carefully builds up an identification of zār inflicted women with infertility using possession vocabulary. Actively and ongoingly, she constructs Aisha as less woman because she does not have a child capital on which to build her female career. It is not Aisha's fault of course and there is a remedy for it. I propose that Dada forces Aisha to actively learn to be a Muslim Egyptian woman through zār. The most notable thing in this relationship is that Soueif does not give Dada a background except for the fact that her people are butchers –an intriguing parallel to the butcher who raped her. We do not know if Dada ever experienced fertility problems or set up a zār of her own. For Dada, zār is the only way to assimilate Aisha's body to the culturally appropriate gender image and we assume she belongs to this heterotopia because she is familiar with it. For instance, she reprimands when Aisha asks about a girl in trance "'She's seen a doctor? That was the wrong thing to say.' 'A Doctor? What would a doctor do? This isn't a matter for doctors.'" (Soueif, 1995, p. 154). For Dada, zār will re-sexualise Aisha and put her within home

(Egypt) and raise a family. Her failure to meet Egyptian ideals must be corrected by zār. Zār is not as punishing for her as it is for Aisha. This is her space, and the reader feels that Aisha is at most be prisoned in it.

Zār is closely linked with fertility, but it turns into a viable way of protest for Aisha. She wants to inhabit this space and fertility dysfunction is not a significant factor in doing that. Its ritualized behaviour, informal logic, idiom, history, and metaphors are not her concern. Aisha articulates her experience via the idiom of resistance:

> [l]et things come to a head. Let them all know she would do as she pleased and there was no harm in it. Let them know more ways of being in this world than the way they chose. And let them know she was content with the way mapped out for her. Not that she wanted to go to Presences and dance everyday of her life. Just that she wanted them to know that there were people, thousands, maybe millions who spoke to their demons with more familiarity than she did to her husband. (Soueif, 1995, p. 169).

The issue is no longer marriage and a healthy pregnancy, but what they signify and do not signify for Aisha. She is not allured to the fertility facet of zār rituals and appropriates the spirit idiom for her cultural and religious unbelonging. One might question the preferability and appropriation of zār as cultural compromise for Aisha because the ending does not resolve the issue. This, I believe, explains Soueif's ambiguity towards zār in the story. Aisha is about to die on the operating table though she proves herself fertile. The gender of the baby is not declared and Soueif makes the motif of expected son superficial. We feel throughout the collection that female children are not as socially desirable as male ones and zār that presumably protects and sustains the fertility of Egyptian society is disguised as rebellion. The Nativity event reveals the sacrificial nature of Aisha's experience, perhaps arising from her female disadvantage, and there are numerous references to sacrificial animals. The conventional sacrifice that completes a zār ritual to spare the life of the host makes the host the sacrifice. We feel that Aisha is defeated in the end leaving power to men and her society despite her attempts to reverse zār as lived by Egyptian Muslim women.

Zār in fact mobilizes Aisha and allows her to manoeuvre through indeterminacies in her married life. She is confronted by paradoxical demands and circumstances and zār is her response at it as it is the response of Egyptian women during Islamic resurgence. There are limits to what zār achieves for Aisha and I argue that she is less circumscribed by cultural and religious constraints on her life and her behaviour. Egypt is not isolated and self-sufficient but a part of a wide political, economic, and religious systems due to its long history. In this situation, zār shows that notions of the controlling, hegemonic groups regarding Islam proper are a fiction. There are discordant female voices and zār is one of these.

Women are more materially subjected in a Foucaultian sense with respect to their fertility and the possession performance attests to the compelling images that discipline and shape their lives. Clearly, Soueif shows that women phrase their experiences through zār illnesses in the face of the fertility mandate. Women, who are ill or claim to be ill, find a heterotopic space and new idiom to articulate their dysphoria. They hold zayran responsible for their procreative catastrophes and negotiate with their spirits via a process of religious socialization limited and special for women.

Similarly, Aisha challenges her subordination and fertility mishap in a self-conscious way by performing zār. With zār, there is an oblique admission that fertility is normative women activity, but I suggest that Aisha reverses the aetiology of zār – this is very revolutionary. Soueif directs query from the control of fertility to the therapeutic function zār and its being a religious outlet for Muslim women's predicament in Egypt. For Dada, zār provides an idiom to communicate her fears and expectations as a Muslim woman when communication is constrained by hegemonic Islam. She maintains, revitalizes, and embodies Muslim female qualities through zār. This takes some doing for Aisha of course and the lines are not clearly drawn for her. With zār, Aisha neither takes fertility for granted nor neutralizes her relationship with Islam and Islam proper. Still, Soueif permits for a negotiation and provokes the reader to realize that religious and cultural belonging is an arena of conflict.

Reference List

Abahsain, M. M. (1993) "The Supra-Symbolic Moth in Arabic Religious Poetry from the Late Ottoman Period." *Journal of Arabic Literature*, 24(1), pp. 21-27. Available from: https://www.jstor.org/stable/4183287. Accessed 15/6/2022.

Adamec, L. W. (2009) *Historical Dictionary of Islam. 2nd Edition.* Maryland: Scarecrow Press.

Ahmed, L. (2011) *A Quiet Revolution, The Veil's Resurgence, from the Middle East to America.* New Haven and London: Yale University Press.

Al-Arian, A. (2014) *Answering the Call, Popular Islamic Activism in Sadat's Egypt.* New York: Oxford University Press.

Alharthi, J. (2018) *Celestial Bodies.* Dingwall, Roth-shire: Sandstone Press.

Amigoni, D. (2000) *The English Novel and Prose Narrative.* Edinburgh: Edinburgh University Press.

Andrea, B. (2007) *Women and Islam in Early Modern English Literature.* Cambridge: Cambridge University Press.

Armanios, F. (2002) "The 'Virtuous Woman': Images of Gender in Modern Coptic Society." *Middle Eastern Studies,* 38(1), pp. 110-130. Available at: https://www.jstor.org/stable/4284213. Accessed: 20/6/2022.

Bernal, V. (1994) "Gender, Culture, and Capitalism: Women and the Remaking of Islamic 'Tradition' in a Sudanese Village." *Comparative Studies in Society and History.* 36 (1), pp. 36-37. Available from: https://www.jstor.org/stable/179326. Accessed: 16/6/2022.

Boddy, J. (1989) *Wombs and Alien Spirits, Women, Men, and the Zār Cult in Northern Sudan.* Wisconsin: The University of Wisconsin Press.

Boddy, J. (1994) "Spirit Possession Revisited: Beyond Instrumentality." *Annual Review of Anthropology,* 23, pp. 407-434. Available from: https://www.jstor.org/stable/2156020. Accessed: 16/6/2022.

Boddy, J. (2003) "Barbaric Custom and Colonial Science: Teaching the Female Body in the Anglo-Egyptian Sudan." *Social Analysis: The International Journal of Anthropology,* 47 (2) pp. 60-81. Available from: https://www.jstor.org/stable/23170055. Accessed: 16/6/2022.

Boddy, J. (2007) "Clash of Selves: Gender, Personhood, and the Human Rights Discourse in Colonial Sudan." *Canadian Journal of African Studies,* 41 (3) pp. 402-426. Available from: https://www.jstor.org/stable/40380097. Accessed: 16/6/2022.

Boddy, J. (2013) "Spirits and Selves Revisited: *Zār* and Islam in Northern Sudan." In: *A Companion to the Anthropology in Religion.* Boddy, J., and Lambek, M. (eds.) Oxford: Wiley Blackwell. pp. 444-469.

Brennan, T. (2021) *Places of Mind: A Life of Edward Said.* New York: Farrar, Straus, and Giroux.

Campion, K. (2019) "'You think you're Black?' Exploring Black mixed-race experiences of Black rejection." *Ethnic and Racial Studies,* 42(16), pp. 196-213. Available at: https://www.tandfonline.com/doi/pdf/10.1080/01419870.2019.1642503?needAccess=true. Accessed: 20/6/2022.

Constantinides, P. (1985) "Women Heal Women: Spirit Possession and Sexual Segregation in a Muslim Society." *Social Science and Medicine,* 21(6) pp. 685-692. Available from: https://www.sciencedirect.com/science/article/abs/pii/0277953685902084. Accessed: 16/6/2022.

Edelstein, M. D. (2002) "Lost Tribes and Coffee Ceremonies: Zār Spirit Possession and the Ethno-Religious Identity of the Ethiopian Jews in Israel." *Journal of Refugee Studies,* 15(2), 15-2. Available at: https://academic.oup.com/jrs/article-abstract/15/2/153/1579111. Accessed: 20/6/2020.

Ejibadze, N. (2011). "The Zār Ceremony in Egypt." *Bulletin of the Georgian National Academy of Sciences,* 5(2), pp. 137-143. Available at: http://science.org.ge/old/moambe/5-2/137-143%20EJibadze.pdf. Accessed: 17/6/2022.

El-Aswad, E. S. (2002) *Religion and Folk Cosmology, Scenarios of the Visible and Invisible in Egypt.* Westport, Connecticut: Praeger Publishers.

El Hadidi, H. (2006). *Survivals and Surviving: Belonging to Zār in Cairo.* Ph.D. Theis, University of North Carolina.

Elhassan, M. N., Al Safi, A. and Khairi, A. B. K. (2019) "The Zār (Bori) Cult: A Proposed Integrated Psychotherapy Model." In: Weber, A. S. and Verjee, M. A. (eds.) *Proceedings of the 1st International Conference on Medical Humanities in the Middle East*, pp. 33-35. 2018 Nov 17-18: Doha, Qatar: Innovations in Global Health Professions Education; 2019 March. [Innovations in Global Health Professions Education; vol. 2019, spec. no.: 1]. Available at: https://journal.innohealthed.com/index.php/ighpe/article/view/77. Accessed: 14/6/2022.

Fakhouri, H. (1968) "The Zār Cult in an Egyptian Village." *The Anthropological Quarterly*, 41(2), pp. 49-56. Available at: https://www.jstor.org/stable/3316878. Accessed: 15/6/2022.

Foucault, M. (1984) *Of Other Spaces: Utopias and Heterotopias*. Translated from French by Miskowiec, J. *Architecture /Mouvement /Continuité.*

Grotberg, E. H. (1990) "Mental Aspects of Zār for Women in Sudan." *Women and Therapy, 10*(3), pp. 15-24. Available at: https://www.tandfonline.com/doi/abs/10.1300/J015v10n03_02. Accessed 13/6/2022.

Hebdige, D. (2002) *Subculture, The Meaning of Style*. New York: Routledge.

Ingham, P. (2006) *The Brontës*. New York: Oxford University Press.

Keener, C. S. (2010) "Spirit Possession as a Cross-Cultural Experience." *Bulletin for Biblical Research*, 4, Winter 1967, pp. 185-194.

Kennedy, J. G. (1967) "Nubian Zār Ceremonies as Psychotherapy." *Human Organization*, 2(2), 215-236. Available at: https://www.jstor.org/stable/26424297. Accessed 15/6/2022.

Kenyon, S. M. (2012) *Spirits and Slaves in Central Sudan, The Red Wind of Sennar*. New York: Palgrave.

Kenyon, S. M. (2019) "Memory and Alterity in Zār: Religious Contact and Change in the Sudan." *Entangled Religions*, 8(2019). Available at: https://er.ceres.rub.de/index.php/ER/article/view/8323. Accessed: 15/6/2022.

Mahmood, S. (2006) "Feminist Theory, Agency, and the Liberatory Subject: Some Reflections on the Islamic Revival in Egypt." *Temenos- Nordic Journal of Comparative Religion*, 42(1), pp. 31-71.

Mahmood, S., (2016). *Religious Difference in a Secular Age, A Minority Report.* Princeton: Princeton University Press.

Manning, S. (2015) "Zora, Zār, Ohad, and Nubia: Research Memos for Reggie Wilson's 'Moses(es)'." *TDR 59*(1), pp. 55-66.

Masahiro, Y. (2011) "Elizabeth Bowen's 'The Demon Lover': Into the Hinterland with the Demonic Wakefield." *Journal of Nagoya Gakuin University*, 23(1), pp. 15-21. Available at: https://core.ac.uk/download/pdf/51458048.pdf. Accessed: 15/6/2022.

Mattar, P. (ed.) (2004) *Encyclopedia of the Modern Middle East and North Africa: Laabi-Shamlu. (Vol. 3).* New York: Macmillan Reference.

Melman, B. (1992). *Women's Orients: English Women and the Middle East, 1718-1918.* London: Macmillan Academic and Professional.

Mirza, S. M. and Meetoo, V. (2018) "Empowering Muslim Girls? Post-feminism. Multiculturalism, and the production of the 'model' Muslim female student in British schools." British Journal of Sociology of Education, 39(2). Available at: https://www.tandfonline.com/toc/cbse20/39/2. Accessed: 20/6/2022.

Muhammas, B. B. (1993) "The Sudanese Concept of beauty, Spirit Possession, and Power." Folklore Forum, 26(1-2), pp. 43-67. Available at: https://scholar

works.iu.edu/dspace/bitstream/handle/2022/2192/26%281,2%29%2043-67.pdf?sequence=1. Accessed: 16/62022.

Nash, G. (2007) *The Anglo-Arab Encounter, Fiction and Autobiography by Arab Writers in English.* Bern: Peter Lang.

Nash, G. (2016) *From Empire to Orient, Travellers to the Middle East 1830-1926.* London: I. B. Tauris.

Natvig, R. (1987) "Oromos, Slaves, and the Zār Spirit: A Contribution to the History of the Zār Cult." *The International Journal of African Historical Studies,* 20(4), pp. 669-689. Available at: https://www.jstor.org/stable/219657. Accessed: 16/6/2022.

Natvig, R. (2013) "Umm al-Ghulam: Zār Spirit or Half-forgotten Saint? Making sense of an Egyptian Zār Song." *Folklore,* 124(3), 289-306. Available at: https://www.tandfonline.com/doi/abs/10.1080/0015587X.2013.812417. Accessed: 17/6/2022.

Nelson, C. (1971) "Self, Spirit Possession and World View: An Illustration from Egypt." *The International Journal of Social Psychiatry,* 17 (3), 194-209. Available from: doi: 10.1177/002076407101700304. Accessed: 16/6/2022.

Nyhagen, L. and Halsaa, B. (2016) *Religion, Gender, and Citizenship: Women of Faith, Gender Equality, and Feminism.* London: Palgrave.

Reed, T. (2009). *Demon Lovers and Their Victims in British Fiction.* Kentucky: The University Press of Kentucky.

Ross, S. (2019) *Youth Culture and the Post-War British Culture, From Teddy Boys to Trainspotting.* London: Bloomsbury.

Sadler, M. E. (2021) "Revenant Narratives, and the Representation of Demonic Lovers in English Gothic Ballads." *Inquiries Journal,* 13. Available at: http://www.inquiriesjournal.com/a?id=1895. Accessed: 20/6/2022.

Said, E. W. (2012) *Reflections on the Exile and other Essays.* London: Granta.

Seligmann, B. Z. (1914) "On the Origin of the Egyptian Zār." *Folklore,* 25(3), pp. 300-323. Available at: https://www.tandfonline.com/doi/pdf/10.1080/0015587X.1914.9718826. Accessed: 15/6/2022.

Shukrallah, H. (1994) "The Impact of the Islamic Movement in Egypt." *Feminist Review,* 47, pp. 15-32. Available at: https://www.jstor.org/stable/1395251. Accessed: 15/6/2022.

Soueif, A. (1995) *Aisha.* London: Bloomsbury.

Tally, R. T. Jr. (2013) *Spatiality.* New York: Routledge.

Werbner, P. (1996) "Allegories of Sacred Imperfection: Magic, Hermeneutics and Passion in *The Satanic Verses.*" *Current Anthropology,* 37(1), Supplement: Special Issue: Anthropology in Public), S55-S86. Available at: https://www.jstor.org/stable/2744234. Accessed 14/6/2022.

Chapter 7

Reflection: Our Belonging

Abstract: The final chapter of this book looks at our own journeys, as women, as academics and as co-authors. We come from diverse backgrounds, both religious and academic, yet working through this book has brought us a degree of belonging, both spiritually and professionally. We too have lived religious experiences and as such, have chosen to examine our own spiritual healthy belonging.

This book came to fruition after a standard call for papers. I (Yvonne) was completing my PhD thesis and had realised as I analysed the data that religion, for my research participants, had a different effect on the women's lives than it did on men. When carrying out the literature review for my thesis, there was much written about women and religion in America but little about women in Britain. The seed for this book was sown.

The call for papers brought a diversity to the topic. It brought together a group from different academic fields, with different academic focuses. We formed and now belong to a new peer group. Chin wrote that:

> [b]elonging concerns the cognitive and affective attachments to others that cement our various forms of "groupness"...To belong is to feel natural and unthreatened in a group. It is to understand and be understandable to other members of the group; to be able to recognise and be recognised within. (2019, p. 717)

This diverse group of women confirms Chin's views; we belong to a group that understands and recognises each woman as an individual and as an equal. Our belonging has been the glue that has bound this book.

Yet this new group has also been connected by one of the threads running through the chapters. As we worked through the book, we initially met regularly via video conferencing. Although we did not set out to do so, we too, by circumstance not design, ended up with a *women only space*. The call for papers was open to all, yet no men submitted a proposal. Miles joined us later in the process, at a time when we no longer met due to family and work commitments.

The experience of working together, discussing our different academic and religious positions made us focus on how we, as women, were affected by religion and spirituality in our daily lives. This recalled King's proposal that spirituality "relates to an intellectual discipline of critical study and reflection" (2017, p. 669). From these discussions, and with King's view to the fore, we decided to use Nicole and Miles's chapter as a focus for reflection as well as a way of drawing the book to a conclusion. We have written our answers to the question: **"What are some of the complexities of belonging as a spiritual and healthy woman in Britain?"** before and after engaging with the chapter.

Keywords: belonging, Christian atheist, Complex Reflective Technê, feminist, health, meditation, Muslim, non-religious, reflection, spiritual.

***

Nicole

Before:

For me, as a white woman born in England, I grew up in a non-religious household, as a teenager, I had a lot of anxiety. In my past, to help deal with this, I went to meditation classes, which is where my love of people's spiritual beliefs and practices started to develop. Following the 1990s aerobic fitness trends, many entrepreneurial-minded exercise gurus took to the airwaves with the goal of convincing the public to buy their complicated contraptions, such as *Thighmasters*. Then, in the early 2000s, Mindfulness-Based Cognitive Therapy became popular. Public health messages about improving a person's health were regularly promoted. All these factors shaped my upbringing and personal philosophy and led to my interest in spirituality and my development as a public health practitioner/researcher within this field. Being a woman, and now identify as someone who is SBNR (Spiritual but not Religious) but also a public health researcher, spirituality and health is an important topic to me. I have been in this field for over seven years now. I regularly examine the literature looking at the relationship between spirituality and health. SBNR is understood as self-identified, a life stance of spirituality that takes issue with organised religion as the sole or most valuable means of furthering spiritual growth (Mercadante, 2020). For me, SBNR means I engage with spiritual activities (in my case, yoga, and meditation), without any of the formal connections to religion. For me, there is no supernatural element. I engage with yoga and meditation every day. I perceive these to be spiritual but not religious activities. When I talk about health, I tend to think of it from a public health perspective and public health is generally defined as "the art and science of preventing disease, prolonging life and promoting health through the organised efforts of society" (Acheson cited in Anugwom, 2020, p. 3).[1] It focuses on the social, economic, and cultural factors that shape the health of populations (Scriven, 2017; WHO, 2019). Public health encompasses health promotion and health education (Scriven, 2017; WHO, 2019).

After:

Through the development of this technique, I now recognised my own bias in addressing the complexities of achieving and maintaining a sense of healthy belonging as a spiritual woman. I acknowledge the power the academic field play in making me think in a very linear way but, the world is far more complex than that. That is what developing Complex Reflective Technê (CRT) has made me realise, as well as how I got stuck into one way of thinking. It is very hard to unlearn what you already know. Applying CRT (and discussing this process with Miles) has enabled me to approach philosophical questions in a different way from before. It challenges my perceptions and my understanding of how this plays out, particularly in the field of education (it makes me realise that university settings can be quite limiting for creativity). This approach is trying to move people away from the structure and be more reflective. Looking back on my own journey, I can see my own limitations and lack of power. The CRT also helps us to reflect on our own personal belonging within the world, which also acknowledging the complexity of doing so. CRT attempts to make these relationships clearer.

Miles

Before:

Applying CRT, my active common heuristic emphasises being as a woman, within a context of being women, and more broadly, being women spiritually whilst achieving and maintaining a sense of healthy belonging. Being a man, I cannot speak to being a woman. I can speak, however, my response informed and influenced by my particular male perspective, in relation to highly complex individual women and highly complex clusters of women, in extremely complex relationships and contexts. My response being an extremely restricted and bounded reflective dialogue.

---

[1] The quote cited is from a report in 1998 commissioned by the World Health Orginisation (WHO).

After:

Writing and engaging with the chapter resulted in my reflecting back on so much I have experienced. It has aggregated up to CRT as a response. This, in recognition of what has evolved to become my fluid implicit response to questions relating to spirituality. It forces me back on myself time and time again, to compare and contrast my own experiences with academically presented findings in nursing. I recognise I have been enacting informal variants of the above CRT that aggregate and start to solidify into our jointly (with Nicole through dialogue, testing and adapting) crafted CRT shared here. It is a key aspect of my response to the initial question. I recognise, through experience combined with multiple trials and errors, the significant challenges associated with even attempting to recognise how asking the question of being spiritual practically poses. A simple response is a common heuristic one presented as "real" when put through the academic processes of research/inquiry. The processes constructing an artifact of an individual's common heuristic response sometimes presented authoritatively as "objective fact". CRT does not overcome this but merely makes it clearer. In so doing, trying to model and facilitate actions, rather than claim direct objective fact. Actioning processes within CRT guiding journeys that generally start at our common heuristic but offering orientation processes through CRT to go wider, deeper, and more complex. In our so doing maybe finding through CRT what our aggregated responses to questions related to "being spiritual and healthy" are, how we act with this and maybe transform as well as strengthen our resilience? It may take us on a circular route back to where we started, but we expose ourselves to the experiences associated with our journey.

Yvonne

Before:

I wrote my thoughts at the beginning without thinking too deeply. As a social researcher, at a very early stage in my academic research journey, I was compelled to examine my own religious beliefs. I had to work out how best to recount (or not) these personal beliefs to participants. My own religious identity is that of, and here I am appropriating Phillip Pullman's phrase, a "Christian Atheist"[2] I enjoy church services from the sermons to the hymns and psalms. I enjoy the sense of community and belonging but have no personal faith.

[2] Pullman is often referred to as being a new atheist, alongside Christopher Hitchens and Richard Dawkins. Although Pullman has atheist beliefs, he does not denounce

As a woman, I feel that I belong to a group of individuals that is spiritual in its very design. I may have no personal conviction of a greater, singular omnipresent being, but I have always believed in a second sphere. We are more than just flesh and blood. Death is not our end and I have always been interested in spiritualism and mysticism. I strongly believe that if I am not happy spiritually then I am not happy physically, however, as I read Nicole and Miles's chapter, I began to think that the link between my physical and the spiritual health was an area I overlook or perhaps just take for granted.

After:

Reading Nicole and Miles's chapter highlighted for me that we are all affected by different elements. Biology, nature, nurture, the environment, and our social interactions all combine to make us who we are. From our actions and interactions with others, we build up a sense of what another person is like yet how do I build up a sense of what I am like? Where do I belong in my healthy spirituality?

Physical and emotional components encompass our views, beliefs, and attitudes. As I worked through the chapter, I came to better understand that I do take for granted the spiritual beliefs I hold. I rarely think of them, rarely confront or challenge them. It is not something I, nor my friends, vocalise. I was steadfast in thinking that my physical and spiritual development were linear. That I grew from the people I met and the things I read. Yet experiences and beliefs are not linear, they are not set in stone.

Time may pass, but that does not mean that we cannot travel back. Working on this book with a group of individuals with different spiritual and religious beliefs alongside different academic interests made me think back and work through events in my own life. I circumnavigated my life and by doing so, I was able to strengthen my spirituality and healthy belonging. One way in which I did this was to orientate myself in the here and now when under stress or feeling overwhelmed by workload or family problems. I made use of a breathing app to ground or orientate myself, to tap into an inner space of calmness.

I look back on my spiritual journey and try to gain a better understanding of where I moved paths from an all accepting non-questioning belief in God to, what I now see was, a spiritual awakening. I was raised as a Presbyterian and joined the Church of Scotland so that I could have my children baptised.

Christianity and describes himself in interviews as a "Church of England Atheist" (Catholic Herald, 2017) or a Religious Atheist (Peter Jukes, 2014).

When I now analyse my decisions, I realise that all of this, and my church wedding, were undertaken because it was what was expected of me by family. I have spent a lot of my adulthood working in religious environments. I was a nurse in a hospice run by Roman Catholic nuns, I was a preschool teacher in a Roman Catholic school. I work with a group for vulnerable women which is run by a Methodist missionary, yet I have no faith. Working through this book and listening to and reading the work of my co-authors has made me grasp that I study religion from a sociological perspective because I want to understand not only why people believe and belong to religious groups but also why I do not.

I understand that I must take the time to tap into my spirituality. To work on a healthier understanding of what I believe. I try to maintain my physical health, but this is nothing without maintaining a healthy spirituality. For much of my adult life, I have worked and studied groups that I have no religious affiliation with, yet I have always felt a degree of belonging.

Amanda

Before:

I aimed to approach my reflection from a personal rather than academic perspective to try and retain an authentic voice. In responding to being a woman spiritually and with a healthy belonging I reflect on what this means to me personally as an adult. As a young woman, through to my thirties I believe I was in the process of developing a sense of self, influenced by my personal circumstances, the people I met and the cultural time. Certainly, my sexuality, femininity as a young woman during a rave culture, amongst new age travellers and staying in caravans, sofa surfing as a student impacted on my growing spiritual self and healthy belonging. My external persona was less feminine and more feral than I dress today, and my healthy belonging included a diet predominantly based on coffee and roll-ups, with little room for organised sports. Although fresh air, long walks, and the outside space with like-minded friends, spiritually connected gave a feeling of healthy living as we approached the millennium.

Tall, extremely thin with long black hair, heavy boots, and long dresses, not hiding but also not revealing my inner self, I think about my spiritually and healthy belonging today. I remind myself of that earlier time. I made friendships with those that I would consider more spiritually awake than I was and how inviting, warm and welcoming they were. In studying religious studies and then psychology, I was exposed and educated about alternative ways of beliefs and faith. This included a form of prayer but also the way people lived their lives and developed a sense of community through food, meditation, rituals, and song. This stays with me and today I feel spiritually connected to the here and now and my responsibility to the environment and the way I ethically live my life. How I share and model these ideas and actions with my children is equally important. I no longer turn to a God but feel a sense of spirituality all around me. By experiencing pregnancy and childbirth, with multiple health concerns and barriers to success, I view spirituality as part of physical and mental health. This also continues to align with my work, researching infant care and the impact of adverse childhood experiences with the potential long-term health implications. My spirituality as a woman and healthy belonging is defined by my community, my family, my friends and knowing I have the privilege to dictate personal lifestyle choices about how I want to live and where I want to live, bridging spirituality with good health.

After:

I am aware being a woman spiritually and healthy belonging is, for me, a personal and privileged choice having obtained good education, with some personal time for myself and financial affordances. I view health to include good mental health, spiritual health as well as physical health. Personal habits regarding diet and vices such as smoking are no longer part of my every day. I also recognise the transitional and temporal states of understanding what spiritually and healthy belonging mean as an older woman. Through life experience, lifelong learning, and the people I meet. I recognise how I reshape and shift my personal views about being a woman spiritually and healthy belonging.

By following this technique, I recognise, in simplest terms, a white female English-speaking woman, probably considered middle class and not considered very healthy. However, this external representation reminds me that I am more than an equal opportunity monitoring form. I consider my life to be much more layered and complex. However, it is a timely reminder of the way generalised viewpoints are made about others but also about me when faced with looking inwards. In approaching the chapter, I had the space to explore my personal journey as a mother and a woman. Is it based on who we are or what we do? In creating a narrative to reflect in meaningful ways, I remind myself how my life journey is shaped by those around, never static as I have passed through maiden, now as a mother and moving towards crone, within feminist spirituality.

Sharon

Before:

As with other contributors, the connections between health (in all its meanings) and spiritual belonging have been neglected in my reflexivity. My thinking in this exercise is made more complicated because I never felt a sense of belonging in the Church of England, despite being part of a congregation from birth. So, I approach this idea of health and spirituality from a profound feeling of alienation. I usually think of my non-belonging in Christian communities in terms of how I see feminism as incompatible with the Church's masculinised symbol system – and I am, first and foremost, a feminist. However, this thought experiment also reminded me of how class has affected my sense of religious and spiritual belonging. Reading the work of French sociologist Pierre Bourdieu has profoundly influenced how I understand the process of belonging as a working-class woman. Reflecting on my years within a Church of England environment, my working-class habitus – a word coined by Bourdieu to mean the environment which shapes us in early life – did not fit the middle-class ideology and culture of the Church of England. There is complexity for me here: on the one hand, I have only experienced non-belonging in the Church, and on the other, I was deeply shaped and influenced by its discourses – I did not belong, but I obeyed the rules around gender, sexuality, and practiced prescribed mental, emotional, and spiritual habits. On reflection, I do not believe this tension delivered holistic health benefits for me. Religious belonging may be regarded by some as a way of enhancing mental and emotional health, but what if belonging is compromised because of gender, class, race, and sexuality? A discussion on the damage such (non)belonging can inflict would fill another book. However, in my chapter, I attempt to trouble this correlation by exploring ways in which non-belonging can be seen as a far healthier place for women priests. It is better, perhaps, to not belong, than to belong to a masculinised paradigm that obliterates sexual difference, to paraphrase French feminist philosopher, Luce Irigaray.

After:

Heuristically, I am excavating a past self who at one time embraced a certain set of beliefs – my present self-interprets this embracing as part of the attempt to belong. I am reminded by the chapter offered by Nicole and Miles of what I learned when studying feminist research methodology; that the memory of a past self is tricky and rarely an accurate reflection of real events. I am reaching back to past experiences of non-belonging in church life to make some sense of my present positioning. I remember two stories from my childhood that I acknowledge are reified into vignettes that act as shorthand for my feelings of gender and class non-belonging. On one occasion, my local vicar told me women could not be priests because they menstruated (and my proto-feminist self became an active feminist overnight!) The second memory influences my feelings of class-based alienation. During a coughing fit in church, I was handed a delicate laced handkerchief by a woman I considered well to-do ("posh"), when I really needed a glass of water. When I offered the handkerchief back, she visibly recoiled and told me to take it home to wash it first. The details of both memories may be mis-remembered, but what I am actually remembering is the profound feeling of shame they each generate (then and now), menstrual and gender shame and working-class shame. My point here is – and I take my lead from the heuristic technique of troubling reflexivity – that I have located an overriding feeling which I now name as shame, that is woven through my memory of attempting to belong in a religious institution that reproduces class and gender hegemonies. In this sense, my chapter reflects my own desire to make sense of a chequered spiritual journey that features non-belonging and to find ways to validate a sense of self outside prescribed religious boundaries. Shame is a corollary of non-belonging: working-class shame, menstrual shame, sexual shame, somatic shame, marginal shame, spiritual shame. These personal reflections about believing and belonging are, of course, woven through my research, and I recognise there is an auto-ethnographic shadow accompanying my study of the experiences of other women who also find themselves in a position of non-belonging.

Ayşe

Before:

Religion is an identity signifier, and it is difficult to dissociate misrepresentation from representation as anti-Muslim hatred rises to endemic, or epidemic proportions. It is no surprise that Muslim scholars and journalists write and speak about underrepresentation and misrepresentation of Islam a lot because the collective memory of Muslims is saturated with terrorism stigma. Perhaps, as Edward Said states, representation is a matter of proportion, and this makes discrimination inevitable. Though not an observant Muslim, I have always felt that it is easy for some non-Muslim people to define Muslimness although it is very difficult for me to do so. These people I talk about have perceived knowledge about Islam, or more prominently Islamism. I feel they define Islam, Islamism or Muslims for themselves and, in doing so, they define themselves.

There are too many terms and sometimes I find myself amid a crisis: is it Islamicist or Islamist; how can I avoid the loaded history of *jihad* while talking about the resistance against imperialism; why does my computer correct *hareem* into *harem* each time I type the word? Is it because of the repeated, copied, essentialist and reproduced attitude in the West, in other words, the learned and overdetermined Orientalist discourse that was centuries in the making? Is the Islamic world militant and unchanging as represented in mainstream media? Is it dangerously threatening to respond as people located historically and geographically? Why do certain people still have the urge to correct definitions in a world of increasing mobility and universal literacy?

After:

These questions never stop when I write. The reason I study religion in post-colonial literary representations as an early career female researcher is because I grew up in a world where Islamic resurgence was (and still is) a reality. There are strict barriers around and classifying religiosity and being spiritual. On the one hand, I cannot situate myself outside any religious realm because I live in a state where Islamic rhetoric is widespread. On the other, this risk space allowed me to create my own Muslimness as a female. In my country, we started to talk about national and religious identity more with the arrival of millions of Syrian and Afghan refugees and, although a hostile environment is in the making, we contest it. We write and speak against it. The refugees taught us that homesickness should be our guide and I feel the religious revival in my home country, Turkey, in the last three decades that made my homeland a place I cannot recognise anymore deserves attention. Homeland has turned into a place of homesickness for many of us – including myself – but we know this is a shared human reality and this helps us tolerate. In this world of contested definitions and redefinitions, I recognise a similarity when I read about distant places such as Egypt, or Bangladesh, or the Sudan, where Islamic activism shaped affective attachments to home. When I study religiosity and religion, I think I write about home, and home is a distant past.

Nazia

Before:

I identify as a Muslim woman living in Britain and share here my personal rather than academic perspectives on religious belonging. Being raised in a conservative Muslim household and educated in a religious school has undoubtedly influenced my views on religion. As an observant Muslim, my religion guides my day-to-day life and impacts the decisions most, if not all, the decisions I make each day. It is probably for these reasons, that I view both components of spirituality and health as being interrelated factors and I regard my spiritual belonging as a direct cause of my positive emotional state. My religious outlook requires me to take the best possible care of my physical and emotional wellbeing, which encourages me to eat healthily, exercise regularly and "feed my soul" with only good.

After:

Engaging with Nicole and Miles's chapter was an interesting way to think about my personal religious practise. Whilst I have engaged in reflective practise in my professional work, I have not previously done so in my personal life, and certainly not with regard to my spirituality. Reading Nicole and Mile's perspectives, and those of the other contributors encouraged me to unpick the strong sense of religious belonging and spirituality I take for granted. The process allowed me to reflect upon how familial, educational, and cultural environments might influence the extent and degree of an individual's religiosity, and whether this can also impact the choices we make on spirituality or healthy belonging. The reflective process identified for me that at a very personal level, I feel a close connection with God. The close connection I feel seems to promote my positive well-being, not necessarily to fulfil the "need to belong" but it maps out my purpose and journey in life, in which I find great comfort. Whilst I do often encounter some inner struggles, in light of the fact that my interests relate to addressing gender discrimination and social injustice more widely, I am able to respond to the conflict through adopting a liberal, rather than conservative interpretation of religion. And thus, in the end, the reflective journey and liberal religious outlook result in me having a greater connection with my religion, a greater sense of belonging and positive spiritual and emotional wellbeing.

Conclusion

This book brings to account some of the current complexities of women being spiritual within Britain today. It raises how we all hold a sense of belonging within our culture and subcultures, whether it be to our faith, our communities, ourselves, and sometimes a bit of all three. While writing this book, a major global pandemic occurred (Covid-19), alongside Brexit and the pressing issue of climate change. These significant life-changing events, not only affect us all, but they will also really shape our beliefs, belonging and sense of connection in the future. As stated in the first chapter, Schudson, Beischel and van Anders noted that "belonging and bonding were uniquely associated with increased life satisfaction" (2019, p. 552). For many women in Britain, religion remains an essential aspect of their lives and belonging helps foster meaningful interpersonal connections.

Within the field of women and religion, currently, research predominantly examines the role of women within religious faiths and religious doctrines, relating to gender, gender roles, and women in religious history (Morin and Guelke, 2007). Even today, many religions elevate the status of men over women, have stricter sanctions against women, and require them to be submissive (Morin and Guelke, 2007). However, this book highlights the extant role women and religion play in current society. We have come together to collaboratively write a book from a very different stance, alongside establishing a sense of belongingness together. At the same time, we have attempted to enable the women we represent and our own voices, to be clearly heard and thought about more critically. We hope this book has helped to contribute further and create a sense of community (like waves identified by CRT), and thus give more consideration and thought for women within these traditions. Although this approach to women and religion is not without its critique, with the status of world affairs, it is felt to be most relevant for us.

To conclude, the book aimed to bring shared insight into some of the roles religion plays within our contemporary society from a woman's perspective. We wanted to highlight that we shared a sense of belonging throughout, and as authors, we also share a sense of belonging to each other. Our faith/or lack of it, in some cases, not only defines us, but also brings us closer together, even if distance-wise, we are hundreds of miles apart.

Reference List

Anugwom, E. E. (2020) "Public Health, Afflictions and Challenges in Developing Countries." In Anugwom, E. E. and Awofeso, N. (eds.) *Public Health in Developing Countries: Challenges and Opportunities.* London: Intech Open, p. 3.

Chin, C. (2019) "The concept of belonging: Critical, normative and multicultural." *Ethnicities,* 2019, 19(5), pp. 715-739.

King, U. (2017) "Spirituality" In Hinnells, J. R. (ed.) *A New Handbook of Living Religions 2nd Edition.* New Jersey: Wiley Blackhall, chapter 6.

Mercadante, L. (2020) "The Hard Way." *Dialog.* 59 pp. 195-196. Available at: https://onlinelibrary.wiley.com/doi/epdf/10.1111/dial.12591?saml_referrer. Accessed: 16/6/2022.

Morin, K. M. and Guelke, J. (2007) *Women, religion, and space: Global perspectives on gender and faith.* New York State: Syracuse University Press.

Schudson, Z. C. Beischel, W. J. and van Anders, S. M. (2019) "Individual variation in gender/sex category definitions." *Psychology of Sexual Orientation and Gender Diversity,* 6 (4) pp. 448-460. Available at: https://psycnet.apa.org/record/2019-42958-001. Accessed: 16/6/2022.

Scriven, A. (2017) *Ewles and Simmett's Promoting Health: A Practical Guide 7th Edition.* Edinburgh: Elsevier.

List of Contributors

Dr Yvonne Bennett has just completed a PhD at Canterbury Christ Church University. Her research area of interest is conservative Presbyterianism in the *Gàidhealtachd* (Highlands and Islands) of Scotland. She has published a book that examines the ways in which churches in Britain help the vulnerable in their communities. The book *The Church Who Needs It? We Do!* examines the difficulties a group of South London women experience with Universal Credit and life under lockdown during the Coronavirus pandemic.

Dr Ayse Çırçır is an assistant professor and earned a doctorate from Ataturk University in Turkey specialising in contemporary fiction written by Arab women. Dr. Çirçir received a TUBITAK research grant for her doctoral thesis in 2015 and was offered a place as a visiting DPhil at St Antony's College, the University of Oxford. As part of her sponsored research, she travelled to Egypt and stayed in Cairo for a long period. Her research interests are Orientalism in literature, Muslimness in British literature and culture, neo-Victorian fiction and literature in English and postcolonial literature. She is currently working at Erzurum Technical University, Turkey, English Department teaching courses at all levels of the curriculum. In addition to her teaching and research, she writes fairy tales for children and young adults that discuss patriarchy, immigration, and the climate change crisis.

Miles Greenford is an independent Public Health researcher in the field of spiritual health. He is currently involved in conceiving a free-at-the-point-of-access online social enterprise to act as a catalyst to advance research relating to applied spiritual health promotion. This research is supported by an MA in Nursing Studies (2002), and a Diploma in Community Health Studies (1995) to support his professional qualifications: Enrolled Nurse (General) (1989), Registered General Nurse, (qualified 1991), Registered Health Visitor (1995), and Nurse Prescriber (2000).

Dr Nicole Holt is a lecturer in Public Health at Canterbury Christ Church University UK. Nicole has just completed her PhD in Spirituality and Public Health. She has completed her PhD titled *The significances for Public Health of the relationship between spirituality, and health, as reported by people identifying as "spiritual but not religious"*, awarded by Canterbury Christ Church

University. She has won several academic prizes, in particular the David Steers Award and Dean of Canterbury's Prize for Christian Theology. Her specific interests are spirituality, health, wellbeing, animals and children and adults, particularly with additional needs. Her latest collaborative publication was "The neurological symptoms of COVID-19: a systematic overview of systematic reviews, comparison with other neurological conditions and implications for healthcare services."

Dr Sharon Jagger gained her doctorate in Women's Studies at the University of York and is now a lecturer in Religion at York St. John University, teaching sociology of religion and gender and sexuality in religious contexts. Drawing on a background in the Church of England and an academic approach to feminist theory, Sharon's research career began with a focus on gender and the priesthood in the Church of England. This work has expanded into an interest in how women integrate goddess spirituality into their beliefs and practices. Her latest collaborative work is "The Female Music Producer and the Leveraging of Difference".

Dr Amanda Norman is a Senior Lecturer and Programme Lead of the BA (Hons) Childhood Studies at the University of Winchester, UK. Since completion of her doctorate from Southampton University, she has published works about infant care pedagogies in academic peer-reviewed and professional practice articles. She is the author of, From Conception to Two: Development, Policy, and Practice (2019) and Historical Perspectives in Infant Care (2022). Amanda is currently researching spiritual and infant care relationships, from historical and contemporary perspectives. As a trained practicing therapeutic play specialist and early years consultant, she continues to support and liaise with early professionals working in the sector, in addition to her academic role.

Dr Nazia Yaqub has practised as a lawyer in family and child law and has a particular research interest in the area of gender justice. Her doctoral research examines the issues arising in international families and examines the legal response to family disputes, in particular cross-border parental child abduction. As part of that study, she interviewed parents and children affected, as well as professionals involved in resolving the dispute, including lawyers, mediators, and members of the judiciary. The study allowed Nazia to examine the interaction of domestic and international family law and evaluate the impact Islamic law has in matrimonial and custodial matters - and led her to examine the topic of Women and Religion in this text.

Index

E

F

G

H

I

J

L

M

T

V

W

Z

CPSIA information can be obtained
at www.ICGtesting.com
Printed in the USA
LVHW082128041222
734160LV00028B/312/J

9 781648 892226